LE CHATEAV · RICHELIEV

Much Depends on Dinner

(THE TABLECLOTH GAME)

Peter J and Frances Diane Roberts

Peter J. Robotti

GUEST EDITOR OF THE CHEF MAGAZINE
(CULINARY REVIEW)
*Official Publication of Friends
of Escoffier Society*

MUCH DEPENDS ON DINNER
(*The Tablecloth Game*)

Frances Diane Robotti

CHRONICLES OF OLD SALEM
(*A History in Miniature*)

WHALING AND OLD SALEM
(*A Chronicle of the Sea*)

MUCH DEPENDS ON DINNER
(*The Tablecloth Game*)

T O N I N O   M A L N A T I

This book is affectionately dedicated
by one of his appreciative pupils.

Much Depends on Dinner

(THE TABLECLOTH GAME)

By Peter J. Robotti

(with Frances Diane Robotti)

INTRODUCTION BY CHARLES COLLINGWOOD

FOUNTAINHEAD PUBLISHERS, INC.

475 Fifth Avenue, New York 17, N.Y.

© *1961 by Peter J. Robotti*

1789

Library of Congress Catalogue Card Number: 61-13472

Manufactured in the United States of America

Van Rees Press • New York

CONTENTS

Contents

LIST OF ILLUSTRATIONS

List of Illustrations

following page 130

President John Fitzgerald Kennedy and other dignitaries.
Governor Thomas E. Dewey with the co-authors.
Vincent Price and Arlene Francis with the author.
Charles Collingwood and Peter Robotti.
General and Mrs. Omar Nelson Bradley.
Fredric March.
Mrs. Drury W. Cooper III and Mrs. John Blair Richardson.
Mr. Robotti welcomes the Hon. Abe Stark, President of the New York City Council.
Mr. and Mrs. Fritz Kreisler celebrate a wedding anniversary.
Actress Tina Louise and Mr. Robotti.
New York socialites Mrs. Robert A. Hendrickson and Mrs. Pamela D. Law.
Mr. and Mrs. Rudy Vallee, Mr. Robotti.
Actors Stubby Kaye and Peter Palmer of "Li'l Abner."
Actor Edward Everett Horton and actress Lila Lee.
Executive Chef Raymond Richez, William Gaxton, Walter Pidgeon and Peter Robotti.
Mallard Duck l'orange by Executive Chef Raymond Richez.
Owner-host Peter Robotti presides over dessert course for party which includes Ginger Rogers.

following page 226

Aging Cellars of The Christian Brothers Winery in Napa Valley.
Vineyards of The Christian Brothers of California.
Kentucky Hunt breakfast arrangement at Tiffany's for the Bourbon Institute.
"The Vintage in California" by P. Frenzeny, 1878.
Beaulieu Vineyard, Rutherford, Napa Valley, California.
Fred C. Taylor, Greyton H. Taylor and Clarence Taylor, executives of the Taylor Wine Company, Inc.
Monastery of Le Grand Chartreuse near Grenoble, France.
Carthusian Monks tend barrels of Chartreuse Liqueurs.
The author in his fabulous Wine Cellar at Le Chateau Richelieu.
Peter and Frances Robotti on board the S.S. *Independence*.
The Peter Robotti School in Fubine, Italy.
The author in his ancestral vineyards.
Fubine, Italy with the Cathedral's spire.
The Old and the New Waldorf-Astorias.
Building housing Le Chateau Richelieu.

viii

ACKNOWLEDGMENTS

THIS BOOK WAS MADE POSSIBLE BY A NUMBER OF GRACIOUS people who have been most cooperative in contributing authoritative material which has given it the touch of authenticity. I would like to thank the authors of the reference books consulted, the magazine and newspaper writers whose timely articles were pertinent as well as the staff of the New York Public Library who assisted us with reference books and pictures.

Appreciation is gratefully expressed to the following in London, England: Mr. André L. Simon, President of the Wine and Food Society; the Savoy Hotel; the House of Sandeman and the Fortnum and Mason Department Store in Piccadilly. In Paris, France—the Bordeaux Information Bureau and the Etablissements Marnier Lapostelle. In New York—the Bourbon Institute, Duncan Hines Institute of Ithaca, Fromm & Sichel, Munson & Shaw, Sugar Information Service, Inc., Schieffelin Importing Co., Frederick Wildman & Sons, the Taylor Wine Company of Hammondsport, the Waldorf-Astoria Hotel. In California, the California Wine Association of San Francisco, the Wine Institute, and the Wine Advisory Board; Almaden' Vineyards, Beaulieu Vineyards, Louis M. Martini, Wente Brothers (who were so cordial to my wife and me on our visit to their wineries).

Acknowledgments

Appreciation is due to Mr. Robert Audelan, President, Academie Culinaire Francaise d'Amerique, Mr. Raymond Vaudard, President, La Tripiere d'or aux U.S.A., Charlie Berns of the "21" Club, one of the first to express the need for a book such as this, Gaynor Maddox, Mr. and Mrs. Ward Morehouse, Ted Saucier and Robert Brennan, Herbert Kupferberg, Clementine Paddleford and Isabel A. McGovern of the New York Herald Tribune, Craig Claiborne and Gilbert Millstein of the New York Times, Robert Dana of the New York World Telegram, Colonel Serge Obolensky, Mr. and Mrs. Allen Stevens of the Socony Mobile Guide, George Serra of Culinary Review, Catholic Digest, Esquire Magazine, Life, Earle R. MacAusland and Alvin Kerr of Gourmet Magazine, Ted Patrick of Holiday, Miss Edith Evans and Miss Gloria Spitz of Living for Young Homemakers, Miss Pat Coffin and Miss Marilyn Kaytor of Look, the New Yorker, the Park Avenue Social Review, Theatre Magazine, and Henry Sell of Town and Country, Charles Collingwood, distinguished CBS commentator, who takes a lively interest in the culinary arts, for reading the manuscript and writing the introduction; my faithful staff—for whom the food show must always go on—and the clientele over a period of thirty years who have been aware of our efforts to please them; Hal G. Vermes for his editorial suggestions; Fountainhead Publishers for constancy and infinite patience, and finally deep gratitude to my wife Frances Diane, whose observations on our various travels were tucked away in numerous notebooks and whose literary skill and devotion clothed my dictation and molded our discussions into narrative form, imparting to the whole the special magic of the historian's touch.

PETER J. ROBOTTI

48 East 52nd Street,
New York City, New York

INTRODUCTION

By Charles Collingwood

I HAPPEN TO LOVE RESTAURANTS. THIS IS JUST AS well since a life of travel has made them indispensable to my well being. There are those who, when they think of a distant city, conjure up its monuments, its art galleries, its orchestras. I think of its restaurants. They are as evocative as historical glories, as well remembered as friends. I have been cured of more ills in restaurants than I have in hospitals. I have had more good evenings in restaurants than in the theatre. Indeed, no opening curtain is as exciting to me as the entrance into a fine restaurant with the silver glowing and the glasses shining, the good things spread out, and a friendly figure to guide you to your table. Peter Robotti has devoted his life to providing these pleasures. As such he is a man after my own heart and so is his book.

There is much talk these days of the decline of standards. The complaint is nowhere more true than in the world of restaurants. While it is doubtless the case that more people eat better than ever before, it is also a fact that it is more difficult for a few people to eat supremely well than it used to be. This is not entirely the fault of the restaurants, at least of the good ones ... It is not true that there is no excuse for getting a bad meal. There are many excuses. But there are fewer excuses in a good restaurant. Mr. Robotti's book is frankly addressed to those who dine in good restaurants, and those who read it will have fewer excuses still.

Our more casual age is less demanding than the days in which a gratified gourmet could exclaim "With this sauce one could eat one's grandmother!" This is obviously a matter of some pain to Peter Robotti—not that he advocates enthropophagy, but rather that he is acutely aware that the standards of cultivated dining which he so jealously upholds depend upon cultivated diners. Indeed, not the least of the lessons imparted by this volume is that the proper enjoyment of a great restaurant is a vocation as demanding as its creation.

He is not stuffy about this, nor doctrinaire. But Mr. Robotti writes from the profound conviction that a meal is more pleasurable if one knows what one is eating, what one is drinking and something of what is involved in their preparation and presentation. A simple premise, but what a wealth of lore and cornucopia of information are made to flow from it.

The contemplation of the act of dining out leads our host to explore many a curious by-way of history and oddity of manners. He parades before us the great chefs and restaurateurs of past and present. He advises on tipping, discourses on the history of New York, analyzes the chemistry of sugar, describes the organization of a good restaurant from the kitchen to the hatcheck girl. And whether he is discussing the influence of air travel on the palate or the epicurean standards of the inhabitants of New York's West Side, he talks rare good sense. A successful restaurateur must be a practical man. Mr. Robotti is a successful restaurateur and this is a practical book. It contains much food for thought because it is based on much thought of food.

Charles Collingwood

Much Depends on Dinner

(THE TABLECLOTH GAME)

CHAPTER

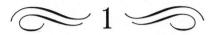

The Ancient Art of Gastronomy

"All the arts are brothers;
Each one is a light to the others."
—VOLTAIRE (1694-1778)

ONE OF THE MOST QUOTED EPIGRAMS ABOUT food is that of Moliere, the seventeenth century French playwright, who affirmed that "We should eat to live, not live to eat." The premise of this book, however, is that there is much more to eating than just filling one's stomach. My contention, as a restaurateur, "the keeper of an inn," is that food, in addition to being necessary for the sustenance of life, can be a most gratifying pleasure. Not only does good food, properly prepared and perfectly served, delight the senses, but it also soothes the soul.

The American woman is a good cook, and many excellent meals are concocted in the home. However, for the epitome in fine dining —without incurring any culinary problems—I recommend any of the well-conducted restaurants to be found throughout the nation and the world.

A restaurant offers not only the well-prepared dish but leisure pleasure, atmosphere and excitement. If your visit is well-planned, your menu selections wisely made, you understand what is expected and what to expect, the whole can be made a rewarding experience and a pleasurable memory, whether you dine out frequently or only upon occasion.

I

The title of this book is from one of Lord Byron's quips: "Since Eve ate apples, much depends on dinner." To be sure, the pleasures of food (and the vast machinery involved in the creation of those pleasures) are intimately related to the most satisfying experiences of life. It would be possible, in unfolding the chronicle of manners and customs associated with social dining, to reveal a faithful picture of a whole chosen epoch. Such a chronicle would reflect the basically human version of that era. If you think about it, you will agree that the standard of cookery and table manners constitutes a gauge which points directly to the individual characteristics of a nation or race. If one considers only superficially the consumption of food and drink as self-gratification, one misses the whole of their significance in the art of living, which implies a cultivated appreciation of life's meaning and pleasures.

A desire to experience the joys of the senses contributes markedly towards creative achievement. Is it true, as is commonly believed, that an artist must starve in a garret in order to be inspired to create? It is easy to disprove this view. Let us take, for instance, the people of Vienna. They consider the culinary arts as an inexhaustible source of the Austrian people's artistic gifts. Food and wine for them led to stretching the hand towards violin, palette and brush. This became known across Europe as "Wiener Lebensart"—the Viennese manner or art of living—giving rise to the vagaries of fashion, art and a style which was called "the life of the Phaeaces." The Phaeacians of the Greeks were those mythical ancestors, who were a gay, seafaring people, described in Homer's Odyssey and other classical literature.

Generally in France, England, and Europe as a whole, one cannot speak of a culinary art prior to the arrival on the scene of the Romans, who borrowed heavily from the Greeks. In their turn, the Greeks borrowed from the Egyptians and other early cultures. Germany was influenced by the past as much as other countries. Two principles have been handed down by the Teutons and their early Germanic tribes:

Nothing should be begun on an empty stomach.

Hospitality is a first duty.

2

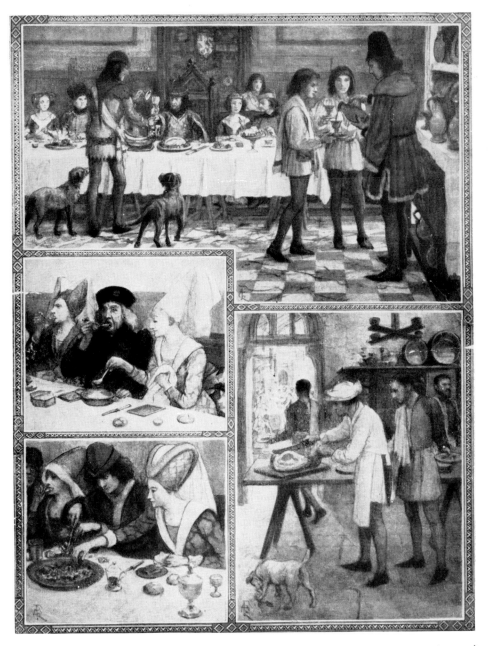

In the "Fingers Before Forks" period of the Fourteenth Century. Preparation, service and dining of elegantes. By A. Forestier.

THERE WILL BE FEASTINGS
IN THE CASTLE HALL:
Music will sound and good wine freely flow;
Joustings and tourneys. The old seneschal,
Clanking his heavy keys, goes to and fro,
Distracted by his master's latest whim.
Now on the market-square whole oxen smoke,
Monks, in the church, rehearse the nuptial hymn.
The Fool evolves some unfamiliar joke.

JUGGLERS AND TUMBLERS.
ERRANT TROUBADOURS
Seeking their recompense for tricks and song,
Beggars and priests, town-bred and country boors,
Surge round the castle gates. And all this throng
Shouting and laughing, are wild for pleasure.
The people are agog this Christmastide;
They reck not, if spent his lordship's treasure,
The heartbreak of the lovely, tragic bride.

AT HER HIGH CASEMENT.
ALONE and LILY-WHITE
She stands. A red rose to her lips is pressed.
Her thoughts are with her faithful gallant knight;
The red rose is a querdon for his quest.
She casts it outward on the morning air;
Swift as a stricken bird it flutters down.
Her eyes are shut, her pale lips form a prayer,
For him whose love she forfeits to a crown.

THE LABOURED SHUNTING
OF A DISTANT TRAIN
Shatters my dream of an imagined day.
The curious spell is broken; once again
The dim romantic past is far away.....
Clouds reappear, the midnight air blows chill;
The moon no longer lights the walls and towers
Of this old city set upon its hill.
Which draws such magic from the darkened hours

Banquet in the courtyard of a Roman tavern in the Sixteenth Century. Painting by Francesco Ricci exhibited at the World's Columbian Exposition in Chicago in 1876.

Fine hunts of the Emperor Maximilian of the Teutons. Luncheon in the forest. Original painting by Bernard Van Orley in the Louvre, Paris.

←————————————————

Feastings in the Castle Hall in the Middle Ages.

Napoleon Bonaparte being presented by his Minister of the Interior with loaves of beet sugar made in France. First developed by a German chemist, extraction of sugar from beets became a full-fledged industry by decree of the French emperor who needed quick energy for his armies. Exhibit of the painting by an unknown French artist stimulated widespread planting of sugar beets.

Western Beet Sugar Producers, Inc.

Parade of the Pheasants by costumed and be-wigged waiters, supervised by Captain Peter Zuliani at the Seventeenth Century Dinner. The roast pheasant was prepared from a 1640 recipe. Every dish was researched by Frances Diane Robotti as the Robottis recreated, for the first time in America, an authentic French dinner of over three centuries ago.

Photo by Standard Flashlight Co.

"An itinerant Italian artist painted The Three Musketeers of the Alexandre Dumas classic for the first Richelieu in its modest old brownstone step-down where the gay, well-fed trio—Porthos, Aramis and Athos—lent an air of Parisian enchantment to the little place."

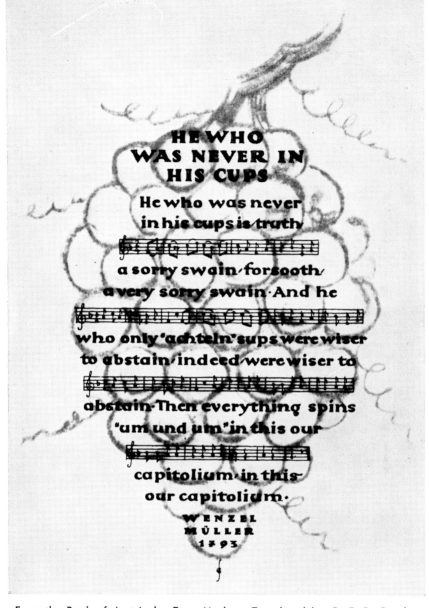

HE WHO WAS NEVER IN HIS CUPS

He who was never
in his cups is truth,

a sorry swain forsooth,
a very sorry swain. And he

who only 'achteln' sups were wiser
to abstain indeed were wiser to

abstain. Then everything spins
"um und um" in this our

capitolium in this
our capitolium.

WENZEL
MÜLLER
1593

From the Book of Austria by Ernst Marboe. Translated by G. E. R. Geyde, 1948, Vienna.

← ─────────────

Captain Peter in yellow brocade and lace collar and cuffs proudly presents a choice dish—*la croute de soufflé de fruits de mer a la cinq Mars* with sauce Cardinal—at the Richelieu's famous Seventeenth Century Dinner tendered on December 1, 1959.

Photo by Standard Flashlight Co.

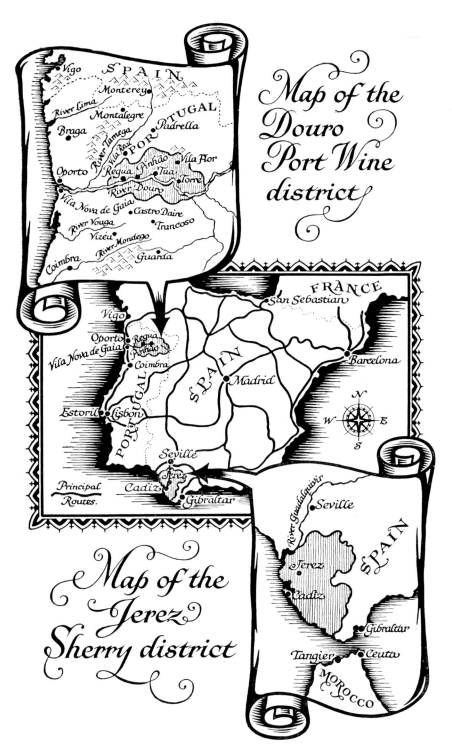

Map of the
Douro
Port Wine
district

Map of the
Jerez
Sherry district

From the "Story of Port and Sherry" by G. Sandeman and Sons,
London, England.

The Ancient Art of Gastronomy

Tacitus, who was conversant with these customs, mentioned them in his *Germania:* "No other race is so eager to offer unlimited entertainment and hospitality. For these people it is wrong to close one's doors to anyone, no matter whom." These precepts eventually spread throughout Europe.

In classical literature, gastronomy plays a leading part. The Roman way of life was centered around the kitchen and the table. In ancient Rome, dining was a science, as well as an art, in which delicate tastes were combined with unlimited luxury, based on painstaking detail. The spirit of the culinary arts hovered over the city on the Tiber. According to Plutarch, Julius Caesar planned banquets with the same attention and care he devoted to his battles. The poetry of Horace and Ovid shows the great interest given to the refinements of eating and drinking. Ovid (circa 1 B.C.) usually associated food with love and, in a charming fragment, he describes how a young man dipped his fingers in red wine during a feast in order to write a declaration of devotion to his lady love on the table linen. "It warms the blood," wrote Ovid, "adds luster to the eyes, and wine and love have ever been allies." Another famous Greek poet was even more emphatic. He declared flatly that "Where there is no wine, there is no love." The feasts of Lucullus are proverbial for extravagant dining and have added an expressive word to our language. Lucullan, more than anything else, describes the most opulent in banqueting.

Trimalchio was a gourmandizer and his feasts were gluttonous orgies of the *nouveau riche,* known to us through the tales of Petronius. Trimalchio's Feast of the Zodiac is still famous. To each of the signs of the heavens he related a selection of foods. Cato, too, loved the delights of the table and complained of his inability to resist the many temptations placed before him: "How hard a thing it is to try to talk to one's belly, which has no ears to hear."

It was natural for the Romans to trace many foods back to mythology. The humble cabbage, which was given its name by the Latin *caput*—meaning head—is said to have originated from the tears which the Thracian Prince Lycurgus shed when Bacchus bound him to a vine-pole for frivolously destroying grapes. The

3

ancient Egyptians consumed quantities of beer and wine without getting drunk because they ate cooked cabbage before their drinking bouts. The observant Cato recommended this preventive to Roman indulgers. Moderns are urged, on the other hand, not to *mix drinks,* meaning in particular not to cross malt with grape; to follow beer with whisky and to follow wine with brandy. We are reminded that lettuce was sacred to Aphrodite (Venus, goddess of love) because she once hid the new-born Adonis among the lettuce. And did you know that to the Greek gods salads were third among their favorite foods? Their first choices were nectar and ambrosia. To create a good salad, one must still employ qualities required by those who served the gods—imagination, perseverance, instinct, and the gift of composition. In fact, the most difficult thing to procure today is a good salad, properly concocted and appetizingly presented.

According to Pliny, the Romans first obtained sugar cane from Arabia. Before that they used honey for sweetening. The Crusaders rediscovered sugar cane near Tripoli and brought it to Europe. It was a long and arduous journey and cane sugar was, therefore, expensive and beyond the reach of most people during the fourteenth century. Sugar in the Middle Ages was used almost exclusively for medicinal purposes, and was found in the laboratory of the chemist. Confectioners did not exist until later. It is said that in Austria, Emperor Maximilian I brought the first *sugar-blower* to his Court in 1514. On the other hand, salt, the traditional symbol of hospitality, was found everywhere in Europe since early times. The Romans sometimes paid for services in salt, whence it is said our word salary derives. One still hears the old remark: "He is not worth his salt."

There is a millennium in culinary history between the third century, when Apicius, the Roman epicure, recorded his complicated cooking recipes, and the first records of the thirteenth century. There are only incomplete references and isolated accounts of that period. The Middle Ages saw the deterioration of the culinary arts. The much-touted age of knighthood in Europe was marked for the most part by a poor table which offered simple staple foods of bread, smoked fish and beef. There was emphasis on only one thing: great

4

quantities must be served. While the meals of every-day life were simple, a wedding meant lavish ostentation. Everyone hoped to be invited to a wedding feast.

In an account by the historian Ottocar von Horneck, of the marriage of King Belas of Hungary to the niece of Ottokar of Bohemia in the year 1264, he writes: "There was indeed more than enough. The Danube was scarcely able to bear the ships heavily laden with food, and many a container burst under the pressure of its contents." The same writer speaks of a thousand bushels of wheat going to the bread bakers, and of wine sufficient for the inhabitants of two countries.

Many social customs are inter-related with the service of food. In the first ordinaries, taverns and inns of New York, men and women ate in different rooms. The early hotels, which served meals without menus in boarding-house style, had long tables which seated some thirty persons, both men and women. Yet the idea of separation persisted and women had to enter the hotel through the Ladies' Entrance. The original Waldorf-Astoria on Fifth Avenue ended this restrictive custom, and other hotels soon followed.

Before the twelfth century, it was the strict custom in Europe for the sexes to eat in different rooms. Later, they were allowed to eat in a common dining hall, the noble knights sitting along one wall and their ladies by the other. There was a passage between the tables for the servants to move up and down while serving. Not until the end of the Middle Ages did stoneware come into use; plates previously were made of wood and pewter. As dining took on a social aspect, the host seated each lady next to an admirer. The couple received one plate between them, and the knight was most attentive, tempting his beloved with choice morsels and endearing words.

After the era of the wandering minstrel, who appeared at times to deliver the news in song, the use of the common platter for both man and woman continued until the nineteenth century. It is Italy which is credited, towards the end of the fifteenth century, with the introduction of the fork. The forks we now have were not generally available until comparatively recent times, and were first used only

5

for cooking, and for holding meat while it was being carved. The original forks were long, two-pronged, and made of iron, bone or hard wood. Three hundred years ago, forks were still a curiosity in Europe. In France, until the seventeenth century, everyone ate with the fingers. The magnificent court of Louis XIV held sumptuous banquets at which guests dined with spoons, knives and fingers. Fine linen serviettes were provided, and it was considered quite proper to wipe one's fingers on the generously overlapping tablecloths.

Until the middle of the fifteenth century, it was the custom to cover the festive board—which was placed loosely on supports and removed at the end of the meal—by enormous tablecloths. These extended over the table and protected the knees during the meal. Before dipping into the dishes, the hands were wiped each time on the cloth; consequently it had to be changed several times during great feasts. Table napkins were introduced in 1450, but were more decorative than practical. At the Court of Leopold II of Austria, they were luxurious squares of colored velvet.

A chronicler tells of Anne of Austria (who was born in 1601) plunging her whole hand into the ragout. It was not until later that the fork came into general use in Europe. The eighteenth century brought the three-pronged and then the four-pronged fork. As for the spoon, the cupped hand was the first, of course, and actual spoons date back to the Stone Age. Yet until nearly 1500, soup was sipped from hollowed out rings of bread, spoons being used only as ladles to fill them. The knife as a tool has a long history, and cutlers are mentioned in the tenth century; but at the table, only the head of the house used the knife for carving. It is strange that tooth-picks have been found even in pre-historic graves, and were carried in costly cases in the Middle Ages. Recently, a golden toothpick was advertised for "the man who has everything."

Old woodcuts show people of Italy enjoying spaghetti while standing up and eating the long strands with their fingers. This is the way pastas were then consumed. It was their popularity, some authorities feel, which gradually increased the use of the fork. As is usual during any social advance, the vanguard of fork users were ridiculed as being too fastidious and dainty. Travelers from Italy

6

brought news of the new implement to other countries. At that time, Venice was the epitome of elegance in living. It was written about a wealthy woman of that city, in the eleventh century, that she had a small golden fork made for her use: "Instead of eating like other people, she had her food cut up into little pieces and ate the pieces by means of a two-pronged fork." Five hundred years later, fork users were still described as being rather peculiar in their eating habits.

Journalists wrote: "At Venice, each person is served, besides his knife and spoon, with a fork to hold the meat while he eats it, for they deem it ill manners that one should touch it with his hand." When the English Puritans settled along the Atlantic Coast of America in the early 1600's, it was written of Governor John Winthrop that he had a fork which he always carried with him.

From the seventeenth century on, table manners developed along stricter rules of dining etiquette. However, certain customs were observed even in earlier times. For example, an Italian manual of the year 1480 warns its readers: "Do not stuff too large mouthfuls into both cheeks. Do not keep your hand too long in the platter, and put it in only when the other has withdrawn his hand from the dish."

Some degree of elegance was gained by using three fingers only for dipping. And the drinking glass was supposed to be held in three fingers. The common drinking glass was in use until the 1500's. Before using it, the glass was wiped with the tablecloth, as was the mouth. When a lady of the court drank, a serving man held a bowl under her chin. All food was covered with a serviette until actually eaten to prevent the powder on wigs and faces from falling into it. In Italy, the land of its origin, silver forks began to appear among the well-to-do and, by the end of the eighteenth century, the fork was accepted as a necessity in the homes of most cultivated people of Europe. Gradually forks came into general use and were welcomed by those affluent enough to afford them.

In any discussion of the good life, one should not overlook Vienna. In the fifteenth century, the cookery of Vienna was considered to be among the best in Europe; and when a Viennese went to war, he took his best cooks to camp. The doughty Capuchin monk Abraham a Santa Clara often flew into a passion over Viennese gourmandizing. In one of his sermons he said he was not surprised that house and farm were often ruined because of the owner's gourmandizings and that the noble soul was suppressed by the fat paunch. The splendor and luxury of Vienna reached their climax in Leopoldan times under Karl VI, Prince Eugene, and during the period of the Vienna Congress. Table decoration was an important part of every official banquet. While there are many references to the culinary artistry of the French, very few writers mention that of the Austrians. Chefs once prepared fantastic shapes in sugar-icing, arabesques, ornamentation, and groups of figures in the days of the great court banquets. The arrangement of the dishes competed with the decorations. A pelican, for example, would be made out of baked bread, and around it were grouped roast chickens and doves.

Extravagance reached a high point when chefs gilded the roast suckling pigs. Pastry ships were filled with fruits. Table fireworks competed for attention with the statues, fountains and castles created out of edible materials. Many confectioners were trained sculptors who worked as well in marble. The most luxurious days of the city were those of the Vienna Congress, as historians agree. Entertainment at the Imperial Court cost 50,000 gulden a day. The wealthy Austrian aristocratic families gave banquets to as many as 700 guests at a time, with one day a week being reserved for this brilliant affair. They were the hedonists of that era.

From the Middle Ages on, music was considered an integral part of dining with pomp and circumstance. Perhaps more than any other musician of our times, Fritz Kreisler, who was born in Vienna in 1875, epitomizes the spirit and refinement of the city so beloved of the Austrians. It was a proud moment recently for me to be the host of the aging violinist and his wife. For a long time he has been Austria's cultural ambassador. As a youth of fourteen, he first came to the United States in 1889. After a successful tour, he returned to his own country to study medicine until called to serve as an officer in the Austrian army. At the turn of the century, he re-appeared on the concert stage in Berlin. Again in 1900, a more mature artist, Fritz Kreisler toured the United States in triumph. Then came

World War I. He rejoined his old regiment, was wounded and discharged. Thereafter he devoted himself to his violin. His name was magic. Fritz Kreisler received $5,000 and more for single performances. Now he lives with his memories in New York on the East River.

Those who long for a glimpse of Old Vienna often go to the Café Grinzing where candlelight, and the haunting refrains from the music of the Strausses recall Austria's ancient capital city. There is a certain continuity in this rendezvous. For a quarter of a century, Bela Villanyi and his violin have re-created the romance and charm of Vienna. Like Kreisler, Villanyi was once a medical student. He was advised to pursue his Muse by Ignace Jan Paderewski, the Polish pianist, who told him he could cure people with his music. "An inspired violinist," said Paderewski, "can cure the world's most deadly disease: weariness of the heart." The Teutons call it *weltschmerz*. In his modest way, the dark-haired Villanyi plays his waltzes and the wild gypsy melodies of Vienna in New York's Little Austria.

The art of good living and dining has always attracted the connoisseur. The late Fletcher Pratt, marine historian and gourmet, felt that fashion has much to do with what is esteemed good eating, the reason cookbooks go out-of-date, and why they are always in demand. His theory was that it depended on the availability of foods and upon their popular acceptance. Not even the wealthiest courts of Europe, for instance, made use of sugar when it was difficult to obtain. A supper of nine courses conjured up by Madame du Barry for Louis XV—in answer to his royal remark that no woman could design a good meal—had for its dessert strawberries and liqueur. When the Spanish-American war gave the United States economic or political control of Puerto Rico, Cuba, the Philippines and Hawaii, opening the gates to boundless supplies of cheap sugar, a positive mania for sweets seized Americans and it has never run its course.

Vegetables came into fashion with a lessening in the availability of meat, fowl, wild game, and the seafood in which world waters once abounded. In the sixteenth century and the Renaissance, the sure sign of good birth and breeding all over Europe was the serving of half a dozen meat dishes at one meal, a custom which still prevails in Portugal. In the homes of the wealthy in Italy today, there

9

is served at least two, and often three, meats for dinner. England clung longest to its heavy meat diet. In Germany, the arrival of the potato from America at the time of the Thirty Years War began a vegetable renaissance about the time when wild game was near extinction from constant raids for the table. By 1645 the wild boars were gone, the marching armies ate them up, and Lennant Torstensson was unable to go on to Vienna because his army could find no meat in forest or field. It was about this time that the grains came into wide use, noodles taking the place of meat.

Devotion to family life is as closely allied with gastronomy as fire is to cooking. The ancient Romans worshipped the Penates who were their gods of the hearth, where food for family and guests was prepared. It meant happiness, comfort, euphoria and gratitude for health. The modern Italian calls the person who is blissfully well-adjusted—*simpatico,* and the Spaniards do likewise. The French have a name for the enthusiasm which gives courage to living as *joie de vivre.* The Teutons—especially the Austrians—call the happiness which arises from comfort—*Gemütlichkeit.* For this, to the Viennese, a woman is always responsible. While men presided over gastronomy for sale, it was the woman who early became the unchallenged and particularly respected representative of a well-defined and charming type of culture in the family circle. The home was her salon in which the husband (and father) was the true head of the house.

No homemaker errs in concentrating her efforts on the home, even though she and her husband may entertain in hotels and restaurants. They will be even more appreciative hosts when dining out because of the care and attention given to the culinary arts in the privacy of the home. Those who visit Vienna and are guests of its people will find that even the average middle-class woman of that ancient city has always lavished her imagination, her good taste, her emotions, and her love on the home and its cultural atmosphere. In the days of plenty, it was an easy victory. Even in difficult times, she retains the faculty of lending the poetic touch to the simplest meal. She spreads a snow-white tablecloth, fills a decorative vase with fresh flowers, arranges an old china service, puts out a dainty mat for the wine bottle, and adds a touch of greenery as a decoration, making the plainest offering most attractive. When she serves tea or coffee between meals, it will be on a cobwebby teacloth of the Vienna Jause (tea table) with the hand-painted biedermeier cups, flowers charmingly arranged around a sponge cake in the center, sugary white and crisp "Guglhupf," and the marvelous aroma of freshly brewed coffee combining to make such a simple repast enjoyable.

Since America is a comparatively new country, I am sometimes asked where the oldest operating inn, hostelry or restaurant is located. While New York still continues to enjoy its Fraunces Tavern of historic memories, we must look to Massachusetts for the answer to this interesting query. Longfellow's Wayside Inn at South Sudbury has dispensed its New England variety of vigorous hospitality since 1686. It has offered food and lodging concurrently with the formation of history. The White Horse Tavern in Newport, Rhode Island, has done likewise since the 1700's, but there are no overnight accommodations. In 1956, the Wayside Inn was damaged by fire, and it was two years before its battered old doors could be opened again. The Victorian additions were removed, and the Inn was returned to its old eighteenth century condition.

Henry Wadsworth Longfellow first visited there in 1850. It was familiar to stagecoach travelers on the route west of Boston who knew it as Howe's or The Red Horse. Like many a European stopover, the Inn was simply a farmhouse with a license to take in wayfarers who were put in the family bedrooms and fed simple but satisfying country food. Generations of taverns and inns were dependent on the fine cooking of the wives of the proprietor. Licensed as Howe's Place before 1692, when the poet published his "Tales of a Wayside Inn" in 1863, the roadside resort became popularly known as The Wayside Inn and so remains.

Four generations of Howe housewives went into building the reputation of the place, with controversy even in the old, old days about the best recipe for clam chowder. These American inns were the foundation of home cooking guidance, curiously enough. They bear no relation to the professional cuisine of restaurants, whose culinary art is handled by a masculine kitchen staff and its principles inherited from Europe. The inns are part of an art which

11

flowers in the home and the feminine tea-shop, with a charm apart from the *haute cuisine* of Escoffier.

Some wonderful advances in cookery are found in today's homes due to the knowledge disseminated by food writers, nutritionists and home economic executives who correlate household improvements with better food preparation. More and more dishes, previously obtainable only in restaurants, are now being prepared at home. However, in my professional opinion as a restaurateur, there will always be a need for good restaurants where patrons can dine at ease in pleasant surroundings, assured that the highly trained staff will prepare and serve a memorable meal for their dining pleasure.

A remarkable exhibition of collected works on food and drink was recently made at the Grolier Club, 47 East Sixtieth Street, New York City. We found there a valuable volume, one of two surviving works of Apicius, the gourmet who lived in the time of Augustus and Tiberius. The Roman philosopher Seneca wrote of him that Apicius spent huge sums on his table and when his fortune dwindled, he poisoned himself through fear of starvation although he was still the equivalent of a millionaire.

On display was a first edition of what is described as the first cookbook ever printed—a work by Bartolommeo dé Sacchi, better known as Platina, the "cuoco secreto" to Pope Pius V, whose cookbook is a sixteenth century treasure. It contains detailed illustrations showing cooking utensils and kitchen interiors of four hundred years ago.

London early began the publication of books on cookery. Mrs. Hannah Glasse authored "The Art of Cookery" in 1747, which became the most famous volume published in the eighteenth century, although as one critic put it: "No other treatise on cookery owes its reputation so little to merit, so much to chance."

At a display by the New York Public Library at Forty-second Street, we found a book called "Almanach des Gourmands" published in 1803, which is said to have first given gastronomy an air of intellectuality and made it a study worthy to be pursued in a library. In 1825, Brillat-Savarin published his "Physiologie du Gout" (Physiology of Taste) a classic on cooking written in a delightful style with anecdotes of his experiences in America where he fled from the French Revolution. He lived in the time of large eaters when quantities were consumed which would stagger twentieth century epicures. The day of the large eater is past, but the gastronomic road to fame has not disappeared.

Three years earlier in London was published "The Important Science of Good Living," maxims and opinions of the pseudonymous Launcelot Sturgeon, Esq., which includes one of his golden rules for women cooks: "Never get drunk until the last dish is served up."

America's first cookbook was published in 1796. This was Amelia Simmons' "American Cookery." Many volumes were produced on the subject up to Fannie Merritt Farmers' "Boston Cooking School Cook Book" of 1896. Since then a river of books has flowed from the presses which increases in volume as interest heightens in the culinary arts. What is the secret of this phenomenon? Perhaps unwittingly Joseph Conrad (1837-1924) put his finger on it when he wrote with much wisdom and clarity:

"Of all the books produced since the remote ages by human talents and industry, those only that treat of cooking are, from a moral point of view, above suspicion. The intention of every other piece of prose may be discussed and even mistrusted; but the purpose of a cookery book is one and unmistakable. Its object can conceivably be no other than to increase the happiness of mankind."

Early Americans did not wait long to establish their own customs to carry on the elegant art of dining as practiced by their European forebears. From the letters of Mrs. Samuel Harrison Smith (who was a leader in the first forty years of Washington society), we get a glimpse of dining at the White House during the term of Thomas Jefferson. Jefferson, whose gracious home at Monticello, Virginia, still expresses his good taste, brought practical as well as fanciful ideas with him to the President's house in Washington. He introduced architectural plans and also some favored domestic arrangements.

There was, for instance, in his dining room his invention for serving and removing the food without the opening and shutting of doors. This was achieved by a set of circular shelves contrived in the wall so that on touching a spring, the whole turned into the room loaded with the dishes placed by servants on the other side of the wall in the kitchen. The empty dishes were removed by the same means, being conveyed out of the room without several servants walking in and out.

When the President had guests in whom he was particularly interested and wished to enjoy an unrestricted flow of conversation, he limited the number to four. Then he had placed by each individual a service containing everything necessary to the progress of the dinner from beginning to end so as to make the attendance of servants entirely unnecessary. An individualist in social as well as political areas, the red-haired and angular Virginian believed strongly that much public and domestic discord was produced by what he called "the mutilated and misconstructed repetition of free conversation at dinner tables by those mute but not inattentive listeners."

It is related that to one of these well-planned dinners, two distinguished and well-known citizens of Philadelphia were invited, Mr. William McClure and Mr. Caleb Lowndes. Mr. McClure had just returned to the United States after travelling over a great part of Europe and after a long residence in Paris. Mr. McClure could, of course, impart a great deal of first-hand information not possible through the medium of letters. His discourse was interesting—and even brilliant—and Jefferson gave him his undivided attention, but as closely as he listened, he could scarcely hear half of what the visitor said. To put his guest at ease, host Jefferson remarked smiling: "You need not speak so low. You see we are alone and our walls have no ears." To this McClure replied: "I have so long been living in Paris where the walls *do* have ears that I have contracted this habit of speaking in an undertone." Mr. McClure then went on to describe to Jefferson the system of espionage established throughout France. Its vigilance reached the most private circles and families, among whose servants there was always at least one in the employment of the police.

The President's usual dinner parties seldom exceeded fourteen, which included himself and his secretary. His guests were carefully invited and selected with regard to their tastes, habits and suitability in all respects. Naturally his parties were more agreeable and successful than the average usually are. Jefferson disliked a party which dissolved into little knots and carried on conversations in undertones. At his table, the conversation was general. Each guest was interested in the topic discussed. Each had a chance to exercise his conversational ability. Enriched by such contributions, the conversation flowed on in a rich, animated stream. Of course, Jefferson led and directed it with discrimination and infinite tact, his purpose being to place each of his guests in a favorable light. His strategy was that thus pleased with themselves, they were in turn enabled to give pleasure to others. He was a master at detecting the withdrawn individual and, by a most undesigning manner, able to draw him into the group and make him a participator.

In her letters, Mrs. Smith recalls such an occasion at the White House. There were several distinguished guests. The conversation was eager and interesting. One gentleman who had just arrived from Europe remained silent and unnoticed. He had been abroad so long that he felt a stranger now in his own land. Mr. Jefferson cleverly led the conversation to a certain point, then turned to him and said: "To you, Mr. C. . . . , we are indebted to this benefit; no one more deserves the gratitude of his country." The previously unnoticed guest, now the cynosure of all eyes, was as much surprised as everyone else. Smilingly Mr. Jefferson continued: "Yes, sir, the upland rice which you sent from Algiers and which thus far succeeds, will, when generally adopted by the planters, prove an inestimable blessing to our Southern States." The point was made just as the steaming bowls of rice arrived at the table to accompany the great platters of roast chicken. True to Jefferson's purpose, the previous nonentity became a person of importance and began to converse freely on a matter with which he was intimately familiar. In this way, an early president pin-pointed the most important ingredients to successful dining—guided and intelligent conversation—which he indicated should be mastered for social grace.

CHAPTER

The Master Gastronomer

*"The pleasant talk of the dinner table promotes diges-
tion and prevents the mind from dwelling on the
grinding of the digestive mill that is going on within
us. The satisfaction and repose that follow a full meal
tend to check a disposition to splenetic argument or
too much zeal in supporting an opinion while the
freedom and abandon of the intercourse kept up is
eminently conducive to the feelings of general be-
nevolence."*
—WILLIAM JERDAN (1782-1869)

GREAT PROGRESS IN THE CULINARY ARTS HAS
been made in New York, and other major cities of this country,
since 1910, the year Nino Malnati brought his talents and genius to
America. Without his inspired leadership, New York City would not
today hold its enviable position as the restaurant capital of the world.

Malnati had been made a Commendatore and a Cavaliero by the
late King Vittorio Emanuel III. The great European hotels and
their dining rooms were familiarly known to him. He had served
the late King Umberto of Italy and his predecessor, King Alfonso
of Spain, the King of the Belgiums, the royalty of France, Germany
and England. King George V was a devotee of this great Italian.
Malnati was decorated by most of the crowned heads of the Continent. He had studied in Berlin and Switzerland. He gained a well-
deserved reputation in Paris, and at the Cafe de Paris in Monte

Carlo when it was the ultimate in elegance. No guest was allowed in the dining room unless attired in full dress.

At the turn of the century, the social elite of New York wined and dined at the Knickerbocker, and at Delmonico's or Sherry's, just a few blocks away on Fifth Avenue. It was inevitable that an enterprising American innkeeper should note the career of Malnati and try to engage his services for a New York hotel which aspired to elegance. James Regan is credited with bringing Malnati to America. Regan was the proprietor of the Knickerbocker Hotel, one of the finest and largest in the country, on Forty-second Street between Fifth and Sixth Avenues, opposite the imposing library, and he also owned the greatest number of hotels in America. Malnati began at the Knickerbocker, with an executive salary of $15,000 a year, as its Maitre d' Hotel. Such a munificent income was equal to $50,000 today.

The elegant Knickerbocker was the home of Enrico Caruso, where he occupied comfortable quarters with his young wife, Dorothy Park Benjamin, and their baby daughter Gloria. The bar of the hotel was enhanced by the painting of Old King Cole by Maxfield Parrish and it was there in the cocktail lounge where the great tenor often enjoyed a midnight brandy after his performance at the Metropolitan. When he became ill with pleurisy, which he barely survived, the great lobby was crowded with Italian laborers, businessmen and statesmen who anxiously inquired about his condition. It was from the old Knickerbocker that Caruso departed to die in Italy. We thought of it when we stood in the old circular traffic center in Naples one summer and the American Express Company's guide pointed out the singer's apartment. When news of Caruso's death reached New York City, women walked down Broadway weeping. Caruso had rebelled against the American law which refused him the pleasure of a glass of wine. To him who loved spaghetti and wines, our Prohibition regulations were sheer insanity and he frankly said so.

At that time, London was leader of the world in cuisine and service, with the Claridge Hotel and the Savoy its most fashionable hostelries. From the time of Malnati's arrival in New York, the United States gradually advanced until it outranked the British capital. To gain this eminence, Malnati trained dining room and kitchen staffs gathered from Italy, France, and other European countries.

From the Knickerbocker, Malnati went to the Biltmore, which was opened in 1914. There he served the world's leading figures, men of wealth and power, and women who were the arbiters of society. He served President Woodrow Wilson, and was in charge of arrangements when the President went to Europe, the first Chief Executive of the United States to do so, to attend the League of Nations convening at Geneva, and to defend his famous Fourteen Points at the treaty-making at Versailles near Paris, where the Hall of Mirrors echoed to the deliberations of the Big Three: Woodrow Wilson, George Clemenceau, and Lloyd George. When Wilson visited Italy, a wave of affection swept over that country for America, to which many were emigrating. As a young man in Torino at the time, I shared in the excitement of Wilson's visit, and vividly remember seeing pictures of the American president tacked up in many homes.

Malnati, in his own field, was a leader of society's struggle against low standards, ineptitude, and lack of social grace. His life was devoted to bringing intelligence and order into the realm of elegant entertainment which to him was important in the advance of man's social development.

The Biltmore remained under the guiding hand of Nino Malnati until his death in the late Thirties. It was there that I received my first training in restaurateurship, first under one of his Captains and then under the Maestro himself, whom I was privileged to serve. This was not an easy road as he was a perfectionist and strict disciplinarian. Fortunately, I had the intuition to recognize my opportunity when it came and it was the turning point in my life. Malnati had reason to be proud. He had seen the hotel in its glorious years followed by the disaster of Prohibition, which robbed it of its soul. He, too, suffered the tragedy of serving fine foods without the natural accompaniment of wines to add an atmosphere of conviviality and eclat.

Congress passed Prohibition over the veto of President Wilson. The era after the War was one of prosperity with people spending for jewels and automobiles. Yet, something was wrong, there was the post-war moral let-down. Skirts became shorter, youngsters drank illegal gin; there were payroll robberies and flappers. The cost of living was high. Eggs were $1 a dozen. Maids received $15 a week. Divorce was up 50% and hundreds of persons died of poisoned whisky. Some knew that Prohibition was on the way. Some 30,000 barrels of excellent whisky valued by experts at $70 million was shipped abroad after being held in Kentucky and Pennsylvania for export to save it.

The terror of the raids by federal agents began in New York City in January of 1920. A government man went into Jack Dunston's famous old restaurant on Sixth Avenue at Forty-third Street and asked for a drink. He received one. Then he asked for half a pint of whisky, received it, and thereupon the agent arrested the waiter who had served him as well as the captain and carted them off to jail. This high-handed action of the government was vociferously resented because Jack's place was anything but a vicious resort. The owner, Mr. Dunston, was a prominent and respected citizen. The raid forced him out of business. Dinty Moore's on West Forty-sixth Street was raided in the same manner without finesse or common sense. Proprietor James Moore always took pride in his service of food for which he charged high prices. He was periodically annoyed for years and part of his place was padlocked. In 1922, the papers heralded a raid at Dunston's when $100,000 worth of liquor was taken from an upstairs room. As the raids continued, the customers became incensed when they were rudely disturbed in their dining. At Peter's Blue Hour on West Forty-eighth Street, the patrons threw chairs, hard rolls and spaghetti at the federal agents.

The restrictions of Prohibition were closely followed by the Great Depression, when hotels became indebted to banks and had to try everything to show a profit. The Biltmore opened its doors to the crowds of Broadway, lowering prices to increase volume. Malnati was grieved to witness this pandering to popular taste, and fought valiantly to hold on to some semblance of the old glories. When the management signed contracts with name bands as an enticement to merrymakers, Malnati bitterly voiced his opposition. "We need the revenue," he was firmly advised. "We cannot pay bills on elegance alone."

So it was that Paul Whiteman and his orchestra invaded the Biltmore. A platform was built for the large band which introduced jazz rhythms for dancing. Silenced forever were the soft violins of the Biltmore's splendid era. Malnati was saddened by the changes wrought, but remained loyal to the Biltmore until his death. Thus Prohibition and the Depression marked the end of a distinguished career.

During his lifetime, Malnati had the satisfaction of seeing the rise of the new Waldorf, the success of the Ritz Carlton, the old Plaza, the St. Regis, and the construction of the Pierre, the most recent of the great hotels built in his time. Through his wide acquaintance, he was able to secure the finest French chefs from Europe. His kitchens at the Biltmore were staffed with 500 employees, serving seven days a week, with 500 more on duty in the many dining rooms and on room service. Before the new Waldorf-Astoria came to Park Avenue, the Commodore and the Biltmore were the two largest hotels, capable of serving 2,000 persons at a banquet.

Surely in the annals of gastronomy such a dedicated teacher as Malnati deserves prominence. And in these pages, I shall record some of the precepts he taught, which have been the foundation of whatever success I may have gained in this interesting and complex endeavor. The principles learned from Malnati I have, in turn, taught to younger men, enabling many of them to graduate from the performance of service to ownership of their own restaurants, or to the management of hotel dining rooms. As with Malnati, this has been the most rewarding result of my years in the culinary field.

Dining Room Staff Etiquette

"There is not a person we employ who does not, like ourselves, desire recognition, praise, gentleness, forbearance, patience."
—HENRY WARD BEECHER (1813-1887)

THE KEY POSITION IN THE DINING ROOM IS held by the headwaiter or maitre d'. He is expected to be constantly at the door to greet guests, by name, if possible. This gracious gesture requires a phenomenal memory. He designates the table where diners are to be seated, if they have not reserved in advance. A French restaurant traditionally prefers its clientele to make reservations. An assistant or captain takes a party to the table, while the maitre d' remains at the door. While this is proper procedure, it is most difficult to maintain in practice. The headwaiter becomes interested in the service, or his attention is distracted, and in that moment the post at the door is left unattended. An important patron may find no one to receive him, or a party may arrive and, instead of the customary warm welcome, be forced to await a few moments for the attention of the maitre d' who has his reservation, or who can designate where he is to be seated.

However, when the room is filled and it is past the usual hour when people arrive for luncheon or dinner, then the headwaiter, designating an assistant to watch the door, may leave his post and move around the tables to pay a compliment here, to inquire if everything is satisfactory there, and if the diners are enjoying their meals. The maitre d' is responsible for the smooth, unobtrusive operation of the dining room staff. He hires the captains, waiters and busboys, and keeps an alert eye on all of them to make certain that they properly perform the duties to which they have been delegated. The well-trained and truly dedicated maitre d' may be likened to the conductor of a symphony orchestra. And he must be constantly on guard to avoid having one of his "instrumentalists" play a false note.

There have been a number of headwaiters in New York of international renown. Prominent among them was Theodore Titzi who, from 1910 for a quarter-century, was in charge at the Plaza and then of the Ritz Carlton. Another maitre d' of note was Paul Boyardi of the elegant old Plaza. At the insistence of his brother—the well known Chef Boyardi—Paul relinquished the never-ending responsibilities of the dining room, and they went into the food manufacturing business together, their company having long since become highly successful. And, too, there was Henry Solinyak, headwaiter at the Biltmore, who retired in 1930 with a reputed wealth of half a million dollars, a considerable fortune at that time. I worked with him, and consider him one of the greatest in our profession. Finally, there was Oscar of the Waldorf who was prominently identified with that famous hostelry for many years.

Since the dawn of formal dining, seating has been a constant problem at the table. Different countries observe a variety of seating arrangements. However, the intent is always the same. In being seated, a person is shown the honor which is due him, and also the exact measure of respect to which he is entitled in the opinion of the arbiter who judges the relative degree of his importance. The head of the table has long been assigned to the master of the house, or the one in authority. It is said that King Arthur designed the Round Table to avoid showing any preference among his beloved followers. In Old England, too, whether one was seated "above or below the salt" was an indication of esteem or the class of society to which one belonged.

It is the responsibility of the host to indicate the seating desired, whether at home or in a restaurant. However, the location of the table in a public dining room is within the jurisdiction of the headwaiter.

He decides where persons will be seated to the best advantage of themselves and the house. This requires an uncanny ability on his part to avoid any offense. When a single diner arrives at a restaurant, it is proper to make him feel most welcome. He should not be shoved somewhere in a corner to dine as a social outcast. He should be seated near other people where he will not feel lonely or conspicuous. Two unescorted women should be warmly received and made to feel as important as the other patrons. They may be slightly sensitive in having to dine without escorts, but that uncomfortable feeling can be quickly dissipated by the proper treatment and their dining made most enjoyable.

Usually a restaurant has a certain section in which important people are seated, with another section for the general dining public. However, the separation must be tactful so that patrons do not feel they are being shunted around unceremoniously. It is said that the "21" Club owes much of its success to its finesse in properly seating its clients. The late Jack Kriendler of "21" had not been trained in the field as a restaurateur, yet with native talent and tact, he became one of the most admired hosts of our time. And also my good friend Charlie Berns, one of the founders of "21," is truly one of the most beloved hosts of the world.

This accolade also applies to Ernest Cerruti of the Colony, who worked under Malnati in England, and was with him as well at the Knickerbocker Hotel. Cerruti went on to open the Colony, which in his lifetime was recognized as one of the world's greatest restaurants. His education in the field had been well rounded, and he proved himself a true pupil and follower of Malnati. Since it was against all tradition, it was remarkable that Jack Kriendler should, without restaurant training, achieve so much. Thus he genuinely deserves an accolade for his mastery in the dining room.

It is poor judgment, when receiving a party of executives from out of town, obviously intent on having a good time in New York, to seat them next to persons who wear their dignity heavily and desire to dine in quiet solitude. The visitors want to relax, enjoy the free and easy banter of male companionship, have a few drinks, and perhaps be a little loud. There is nothing wrong about this at all, and it is up to the headwaiter to recognize at once that they want fun with their food. He must know this by sure instinct and long experience. Such a group should be welcomed and seated with the proper attention at a table where they may enjoy privacy to the fullest without disturbing others. A maitre d' is often rewarded for his discretion in the delicate matter of seating each party so that they will enjoy themselves without intruding upon the pleasure of others.

The first step in proper dining room service begins when the client enters the door of an establishment. As he checks his coat or briefcase he receives his first impression of the service. How the receptionist takes care of these seemingly minor details, her attitude and expression are most important. A good receptionist is a definite asset to a restaurant. As the client enters, he should be greeted courteously and —if personally known—warmly, by the maitre d' or host in charge. At that precise moment, he is like a welcome guest in your home. He has come to enjoy your hospitality: the cuisine, the attentions of your staff, the results of all of your painstaking efforts in his behalf. If he is allowed to wait unattended, to look around, he receives the first vague chill of uncertainty. From that moment of neglect, he begins to wonder if this place, after all, will make his visit to your establishment a pleasant memory. However, if he is graciously greeted—by name, if he is known—he is at once put at ease, and thereafter receptive to all further attentions.

When a party is escorted to a table and made comfortable, the captain immediately presents the menus. The guests may linger over them and discuss the various dishes as long as they wish. At this point, however, the captain delicately inquires if an aperitif or a cocktail is desired, but he never insists. Further, he will not suggest certain selections unless the party requests his assistance. Should a captain take the lead in recommending a dish, the diner may be secretly disappointed and feel that he has been served contrary to his own wishes, which leaves him doubtful about his own proper conduct. This is not the patron's fault but that of an inept and poorly trained captain.

The captain should be ready to explain any dish on the menu which is inquired about. He must try to have the diner appear to make the choice himself. Thus the captain begins by saying: "Would you wish something in the line of beef, fish, veal, fowl or game?" This immediately gives the hesitant patron a choice among the main entres. Then the captain—once the diner has expressed himself in favor of a certain classification—can concentrate on the finest in that category to please the palate of the guest.

I have often wondered, as I saw this rule violated even in good places, why a captain will insist on, let us say, fish, when the patron perhaps prefers beef, or suggesting beef when the diner perhaps has veal on his mind. The captains at the Richelieu are always carefully instructed on this important line of questioning to determine the patron's exact wishes. I consider this a most important part of their initial training. Often a guest will say, "What do you suggest?" though he has already made up his mind and is just checking on what the house can offer, or perhaps he is not concentrating on his dinner. The seasoned captain will proceed cautiously by always asking the patron's permission before replying to be doubly sure that he will be more than satisfied with his meal, and with the impeccable service and attention he receives. It is impossible to be too meticulous about these matters, for a restaurant's reputation and success depend not alone upon good food, but also on the occasional diners who become regular patrons, and heartily recommend it to others.

Brillat-Savarin, the famous gastronome, wrote that "An animal swallows its food; a man eats it, but only a man of intelligence knows how to dine." And, may I add, he expects a man of intelligence to serve him.

To please a distinguished clientele of Very Important People is a constant challenge to a restaurant. This type of clientele has been everywhere in America and abroad. Many have been reared in an atmosphere of affluence, graduated from finishing schools, fine academies, and Ivy League colleges, polishing off their education abroad at the great foreign universities. Many have become familiar with good wines and foods. Some have even attained the stature of gourmets. This word, by the way, is often loosely used. It is a French term for one who takes a refined and critical pleasure in good cooking and the delights of the table. Sometimes people, who can afford to eat at good restaurants, have the intestinal fortitude to consume great quantities of expensive foods and wines and so think of themselves as gourmets. Actually they are gourmands, which is far from being a connoisseur of fine viands.

Those who are hard to please have certain qualities in common: they are authoritative; they know what they want, and when they have received it. All of them are very demanding and sometimes difficult. With them, price is never a consideration. It is the cuisine, the ritual, the proper performance by the staff, the ability of the establishment to extend itself in knowledge and service. This class of patronage is always a problem. Very often only the owner-host can meet their demands. If he succeeds in satisfying them, it is a memorable achievement of tremendous satisfaction to the establishment. But one must still be alert on the second visit and even on the third. By then, complete confidence has usually been established. The victory is a happy one for both guest and host.

One day a very imposing gentleman came in and selected a table which he wanted reserved for the following day at one o'clock. Unfortunately, by one of those unaccountable slips, the captain forgot to report the reservation to the headwaiter or myself. As a consequence, when the client appeared at the appointed hour, the table he had chosen was already occupied. The gentleman, in his seventies, one of the elegantes of the old era, came up to me and announced with an arrogant air: "This will be my first and last visit to your place. I had heard a great deal about it, but I want you to know that I am completely disillusioned."

There was nothing to do but humbly ask him to excuse the error and ask forebearance since I was dealing with human beings and such regrettable mishaps do occur. I assured him it would not happen again. However, the man was adamant, would not listen, and said most emphatically that the only reason he would remain was because he had made an appointment with two prominent men, one from Chicago and another of New York. I promised him an even better table than he had previously selected and said that I would take care of his party personally. But this assurance did not convince him at all. When his guests arrived, I seated them in a quiet place and took personal charge of their order. They asked for suggestions, which I offered; and after my recommended beef dish was served, I politely inquired if they were enjoying it.

The gentleman's two guests were so impressed with the food and the service, that they gave me their business cards and indicated they wanted to be recognized when they came again. Still their host did not capitulate. In fact, he spoke to me privately and quietly warned: "Remember, you have competition." However, after serving the dessert and coffee, he, too, had to concede that everything was perfection. After the luncheon, he came to me to arrange privately for payment of the check. I was delightfully surprised when he said: "I have never reneged on a million-dollar deal, but today you have convinced not only my friends, but me as well—here is my card." This surmounting of a difficult situation, requiring the most delicate diplomacy, is a frequent occurrence in the life of a restaurateur. Such little victories are the source of much personal satisfaction.

It sometimes transpires that an owner has to cope with a guest who is a behavior problem. One evening there was a man at the bar who began to sing an operatic aria. He was in a very gay mood, and had a good voice. If he were at the Asti Restaurant, they would have been delighted with his performance. For my part, I could not allow it, as other guests would not welcome the intrusion on their privacy. I explained to him carefully: "We would not like to pay for your performance as this is not the Metropolitan Opera House, and here we prefer to dine in peace and quiet." It was said graciously, and the client was not offended. As a matter of fact, he took my well-meant caution in good grace and didn't even hum thereafter. My inviolate rule in such cases is to treat a gentleman as a gentleman, even when he is not acting like one. In that way, there's no harm done, and our respect for each other is maintained.

There are certain commandments one tries to follow as a matter of good business practice. A client is the most important person to any business. He is not an interruption of our work—he is the purpose for it. He is always part of our business—not an outsider. He is not a cold statistic on the accountant's sheets—he is flesh and blood, a human being with feelings and emotions like our own. He is not someone with whom to argue or match wits. He is an individual who presents us with his personal desires or needs. It is our job to fulfill them. A patron is deserving of the most courteous and attentive treatment we can give him for he is the life blood of our business.

This is especially true in a business such as the sale of hospitality, which is a service industry. No product is created of lasting value, for it is immediately consumed. It is, therefore, something of the spirit which must be imparted. It may be termed the "atmosphere" or "personality" of a restaurant. While the restaurateur has an obligation to the client, he, on his part, also has his obligation as to behavior, appreciation, respect for staff and property, and the non-abuse of extended privileges—otherwise, if he defaults, he becomes an unwelcome guest, a burden instead of a pleasure.

In the well-staffed dining room, a captain generally is in charge of two waiters and one busboy to take care of five tables. This constitutes good service. The captain assists the patron in making a choice and writes the order, which he turns over to the waiter, following through to make sure it is properly executed. Very often the captain, although giving the order to the waiter as usual, personally checks that it is actually carried out as desired from the kitchen. Proper supervision by a captain insures quiet service with dignity throughout the meal. While the captain has no authority to fire a waiter, if he is displeased he can report to the headwaiter. If a situation arises in which the captain can no longer work harmoniously with a waiter, the headwaiter must determine where the fault lies. If there has been a disagreement, the headwaiter can place the man under another captain. When a diner makes a complaint, the captain tries to rectify it and provide the service required. If the patron is still dissatisfied, and the captain cannot placate him, then the headwaiter is brought to the table.

A waiter is under a captain, and his duties are to take the order to the chef, be alert as to timing, and to bring the order promptly to the table. He is attentive to the guest, seeing that the tablecloth is kept clear of crumbs and, if an accident occurs with food, water or wine, he corrects it quietly with a fresh cloth. Before the dining room is open, the waiter on the morning watch sets the tables, arranges chairs and brings the table flowers. He checks the *mise en place* (service

28

table) and replenishes it, when necessary, with sauces, sugar, salt and pepper, English mustard, paprika and other condiments.

The waiter sets the table according to the code of the house. There are certain regulations of proper setting which, if faithfully observed, give a table an impressive appearance. It is really a matter of plane geometry to achieve the difference between a mediocre table setting and true craftsmanship. First, in unfolding a fresh cloth, the crease should run exactly across the center of the table. A regular setting comprises a showplate, two forks, a steel knife, soup spoon and butter knife to achieve an artistic effect. There are many first-class restaurants that believe in setting a table with only one knife and fork to begin with and I fully disagree with this. The setting should be as follows: the showplate is placed approximately an inch from the edge of the table. The fork nearest the plate should be an inch from the edge of the table, the next fork should be half an inch higher; to the right of the plate and an inch from the edge of the table should be the steel knife, the soup spoon should be close in line but raised a quarter inch and the butter knife another quarter inch higher than the soup spoon. This given a harmonious setting.

A very elegant part of table service used by the most famous restaurants in England and in this country many years ago, but no longer in practice anywhere that I have seen, is the use of the butter chip. The silver butter chip, round or square approximately two inches, is placed right above the butter knife. The little bread plate is then to the left of the showplate. The bread and butter in this way remain neat. The butter chip gives an easier performance for the diner and is truly elite.

The busboy must be on the alert at all times. As a patron is seated, he brings bread and butter, water, celery and olives and stands ready to serve more water the instant the diner empties the glass. He also replenishes the bread and butter when needed. The waiter removes the dishes to the service table, and the busboy carries them to the kitchen. A busboy should be observant and learn the service so that he may advance himself and become a waiter. This is really a prospective waiter's training period. During the morning watch, and after luncheon, the busboys help to vacuum and clean up the dining room. From such menial yet important work have many fine waiters, and even maitre d's, risen. While a restaurant staff operates on a strict caste system, anyone, however lowly, can, if he is intelligent, ambitious, and devoted to duty, work himself up to the highest position.

The operation of a restaurant requires tight control of all of the many activities, however insignificant they may seem. Just one careless slip in service by a busboy or waiter may result in the loss of thousands of dollars in patronage. The manager must know the exact duties of each employee, and make certain that they are carried out to perfection. He "sees all and knows all." He must also constantly plan for the future development and expansion of the business. No business can stand still, especially the restaurant trade, where patronage may come and go inexplicably, like the vagaries of the wind. The large percentage of failures in this field is invariably due to the lack of thoroughly understanding the many facets of a highly complicated business.

The manager—or owner-manager—holds the key position and is wholly responsible for the success or failure of the establishment. He delegates important responsibilities to the maitre d', whose principal concern is overseeing the operation of the dining room, and to the executive chef, who is in charge of the kitchen. Nevertheless, should the restaurant fail, the blame rests entirely upon his own shoulders.

The manager must know the merchandise which is bought, prepared and sold, and that the proper percentages of cost are being maintained. He must know food market conditions, understand the handling of clientele in the dining room, and supervise finance, promotion and advertising. He must be thoroughly familiar with the many government regulations on health, sanitation, licenses, taxes, and the many forms which the food business, in particular, must fill out in these days of close regulation and taxes on everything in our age of enterprise.

It is necessary to hire workers with a sense of loyalty, responsibility, maturity, interest in their work plus willingness to learn and the ambition to advance within the organization. One might well point out that such personnel are too costly and not to be found anywhere. Yet these qualities are not rare and it often depends upon the employer how well they are developed. Even indifferent workers can be trained and supervised into becoming top-quality employees. The criticism leveled at the errors of employees should often be laid on the desk of management.

Careful supervision, thorough training, and the willingness to delegate responsibility where merited, usually evoke response from even seemingly indifferent employees. The manager cannot coerce but he can lead. Personnel respect authority when it is based on discipline, long training, and experience. They expect the manager to know what he is talking about before they will faithfully follow his leadership.

The manager must merit the respect he receives. He must be on the job, and have his presence felt as unsupervised employees fall into negligent habits. In the restaurant business especially, firm leadership is requisite because literally thousands of details must be quickly taken care of, and an atmosphere of cooperation and friendly hospitality must always be maintained. At the heart of the organization, defeatism will spread throughout unless buying is shrewd yet honest, merchandise on delivery is checked, high standards of cleanliness and service are maintained, and excessive spoilage and breakage is controlled. While the job of management never ends, it has its rewards. Its presence is felt, and other establishments look upon its success with envy, often trying to entice its personnel away. However, the manager who has won the respect of his staff has little fear of competition. Knowing humanity, as he must, he is assured of their loyalty.

The most stimulating hours of the owner-host of a restaurant are those when business is at its peak. This is the harvest toward which all the careful planning and nurturing have been directed. This is when all of the parts fall into place and the show goes on. The owner or manager gives orders to the captains, greets guests, recommends wines, sees that each key person oversees the activity of his own group of employees. His knowledge, experience, and energy have welded his employees into an integrated team. He is everywhere at once—in the dining room, in the kitchen conferring with the executive chef, keeps an eye on the refrigerators, the wine cellar and on his staff, their appearance and behavior. The patron is unaware of this beehive of activity and only senses that his dining is a delightful experience, the service smooth and faultless, the visit a memorable one.

Today's public has become more conscious than ever before of the fine art of dining. The food writers across the nation, the syndicated columnists who tell the history and legends of foods, give recipes, write of varied cuisines and interesting restaurants, have aroused a tremendous interest in gastronomy. Magazines carry colored illustrations of enticing, well-prepared dishes. There is a greater understanding of nutrition and the effect of foods on the body and on good health. The science of geriatrics has advanced and the effects of nutrition on the aged has reached such importance that national conventions are held annually. Homes for the aged benefit greatly in knowledge of feeding of guests to make the autumn years ones of greater strength and happiness, as we are informed by Mother Bernadette de Lourdes of the Order of Carmel, Mother Superior of St. Joseph's Manor at Trumbull, Connecticut who has been devoted to this field for the past twenty-five years. I have found over the years that people have become more interested in the kitchens of a restaurant, often requesting to be conducted through them. They express amazement at the intricacies of preparing and serving even the simplest meal.

Entertaining guests at a restaurant is a delicate affair requiring finesse on the part of the host or hostess. In the past, fine restaurants drew most of their patronage from the "Four Hundred" of society, the professions, and the arts. Now, however, prosperous times have made it possible for many others to enjoy distinctive dining in well conducted restaurants, and they are welcomed. While the reasonable restaurateur does not expect all of his clientele to be gourmets, they should have some acquaintance with the ordering of food and the selection of wines and spirits. If they do not, they shouldn't hesitate but should express their desires and the staff will be most happy to advise them.

There is a knack in ordering in a restaurant which reveals the experienced host. Fundamentally, the host should always offer the most he can to his guests. He should not repeatedly question his guests about the appetizer they desire. Some actually do not know; others may think of the cost involved and be reticent. The host should order what he thinks is best and what his guests might enjoy to begin the dinner. Guests are also hesitant in the matter of cocktails and it is up to the host to determine *what* would be pleasing. He does not inquire *if* they wish a cocktail. He asks if they prefer an aperitif or a certain kind of cocktail.

The same holds true for wine. If a host asks pointedly whether his guests wish wine, they may decline because of the cost, and thus the opportunity passes to make the dinner a truly elegant occasion. The proper host suggests a variety of wine and, if he receives no response, proceeds to order what may prove pleasing with the meal. The host also does not neglect to order an elaborate dessert. This will be the crowning touch of the evening. He may order *Crepe Suzettes* for the pleasure the captain's showmanship affords, or a delicately prepared *Soufflé*. The dramatic climax of a dinner is often Baked Alaska, arriving Flambeéd.

Tradition has always lent its radiance to a place, being the culmination of the lives of many individuals who have given of themselves. One cannot rely, however, on age alone to keep an institution foremost in the roster of restaurants. Like a person, it is a living character. It either retreats, maintains its status quo, or goes forward. Tradition must be respected and standards constantly kept high. Being in business a number of years exposes a place to many hazards. Décor must be maintained or improved, furnishings replaced as well as tableware. Often major interior changes (which effect its physical aspect) and changes in personnel for better service, will transform a restaurant. That roving connoisseur of good food and fine wines, Robert W. Dana of the N. Y. *World Telegram and Sun,* has seen many places develop over the years. "The coming of age of a restaurant is a fascinating thing to note," he has told us, "like fine wines, many take several years to mature. Others have a short and lively span; then they are gone." Some French restaurants which begin as humble bistros gradually shed their adolescence and grow into an elegant maturity.

Some clients of the Richelieu are charter members. They have watched its progress on Fifty-first Street (just west of Fifth Avenue) from the modest place it occupied in an old brownstone step-down in the early Thirties. The cozy booths there were colorfully painted on black backgrounds by an itinerant Italian artist who knew exactly what he was doing. The Chateau Richelieu had originally been named by an erudite Austrian doctor familiar with his French history and literature. It was most fitting that the story of how the crafty Cardinal Richelieu plotted against King Louis XIII should become a subject for the genius of Alexander Dumas; he had an enormous zest for life and was an expert on culinary matters, all of his voluminous novels overflowing with references to his pet subject. Our artist friend had covered the booths with scenes from Dumas and there was an especially colorful one of the Three Musketeers who, headed by their leader, the dashing D'Artagnan, defended the monarch against the schemes of the Cardinal. For some years the well-fed trio—Athos, Porthos and Aramis—inspired our patrons to eat heartily, and lent an air of Parisian enchantment to the little place.

Thomas Wolfe, the lumbering literary giant, used to come to our place at 11 and 13 West Fifty-first Street and there he would work on some of his wonderful novels like "Look Homeward, Angel" and "Of Time and the River." He would sit over in a corner; never bother anybody and would drink ten or twelve Cointreaus. He loved spaghetti and we used to make it especially for him. He paid his checks all of the time; there was very little charging in those days. Then he would carefully assemble his papers, put them in his briefcase and take the subway to Brooklyn where he lived.

After this place gave way to the Esso building, our larger restaurant was built to specification in 1940, located closer to Sixth Avenue. This was at the beginning of World War II. The little lobby was dominated by the large full-length portrait of Cardinal Richelieu with the murals in the dining room elegantly reminiscent of the French court of his era. Over the Vernon MacFarlane interior was the blessing of a gold-leaf ceiling which eventually had to capitulate to the commonplace of an acoustical installment to absorb sound. Many attachments and friendships were initiated there.

The names of the renowned are legion. There were some intellectual giants such as Keats Speed, the white-haired newspaperman with the old New York Sun, the late Arde Bulova, the watch king, and many from the arts. Charles Laughton was interested in great quantities of good food which he consumed with relish. Fredric March liked simple food and favored steaks when appearing in the Eugene O'Neill

John Malnati (May 29, 1869—October 5, 1938), to whom this book is dedicated, was born in Milan, Italy. Known to his friends and associates as Nino and, sometimes, Jean, he was decorated by most of the crowned heads of Europe. This picture shows him at 35 years of age, when he was maître d' at Cafe de Paris of Monaco.

P. Auguste Escoffier (1846-1935) in the painting by J. Kaplan. The royal chef, who introduced a la carte menus, is renowned as the "Father of Modern Restaurant Service." Dignity was his trade mark. Weekdays he supervised his kitchen dressed in a black dress coat severely tailored. On Sundays, he wore the traditional Toque Blanche and a white coat.

Peter Robotti watches his Chief Patissier preparing the daily sweets. In the foreground are Baba Rum Flambé.

Buffet decorative display of pheasants, fruit and wine for An American Game Dinner served at harvest time, 1960, at Le Château Richelieu.

Photo by Edward Ozern

Le Château Richelieu

MENU

LE CONSOMME' SAINT-HUBERT

Tio Pepe Sherry

——

LA TRUITE DU RUISSEAU ARTEMIS

Bernkasteler 1957 Blue Nun Label

——

LE FAISAN AU CHAMPAGNE
Comme L'Aimait Le Cardinal Richelieu

Chateau Leoville La Cases 1953

——

LE SORBET DES CHASSEURS

Kirsch de Zoug

——

LA FEUILLANTÉE DU CAPUCIN DE LA PLAINE
Dans sa fine gelee au porto

Clos de Vougeot 1949

——

LES SUPRÊMES D'ENDIVE A LA FACON DE L'HOST
LES QUELQUES FROMAGES CHOISIS AVEC RAISONS

Corton 1953 Domaine Lequin-Roussot

——

LA SURPRISE GLACÉE DE DIANE LA CHASSERESSE
Accompagnée de ses frivolités

——

Champagne Cuvée Dom Perignon 1952

——

LA DEMI-TASSE DE MOKA

Hosts :   Peter Robotti

Ted Saucier

MASTER CHEF—RAYMOND RICHEZ

CHEF PATISSIER—Georges Cromarias

Platters handsomely decorated with pheasants in beautiful plumage with inner electrical illumination of a woodland scene with roast pheasants in a nest. Prepared for An American Game Dinner at Richelieu by Sous Chef Henri Thong and his assistants André Delitroz, Rolland Kannengiesser, Francis Laurent and Roger Peron.

Photo by Edward Ozern

From the French Pastry Shoppe of Le Chateau Richelieu, Chef Patissier Georges Cromarias fashions for An American Game Dinner: *La Surprise Glacee de Diane la Chasseresse* with decorations of roses and ribbons in pulled sugar work for which Chef Cromarias holds several prizes.

Photo by Edward Ozern

Sous Chef Henri Thong presides over hors d'oeuvres buffet display centered by caviar and Pâté Maison.

Chef Patissier Georges Cromarias puts finishing touches to his sugar eggs for the buffet's Easter display.

Photo by Edward Ozern

Cold lobster and devilled eggs.

Stuffed ham cones.

Roast chicken in chaud froid.

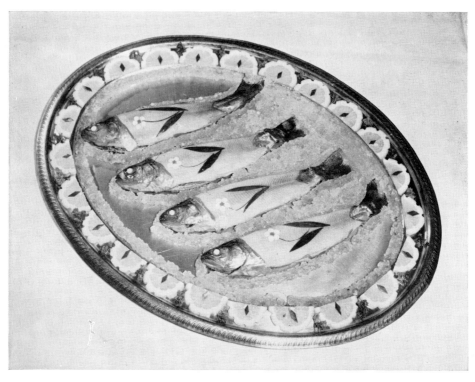

Smoked brook trout in aspic.

classic *Long Journey into Night.* Charming Mary Pickford, who speaks Italian and loves its cuisine, favors snails. Grace Kelly, cool, blonde and lovely, came into the Richelieu once or twice after we moved to 37 West Fifty-first Street and before she became the Princess of Monaco. Regular patrons included Paul Muni, Dick Powell, the late Paul Douglas, Ethel Barrymore, Michael Strange, Arthur Treacher, Desi Arnaz, William Saroyan, Irene Dunne and many other stars.

When we moved to our present address near Park Avenue, the large portrait of the Cardinal could find no space in the dining areas, so it was hung in the Wine Cellar where he presides over the wines and spirits and an occasional party of merrymakers. Some thirty years after the artist had painted his Three Musketeers for the Fifty-first Street place, they were again associated with the Café Richelieu when David Susskind, the guiding genius of Talent Associates, produced for C.B.S. Television's Family Classics (November 30, 1960) the old story of sword play, brave men and glamorous women. Vincent Price, perfect for the part, played the wily Cardinal. He came to dinner several times "in order," he said, "to absorb the atmosphere of French court days" in the present-day *maison* of the long dead statesman.

Many of our patrons have watched Fifty-first Street, from Fifth to Sixth Avenues, lose its character as restaurant row while place after place was reduced to rubble by bulldozers and dynamiters: The Golden Horn, Toots Shor's, the Gloucester House, Rose—all having found new quarters elsewhere—even Hamburgher Mary, whose spirit survives in the many hamburger heavens in New York City. The street once had a small village aspect about it, even after the old brownstones it faced, in what became Radio City, were torn down. Every trace of friendly hospitality eventually gave way to the severe facades of the banking houses facing Rockefeller Center.

There used to be a police officer, I recall, famous on the force for his great size and good nature. Pete Matthews—Big Pete—finally went into retirement. He knew all of the restaurateurs by name, and they engaged in a reciprocal type of courtesy. He sampled their cuisines, and they felt the security of his protection. I remember my own embarrassment over his personal attention. Before the automatic traffic lights were installed at Fifty-first Street and Fifth Avenue, at St. Patrick's Cathedral, he would raise his big hand and say "Come on, Boss!" bringing traffic to a deadstop so that I might safely cross the crowded thoroughfare in recognition of his esteem. To avoid his well-meant attention, which momentarily tied up traffic, I thereafter crossed the Avenue at Fiftieth Street, a block below his station.

The last of the great brownstones to go was the Vanderbilt Mansion, on the corner of Fifty-first Street and the Avenue. One day the caretaker took us through the sprawling house with its large, high-ceilinged rooms, marble stairways, and gigantic hotel-like kitchens. On the grand piano in the Victorian drawing room with its worn, but beautiful Persian rug, were many photographs, including one of Queen Mary and King George VI. As of 1913, there were four huge homes built for the powerful Vanderbilt clan on the west side of Fifth Avenue between Fifty-first and Fifty-third Streets. The National City Bank replaced the Fifty-first Street mansion, the De Pinna store, and the Tishman Building the others. The exclusive Union Club at the north-east corner of Fifty-first Street gave way to the department store of Best and Company.

There are still people who nostalgically seek the atmosphere of the old places, and it is a challenge to the restaurateur to re-create, in a new setting, the best qualities of the older establishment. He will be successful if he adheres to the principles of true hospitality, and keeps deep-rooted faith in his ideal that fine dining is an art to be fostered and to be cherished. The transition is the most difficult period in the life of a restaurant man. While many patrons will be strangers and know nothing of the tradition of the place, they will sense it in the atmosphere surrounding the new décor. It gives the guest the feeling of experiencing genuine hospitality. While it is true that the restaurant sells food and service, hospitality is the spirit in which these functions are performed.

While the old brownstones of New York continue to be demolished and replaced with modern office buildings (which often allot ground-floor space for the sale of hospitality) certain intangibles remain in the musty archives of memory. Some places are impregnable, such as the "21" Club on West Fifty-second Street, a spreading brownstone with iron grillwork fencing, world-famous for its gracious dining and tradition, preserved by the gods of the hearth, with its deep cellars for wines, its narrow corridors and panelled walls, like a book of tales, the leaves bound in old and polished leather, sustaining a precious glow of hospitality in a continuity rare in a metropolis subject to drastic changes from year to year.

Henry Moser was moved to express his protest of change itself in these few lines (*New York Sun,* May 4, 1949)

> DEATH OF A BROWNSTONE
>
> No cry could stop the murderers from
> their task
> But I can close my eyes and I am able
> To see through Time's kaleidoscopic
> mask
> Candles and wine of France upon the
> table
> And reconstruct above each gleaming
> shoulder
> The flashing jewels and brighter flash-
> ing eyes
> One cameo focused when the night
> grows older
> To hold me there as the gay back-
> ground dies:
> Come, wreckers, ply your crowbars for
> a spell,
> A chromium dream shall rise to fill this
> space
> And then some day someone shall pause
> to tell
> A newer version of a different face.

CHAPTER

 4

The Kingdom of the Kitchen

"We may live without poetry, music and art;
We may live without conscience and live without
heart;
We may live without friends; we may live without
books;
But civilized man cannot live without cooks.
He may live without books—what is knowledge but
grieving?
He may live without hope—what is hope but de-
ceiving?
He may live without love—what is passion but pining?
But where is the man that can live without dining?"
—Edward George Bulwer-Lytton (1803-73)

THE CHEF DE CUISINE, OR EXECUTIVE CHEF, is in complete charge of the kitchens. He prepares the menus for the day, tries to have the best key men for each department in order to insure nothing is short of perfection in every type of food to be served. In a first-class restaurant which has seating for 150 or more persons, the kitchen is divided into co-ordinating departments:

Sous chef, saucier, boucher, garde manger, poissonnier, entremetier, rotisseur, potager, patissier.

Each of these men has one or more assistants according to the size of the kitchen. Under the executive chef is the sous chef, his assistant and understudy. In a very large place the boucher actually cuts up the carcass as delivered of the beef, veal and lamb. In a smaller place, a

38

boucher-garde manger performs this duty and is also in charge of fish, fowl and game. In his little shop in the restaurant, he bones the meat and cuts up the whole into parts. He cuts the meat into the portions ready for preparation for the dining room and brings them to the rotisseur, the saucier and the entremetier.

The rotisseur broils all meats, fowl, game, fish, etc. The entremetier prepares vegetables and eggs, handles orders of pasta and secures sauces from the saucier. The vegetable man prepares vegetables for the kitchen. The saucier and commis saucier (assistant) prepares in the morning and the evening all the sauces and everything which is cooked in sauce is their responsibility. In a larger place the potager prepares soups. In a smaller place the saucier and commis saucier prepare the stocks for the great stock pot and the soups. The salad man presides over the salad table and makes up fruit cups, melons, fruit juices, tomato juices, salmon, hams, prosciuto, etc., serves the ice cream and ices, and is in charge of the coffee urns, tea, milk, and prepares all ingredients for mixed salads. The oyster man opens up oysters, clams, etc. and assists the salad man.

The chef arranges his menu according to seasons, with an eye to the buffet display of seasonal offerings. He also arranges a menu suitable to the guests, whether it be a mixed party, or a party of ladies, and whether a fish or meat dinner is desired. A chef should also be familiar with the various styles of serving, whether French, English, American, Russian, for each has its own peculiarities. If a dinner is to be given for foreigners, the chef should have in readiness some of the home dishes of the guests to be honored. He must also have a feeling for color harmony. Meats and sauces of different hues should follow one another with an eye to variety.

For a banquet, the chef issues orders to trained assistants who represent the different departments of the kitchen. The leading hotels and restaurants have assistant chefs, each with a corps of helpers for creation of the sauces and preparation of the roasts, pastries and sweets. All are under the supervision of the chef and they report directly to him. The executive chef personally supervises the work of his assistants. He in his turn is directly responsible to the restaurant proprietor or manager. Sometimes he may imagine himself in complete command, not only of the kitchen, but of the whole operation. This high-and-mighty attitude inevitably leads to violent dissension and eventuates in the resignation—or discharge—of the chef. And when he leaves, he often invites favored employees to accompany him to his next undertaking. In the same way, the incoming executive chef may invite favored employees of his previous post to join him in his new position.

All of this tempest in a tea-pot or "kitchen revolution" is most disconcerting to management and may well disrupt the smooth operation of service to the clientele. Whatever battles may rage in the kitchen, it would be fatal to advise patrons that dinner will not be served because the chef walked off in high dudgeon. It is imperative, therefore, that owner or manager and chef work amicably together, "hand in hand," for the welfare and good will of the establishment.

The executive chef employs the finest staff available and sees to it that each member performs the highest type of cuisine. It is his responsibility to maintain harmony and peace among his assistants, and upon his talents of leadership depends the successful operation of the kitchen. Frequent turnover in the kitchen staff is to be avoided, and the great chef earns the respect and loyalty of a steady crew. He confers with the owner, manager or maitre d' to see what dishes are suitable to the season, and their availability and cost. He seeks to inject novelty in the department of fish or game to dress up the menu. When the chef is put in charge of purchasing—sometimes he designates another man while he is absent—he is responsible for the delivery of food or merchandise of the highest quality obtainable on the market. The manager of the restaurant usually supervises the porters to make certain that the establishment is immaculate at all times.

A good chef is a jewel in the crown of the restaurant. His soundness of personality, his sureness in leadership of his crew pervades the entire establishment with well-being. If, in addition, he is blessed with humor which takes him over the rough spots then, indeed, he is a philosophical fellow and well adjusted to the rigors of the culinary arts. Such a chef is Raymond Richez from Le Grand Véfour of Paris who now presides over the Richelieu, and has justly earned his accolade as one of the best in the profession.

The Kingdom of the Kitchen

Temperament has long been the occupational affliction of the master of the kitchen. There are many true stories about French chefs who were led to disaster by it. Monsieur Vatel, for whom the Vatel Club of New York is named, suffered from temperament. He is generally remembered because he committed suicide when the sea fish he was expecting to prepare for a great occasion failed to arrive at Chantilly on time. He simply could not face the consequent defeat involved. Then there was the saucier in France in the 1920's who became so incensed at a disparaging remark made by an unappreciative dishwasher about his sauce, he grabbed a carving knife and stabbed the wretch to death. On trial for his life and facing the guillotine, the saucier pleaded artistic temperament to such good effect, a Paris Assize Court let him off with one year imprisonment.

The chef of a royal household was held in great esteem. Very often there was reciprocal affection based on the excellence of the preparation of favored dishes unfailingly over a period of time. Such a chef was Louis Enst Ache Ude who served Louis XVI for many years. Going to London he founded a modern French school of England which influenced better cookery in his day while he was attached to the household of the Duke of York. The summer after he left the service of the Duke, he became chef at a prominent London club where word reached him of the death of his previous patron. Monsieur Ude was visibly affected by the news. "Ah, my poor Duke," he mourned, "how greatly you will miss me now where you are gone."

The *artiste* of the culinary family is the chef patissier, an assistant to the executive chef, and chef in charge of his own Pastry Department. He prepares a variety of pastries, strawberry tarts, cakes for the pastry wagon, and a supply of petits fours and after-dinner mints. On order, he devises cakes for festive occasions: birthdays, anniversaries, bon voyage, etc. The patissier also prepares a variety of soufflés.

At the request of the chef, the patissier also prepares patties for chicken a la king, shells for lobster Newburg, pastry for filet mignon Wellington, in which dish, as you know, the beef is completely wrapped in a robe of pastry and baked. He also prepares English muffins for eggs Benedictine, and the rolls and breads for luncheon and dinner. Decoration is the most important art of the pastry chef.

He receives long and careful training in the delicate sugar work of pulled sugar flowers for festive cakes and the art work on the surfaces. He also prepares beautiful little baskets woven of pastry strips and baked brown. In these are served the *pommes souffle,* the delightful little puffed pillows of potatoes. Out of a composition of sugar and flower he creates dish stands on which the petits fours and mints are served. Monsieur Georges Cromarias is the prize-winning chef who graces the Richelieu Pastry Department.

The kitchen, in truth, is the executive chef's own little kingdom. Upon his rule depends the entire welfare of the establishment. Each successful service of the luncheon or dinner period is an achievement. The whole undertaking has aptly been compared to a battle: the raw provisions are the ammunition; the staple courses are the heat of combat; the dessert is the victory or the defeat. And defeats must be rare for, especially in the restaurant business, they are very costly, and a number of them may well write "fini" to the success of a place.

The Service of Wines

> *"What stores of sentiment in that butt of raciest Sherry! What a fund of pensive thought! What suggestions for delicious remembrance! What aids to reflection in that hock of a century old! What sparkling fancies, whirling and foaming from a stout body of thought in that full and ripe champagne! What mild and serene philosophy in that burgundy, ready to shed its sunset glow on society and nature!"*
> —Sir Thomas N. Talfourd (1795-1854)

Timing is of utmost importance in the service of wines. A rich accompaniment to a fine dinner can be ruined by improper timing. Yet even in places of good repute this may occur, though it can easily be avoided by strict attention to detail. Wine should, in the first place, be ordered at the proper moment, which is early in the visit. It should always be served *before* the main course is brought to the table, thus enabling the members of the party to concentrate on the wine and to make a toast. Too often the wine is brought simultaneously with the main course which, from the view of production of the scene, creates disaster, for the guest must divide his attention between the most important dish of the dinner and the excitement accompanying the wine service. He is asked to toast or comment on the wine, and on the entree at the same time. This need not be so.

Smoothness and grace can be achieved by serving the wine by itself. The captain or sommelier gives the host a sample to try, without the disturbance of the arrival of entrees for several people to the table. Toasts are made and the party then awaits the main course. I have always made it a rigid house rule to serve wines *first,* avoiding the indignity of having this ceremonial ritual ruined by the interference of bustling captains and waiters just at the very moment the wine service is in progress.

I have often read releases from wine companies who instruct purchasers to open red wines ahead of time, allowing for "breathing time," saying that wine in contact with the air releases bouquet. There are two schools of thought on this opening of wine in advance. My father, and other vintners of Italy, whose opinions as long-time viticulturists were highly respected, never agreed with the idea of opening the wine too soon. Some chemists I know feel the same way on this question. On the other hand, there are authorities in the field who maintain that it is proper to do so. This resolves itself into a moot problem which very likely will never be settled. As for myself, I am in accord with the classic tradition and believe that there is nothing to be gained by opening red wines some time before they are to be served.

Although taste in wine is an individual matter, wine experts, wine lovers, and generations of gourmets have agreed upon, and formed into a definite pattern, the union of certain foods with a variety of wine which seems pleasant to everyone. When in doubt, serve the wines listed on the left with the foods given on the right.

White wine, light and dry	Hors d'oeuvres, oysters, fish, white meat
Dry white wine; light red wine	White meat and poultry
Red wines	Red meat, game, cheese
All wines (except sweet ones)	Pungent cheese, all cheeses
Champagne and rosé	With all foods and at all times
Madeira or full sherries Sweet white wine. Sweet or dry champagne. Sparkling burgundy, rosé. Natural sweet wines	Desserts and sweet dishes
Dry champagne, sauternes, the fine sweet and mellow wines	With fruit
Cognac, liqueurs	Coffee, espresso or after dinner

44

The Service of Wines

A French dry white wine is always acceptable when served all during a meal, as champagne and rosé sometimes are.

Red wine is drunk at "room temperature," an old term which does not mean exactly what it says. Centuries ago, when this phrase was coined (in French, *chambre*) dining rooms were much cooler than those of today. Huge rooms were heated by a great log fire, which left the atmosphere still chilly. "Room temperature" certainly does not apply to what is accepted as comfortable today in centrally heated dwellings. The right temperature for red wine is about 60° to 65° F. Regional wines may be served even a little cooler. White and rosé wines must not be too cold, but served only slightly chilled. Rosé should be around 60°; white wine 50°. Fifteen to twenty minutes in an ice bucket (well covered to the neck of the bottle with ice) brings the wine to the right temperature. Champagne and sparkling wine should be allowed twenty-five to thirty minutes to cool.

Some restaurateurs feel that white wine should have a different temperature in the wine cellar than red wine. This is a false premise because the wine cellars of Europe, which are natural caves dug out of the ground, provide the same degree for all wines. Red wine is served as it comes from the cellar. The whites and champagnes are chilled before serving, but the cellar temperature is maintained at the same degree for both red and white. Where we do not have natural caves, the room designated for the wine cellar must be maintained by air-conditioning all year around at 60° to 65°, the usual room temperature years ago. People now are accustomed to 70° in their homes, but wine's "room temperature" is fixed at the lower degree. Many establishments—especially hotels—chill white wines ahead of time in their refrigerators, which kills the wine. After twenty-four hours of such exposure, the bouquet suffers, as does the wine itself.

For centuries, tradition has prescribed certain glasses for certain wines. There are different glasses for red bordeaux, white bordeaux, red burgundy, champagne, Alsace and Anjou, as well as many others. But this custom is now held by many to be a charming conceit. It is becoming obsolete to use so many different glasses, and experts agree that there is one perfect glass for all wines which may be used by the

45

homemaker not equipped for extensive wine service. This glass is long-stemmed and tulip-shaped, with the bowl the size of a medium orange, the glass clear and thin, without ornamentation. If the quality of the glass is good: clear, simple, well suited to its purpose, it is right.

The glass usually used for burgundy or claret has a generous bowl, and a mouth which is somewhat smaller so that the wine can be swiveled around without splashing it over the rim. The purpose of the narrowing lip is to concentrate the bouquet of the wine. The Bordeaux Wine Information Bureau of Paris holds that for the real enjoyment of wine most people prefer clear, thin crystal unadorned and without cutting, so that the sparkle of light on the wine, and its true color, can be seen.

Rhine wine glasses, however, have been colored for centuries. The reason for it is that the ferrous deposits so abundant in the terrain of the Rhine Valley produced wines in that region, in either the German Rhine districts, or in Alsace or along the Moselle River, which were not clear; and to conceal this fact, the lords and masters of the Rhine Valley ordered colored glasses from Bohemia. French wines were so golden clear by comparison, that the Germans had to do something, and behind the deep ruby of the Bohemian glass the opacity of the wine did not show.

Now through new and better chemical techniques, Rhine wines are very clear, but the characteristic long-stemmed glasses have remained colored. Connoisseurs prefer even their Rhine wine glass to be clear since the first prerequisite of a fine wine glass is clarity. The second requirement is thinness. A good wine glass should be light and almost non-existent, so to say, in order not to interfere with the pure enjoyment which the real gourmet derives from viewing the beauty of the wine as he sips it slowly and appreciatively.

Size and shape are important qualities. The French master gourmets have devised a different size and shape for every type of wine or brandy. Red wines have more aroma or bouquet than white wines and are usually served in a larger glass with more area in which to move the wine and release the bouquet. A good rule to follow is: a delicate wine in a thin glass, a great wine in a large glass, one-third full.

The Service of Wines

HOW MANY SERVINGS IN A BOTTLE?
(Courtesy of the California Wine Advisory Board.)

The average serving of dinner wine or champagne is 3 to 3½ fluid ounces; of cocktail or dessert wine, 2 to 2½ ounces. The following sizes of bottles give these approximate servings:

Size	Ounces	Dinner Wine Champagne	Cocktail Dessert Wine
FIFTH (⅘ qt)	25.6	8 servings	8-12 servings
TENTH (⅘ pt)	12.8	4 "	4-6 "
SPLIT	6.4	2 "	
QUART	32	10 "	10-14 servings
PINT	16	5 "	5-7 "
½ GALLON	64	20 "	20-30 "
GALLON	128	40 "	40-60 "

There have been numerous books written on the subject of what wines should be served with various foods but, beyond the fundamental principles already given, the best guide is individual preference. Remember, there are certain people who cannot drink burgundy, others who cannot take champagne or port. It is always safest to inquire of your guests what they would like. If they say they do not mind, they will be happy with champagne. If they wish any other kind of wine, they will be specific. The psychology of this attitude is quite evident. Champagne is always expensive, so there is a natural reticence about asking for it outright. Actually, other wines may be more expensive, but since they can be less costly, as well, there is no hesitation in suggesting them.

As in other areas of human experience, there is the question of bidding for status. There are thousands of wine drinkers, points out Leon D. Adams in his *The Commonsense Book of Drinking* (David McKay Company, New York) who mistakenly consider it a mark of discriminating taste to insist that their beverage be "dry." They imagine that dryness somehow signifies fine quality. Vintners, however, know that most people like drinks that taste sweet, so they simply make their wines sweet, but label them "dry." In order to sell a rather sweet champagne to Americans, it is labeled—of all things—demi-sec or "semi-dry." Americans have an inclination toward sweets, so naturally vintners cater to their "sweet tooth."

Wine is a solace and a consolation, given to man for his happiness. To deny the pleasure of vintage is to declare oneself an economist in the fruitful expenditure of time and treasure. There is also the question of manners. When someone invites guests to a festive occasion—for which they dress and anticipate an evening of pleasure—at a restaurant or hotel where wines and liquors are served, it behooves the host to offer cocktails or wine, or both. If he is too unfamiliar with wines to make a choice from the Wine List, he can tell the captain he wishes an appropriate, moderate wine, and either approve it or ask for another. If he feels he is not affluent enough to foot the bill for such an evening, then he should not try to entertain at all in a place where food and drink go together like Omar Khayyam's bread and wine, and Shelley's poetry and love.

The Sommelier

"If a man will be sensible and one fine morning while he is lying in bed count at the tips of his fingers how many things in this life truly give him enjoyment, invariably he will find food is the first one."
—Lin Yutang
And the second—the fruit of the vine?

THE SOMMELIER IS A RELIC FROM OLDEN times. He carries around his neck a broad-linked chain with a large key to the wine cellars, and a cup, an outfit which weighs up to ten pounds. These are the symbols of the great tradition of the sommelier when, in the days of castles and kings, he was responsible for the life of his master. He carried the key on his person so that no one could gain access to the precious wine cellars and poison the wine. It was he who raised the silver cup to his own lips before his master enjoyed the pleasure of the vineyards.

At one time the sommelier was entirely responsible for the selection of wines. He knew every bottle and vintage of an establishment's cellar for it was he who purchased the stock. Therefore, he was in the best position to recommend various labels to the diners. It is now almost impossible to find a man who qualifies for this responsibility, and the situation is made more difficult because today he usually does not buy the wines, and has not interviewed the wine merchants. Thus he lacks the essential knowledge necessary to his profession.

The sommelier used to appear in the dining room proudly wearing the key, his insignia of office, indicating that here was the fount of knowledge with regard to the correct selection of wines as accompaniment to an excellent dinner. While some restaurants do maintain sommeliers and a percentage of them are well versed in their profession, very often this picturesque addition to the dining room is used for conjuring up a respected post which the sommelier of today is not truly qualified to fill. His previous eminence has been reduced to window dressing for the dining room for he has long been deprived of his most important function—that of being allowed to buy the wines, or even to interview or be interviewed as to his needs by the wine merchants. Under such circumstances, what can he do? If a diner asks any questions, he only knows the price of the wines which he quotes from the Wine List. The indication is that the higher the price, the better the wine, and that resolves the problem in a very feeble fashion, indeed.

My experience with sommeliers is that they invariably offer the client the highest priced wines. This is decidedly wrong. A life-long familiarity with wines of many countries yields unexpected rewards. This experience is not to be bought, and the sommelier who does not have it certainly does not deceive the knowing guest, gourmet or connoisseur. To them, he is just a man in costume who immediately reveals his abysmal lack of knowledge. One who knows the reputation of a wine, its vintage, its regional source, and has an instinct for it, can go down the wine list of a merchant and select quite a number of winners. For instance, he will find that there are some wonderful wines which can be sold to the patron for $6 or $7 a bottle, which are equally as good, or perhaps even better, than those priced at $12 or $15 a bottle. Often an expensive wine has only its high price tag to recommend it.

As a matter of actual fact, I have purchased cases of wine which were overlooked by other restaurateurs simply because they were priced too low, and inexperienced buyers were afraid to risk a purchase. I have found these moderately priced wines, in some instances, to be really finer than costly wines but because of insufficient knowledge, they were not made available to the dining public. Carrying out this premise, I have often purchased truly good wines at moderate prices, and have unhesitatingly recommended them at a moderate price to patrons with the authoritative assertion that they were excellent. And may I say that my judgment has been confirmed by gourmets who have received them with exclamations of delight.

Distinguished Europeans from various countries, who know the cuisines and wines of world capitals, have purchased these wines in our dining room and were amazed at their quality. Sometimes they return and inquire for these wines, and I am sorry that even more of them are not available. My policy is that when I do find a wine above the average in quality, I buy as much of the supply as possible. Diners should be cognizant of the fact that, regardless of reputation, not every wine is a hundred percent in quality from one vintage to another. Some are better than others. It is the province of nature herself. There is no monopoly on greatness by one proprietor over another in producing each year the best quality, for vineyards are subject to unstable weather conditions with more or less sunshine, winds or rain. Even a few extra hours of brilliant sunshine, or one day of overcast sky, will be reflected in the grapes, so that qualities differ from year to year.

The wine steward also purchases all liquors for the bar—spirits, brandies, whiskeys, etc. A first-class place makes sure that its Liquor Division buys only the finest type on the market of bonded bourbon, bonded rye, imported gins and Scotch. The wine steward, to please the varied tastes of the clientele, makes sure to carry representative stock. At the Richelieu, we order at least a case of anything the public demands, either native or imported. A first-class establishment should never have to refuse a request, even if it means buying only a small quantity.

The bartender is asked to make a note daily if there has been a request for any brand which the house does not have. This is turned over to the wine steward and two or three bottles are purchased. Even if it is called for only once or twice a year, this is good policy. The restaurant and bar business are highly competitive, and if a place does not have what is called for, the patron will go elsewhere, and often take his friends with him. On the other hand, lifelong confidence is gained by a properly stocked bar and wine cellar.

51

Before we leave the province of the sommelier and wine steward, we shall say something of wine-tasting. In France there is an old and honored organization known as the *Chevaliers du Tastevin* (knights of the Wine-cup) in which the wine regions are represented. Flowing robes are worn (as in the priesthood) for meetings and on the day sacred to St. Vincent, the knights march in the street attired in all of their ceremonious robes and degrees as St. Vincent is the patron saint of the vine growers and wine producers. The American wine producers follow in their footsteps in holding periodic wine-tastings, most of which are exclusive to the trade and restaurateurs. The Astor Wine and Spirits Co. (12 Astor Place, New York) have tastings to which the public is invited and interested people are admitted by writing for an invitation. According to Tom Marvel, Astor's wine consultant, and Raymond Ochacher, Astor's president, the only way to know wine is to taste wine.

The French Government's *Comité National de Propagande en faveur du vin* of Paris has issued a practical guide for the wine-butler and connoisseur, authored by William Bird, which is most revealing. We are privileged to quote the paragraphs pertaining to wine-tasting:

"When an old wine is poured into your glass, reflect for a moment what it has cost in labor and skill and devoted care to bring it to your table. Generations of wine-growers have spent their lives cultivating a vineyard and learning by long and patient experience how to produce a superlative wine. It has been watched and tended like a baby during its childhood in the barrel, and its formative years in the bottle. Now in its maturity, the moment has come for you to savor its stored-up joy. Whether you get from it all that its makers have put in, depends upon your ability to appreciate it.

"Let the glass be large, and of fine clear crystal, and let it be filled rather less than half full. If you have the good fortune to possess a set of those very large tasting glasses, which hold a pint or more, take only as much wine as will generously cover the bottom. The first of the senses to come into play is sight. Hold your wine toward the light and admire its color, its 'robe' as the French say, its gown. You will, with a little practice, be able to tell much by the appearance. If the color is deep purple or rich crimson, you will judge that it is a young wine, or else a very robust old one. If it is brilliant ruby or vermillion, conclude that it has reached its prime. If its tints have mellowed to the tones of autumn leaves, you will judge that it has passed its peak of perfection and yet, if it is a wine of great race, it will have retained most of its charm. Wines, like men, have different virtues at different ages.

"When the eye has appreciated the wine, it is the turn of the nose. But before raising the glass to your eager nostrils, impart a rotary motion to it, in order that the inner walls of the glass may be moistened. By thus creating a larger surface of evaporation, you intensify the aroma. Take several whiffs in slow succession. There is no hurry. The odor of a fine wine is extremely complex, and a single sniff will not tell you all. Scents are difficult to describe in words, but you will detect in some wines a scent approximating that of wildflowers, or of different fruits, or of honey or almonds. Other wines have a scorched smell, or may make you think of fresh hay, or ploughed fields. And several of these scents may be combined in the same wine; but they will not strike you all at once, because usually there is one that predominates and the others reveal themselves slowly.

"Take, I repeat, plenty of time to examine the aroma before you taste the wine, because although smell is not one of our keenest senses, it is one that has a long memory, and sensual memory is the connoisseur's most valued possession. And even after the eye and nose have told you all that they can tell, do not be in a hurry to drink. I assume that you are at table with other lovers of good wine, and now is a good time to exchange impressions. Discuss the color and the aroma. You will find that your companions have noted qualities which you overlooked. All this helps to sharpen your judgment and at the same time to whet your palate.

"Now comes the moment to taste the wine. Take the bowl of the glass in your palm and make sure that the wine is not cold. If it is, warm it gently between your palms for a moment. Then take a small sip and roll it around with your tongue to make sure that all the taste buds have a chance at it. Or purse your lips and draw air into the mouth through the wine, so that the fumes penetrate the head passages.

"This first taste will tell you of the wine's body, whether it is full or light, and it will confirm or upset your previous judgment as to its age and vigor. A ripe and perfect wine will be full of a rich bouquet, made up of a great complexity of tastes, which it will be hard to separate and identify. If it is too young, there may be a slightly acid or bitter savor—rough corners that a few more years in the bottle would have rounded off. If too old, the wine will have lost its power, although there may remain some lingering charm, akin to that of a historic ruin.

"When your first sip has been swallowed, there comes the after-taste, which often is a surprise. Not being an anatomist I cannot explain this phenomenon, but it is a well-known fact that some wines which seem quite undistinguished to the taste, leave a very pleasant sensation in the mouth after swallowing, while others that seem quite perfect leave an acrid after-taste which is most disagreeable.

"We cannot expect every wine we drink to be perfect. If the good qualities outnumber the defects, let us be content. But on the day we are privileged to drink a truly aristocratic wine of a great vintage, which has been properly preserved and presented, let us rejoice, because the table affords no higher pleasure."

CHAPTER

This Matter of Tipping

"A man there was, and they called him mad;
The more he gave, the more he had."
—JOHN BUNYAN (1628-88)

THE TRADITION OF TIPPING HAS BECOME SO
entrenched in our way of life that it has long passed the debating
stage. It is no longer whether to tip or not to tip. Now it is how much?
There was a good deal of grumbling before tipping reached its present
status, but it need not be considered either undesirable or a hardship.
When one plans for certain pleasures and luxuries, tipping, like taxes,
should be considered part of the cost.

As originally intended, a tip was given in gratitude for extra or
particularly efficient service, and as such gave pleasure to the tipper
and the receiver. It should always be an expression of appreciation,
and the giving should be done freely, graciously, and in good spirits.
The tip, however, remains a gratuity, and the size and frequency are
within the discretion of the tipper. Rudeness or willful neglect deserve no tip at all, and the employee who assumes that tips are guaranteed, regardless of his attitude, will soon change his tune when he
sees the diminishing returns.

On the part of the tipper, it is bad manners to tip ostentatiously.
It is embarrassing to the recipient, and unfair to others who perhaps
cannot tip so lavishly. It is also lacking in grace to complain about the
necessity of tipping when visiting an expensive restaurant, taking a

luxurious European cruise, or staying at a high-priced summer or winter resort. Either one can afford the cost, which includes tipping, or one cannot, and should stay at home.

Tipping is not confined to America alone, as stay-at-homes may naively imagine. Quite the contrary, tipping abroad is even more prevalent than in the United States, and more people in foreign countries depend on it for a major portion of their living wage. Some of the most common words one will hear abroad are the French "pur boire," and "drickspengas" in the Scandinavian languages. All literally mean "drinking money" or "for a drink." These expressions shed some light on the custom of tipping, and also serve as a guide in establishing the minimum tip that should be given in various foreign currencies. The normal tip for most minor services, such as performed by bellboys, doormen and the like, would be the least amount one could wet his whistle with.

In Spain, where the standard of living is low, two pesetas (or the equivalent of three cents) will buy a bellboy a thirst quencher. The same applies for the Portuguese escudo. However, it requires about 50 francs (or approximately 13 American cents) as the minimum for which a Frenchman could obtain refreshment at any respectable place. This holds true for 80 Italian lire, a shilling, half a mark, and half a kroner. The multi-languaged guides who tell you about the Italian countryside from a chartered bus, invariably conclude their remarks with the plea "Don't forget your guide, please, before disembarking from the bus." At the Folies Bergere in Paris, the usherette will remind you about her tip in case you have forgotten that in French theaters you tip the one who escorts you to your seat.

No discussion of dining out would be complete without considering the intricacies of tipping. A knowledge of the "Common Law of Tipping" is essential in being the perfect host. When the proper distribution of gratuities is made, the host is insured that his party does not leave dissatisfied and disappointed employees behind, which was not really intended. A host who knows his tipping is a great joy to the staff of the house he frequents.

Let us examine the tipping procedure followed at some of New York's leading restaurants. For an elaborate dinner requiring delicate attention, in which the captain performs even more than the waiter in planning and executing the service, the captain should get 7%. When a patron is a charge account and leaves the arrangement of the gratuities to the owner or manager, it is done in this manner:

1) 15% is allowed for the waiter and 5-7% for the captain, providing the service requires the captain's very close attention. The patron is not obliged to concur in this arrangement, if the distribution does not happen to be agreeable to him. In that event, the restaurateur himself contributes the captain's tip.

2) When the patron, through oversight, does not provide at least 15% of the amount of the check, the house makes up the difference, and also provides for the captain according to the service he has rendered. This policy creates harmony and good will among the staff.

3) When the patron indicates simply "gratuities of 15%," then the waiter gets it all.

4) When a patron indicates gratuities of 20%, 25%, or sometimes even 30%, the waiter gets 15%, the captain 7% and the balance is evenly split between waiter and captain.

Before World War II, 10% was customarily the regular tip. After the war, however, 15% began to be put on checks. This was ill-conceived and wrong, yet it eventually became regular practice. In view of the inflationary trend in prices for food and liquor, 10% was perfectly adequate in rewarding service, and 15% was a mistake, but it has continued ever since. The results are that the income of waiters is out of all proportion to the rest of the staff who receive no tips and the patron is penalized besides. In my decided opinion, 10% of a check should still be adequate, and 15% considered a very good tip.

This position can be clarified by a specific example. Let us say that an average dinner in a leading place was $6.00 per person. Today the price has been increased by inflation to $12. Whereas a couple used to spend $12.00, they now spend $24.00. Previously, 10% of the tab came to $1.20; 10% of today's tab comes to $2.40. Now, the customary minimum of 15% brings the tip on a dinner at $24.00 to $3.60, which means that the price of the meal has doubled, while the size of the tip has tripled. This is out of order and increases the cost of the dinner too much; 10% of $24.00 or $2.40 would be adequate and a good tip for service.

There is also the problem of the restaurateur which complicates this unhealthy practice. He would prefer to promote one of his own men to a captaincy, rather than an outsider who is not trained to the house's particular methods of operation. He finds, however, that waiters refuse his offer of promotion because of the consequent substantial loss in tips. The only answer to this situation is a large base wage for the captain, and the development of a following to reward his efforts.

To insure contentment, and place reward where it belongs, the tipping schedule should be set at 10% to the waiter, and 5% for the captain. It has become the policy of a good place and the Union to remember the captain, when he is overlooked or forgotten, by the house taking care of him. Through unfamiliarity with current practice, a client may have an exclusive party running up a bill for $100 to which he adds 15% for the waiter, but nothing for the captain, whose skill in placing and planning the order, carving and other attentions, have made the dinner a success. The captain performs more work than the waiter in the service. By adding 15%, the host thinks he has taken care of everything, but his captain is overlooked. In such a case the house will assume his tip.

With regard to the busboy, who also feels the injustice of present tipping practice, it should be noted that he used to get 10% of the total of tips made by the waiter, and he is now still getting 10%. The Union has not suggested any solution to correct this inequity. The busboy should get 15% of the take, and not 10%. An example will point up this situation. Previously, when a check came to $100, the waiter got 10%, which was $10 and of this the busboy got 10%, which is $1.00. Under today's method of distribution, the waiter, at 15%, gets $15.00, and at the going rate of 10%, the busboy gets $1.50. On the other hand, if the busboy got what he is entitled to, which is 15% of the waiter's tip, he would receive $2.25, not $1.50. His loss, therefore, on every $100 of revenue amounts to 75¢ which, by the end of the week, becomes a sizeable sum. The gain has been for the waiter alone, not for the captain or busboy, which is unjust.

In Europe, there is in practice an equitable distribution of reward which spreads good will among the staff. According to the standards of the place, the tip runs 13% to 20%, which the client divides between the waiter, the captain, the maitre d' and some to the kitchen and the bellhop. This distribution is not made by the guest, but by the establishment itself. Hotels and restaurants on the Continent, and frequently in Great Britain, add a service charge to the bill, which is theoretically supposed to cover all gratuities. However, in addition to this charge, to avoid embarrassment and insure service in the future, it is wise to add another 3% to 5%.

Many people do not approve of tipping at all, and tip under protest because it has become the accepted custom. But if it is considered as a legitimate part of the over-all cost—which it is—then there should be no objection to the practice. And as to the proper distribution of gratuities, that is a problem which management and the Union will have to work out between themselves.

CHAPTER

 8

The Delight of Desserts

"Happiness is dependent on the taste and not on things— It is by having what we like that we are made happy, not by having what others think desirable."
—DUC DE LA FRANCOIS ROCHEFOUCAULT (1830-1880)

FROM THE TIME OF THE HEAVILY LADEN tables of the ancient Romans and Greeks, as they feasted in celebration of victories in the stadium or coliseums, the display of foods has been part of the elegant banquet. Today there is more emphasis on the value of exposure. The listing on a menu does not conjure up the heavenly delights which display achieves in tempting the appetite. A luxurious restaurant can usually afford the space for display, and a pastry shop on the premises is necessary to produce it. Desserts which will bring the fine dinner to its triumphant climax are attractively arranged on a rolling table of mahogany and silver, perhaps, or on the stainless steel wagon put out by the Legion Utensil Company of New York City, which is the best available and justly famous. The company is headed by A. C. Scavullo, a pioneer in stainless steel.

When the wagon is rolled to the side of the table, the guest has the opportunity to look at the varied array and has the pleasure of making a selection of the day's offering: Floating island, a mousse, a Napoleon, a slice of strawberry-cheese tart. In season, a great silver bowl may be filled to the brim with luscious strawberries, while another bowl contains the crowning touch—zabaglione. This combination brings a light and refreshing end to a dinner, which may then be concluded with a liqueur or brandy.

Fruits may also be exposed in bowls for the guest may wish only an apple, peach or pear, accompanied by one of the cheeses offered on a napkin-covered tray. The European diner invariably finishes a meal with fresh fruit. On rare occasions, he may be induced to take sweets. Americans are finding the delight of eating a Bartlett pear with a slice of cheese. Still the American palate loves the fancy sweet dessert, takes crepes suzettes, soufflé or pastry, and lets his conscience be his guide.

The longing for fruit is a basic instinct. We know that fruits of the tree—from the time of Adam and Eve—predated civilization. Our early ancestors cultivated orchards, constantly trying to produce juicier plums and sweeter oranges. It is said that Cortez, in his explorations, carried the fig from his native Spain to the new land of Mexico. Fruits have always been the children of climates. Just as olives grow well in Greece, Italy, and in the dry valleys of California, apples receive their rosy cheeks in the frosty regions of British Columbia and Oregon. The beautiful colors of fruits have inspired the brush of artists, the glossy deep maroon of ripe cherries, a challenge to the imitator. Fruits delight several senses at a time: sight, taste, smell. Even cooked fruits served flambeéd lend excitement to the dessert, such as the old favorite, Cherries Jubilee.

What can compare with the lusciousness of a true-flavored peach? Perhaps the most difficult fruit to purchase, the peach reveals the secret of its goodness only when consumed. One cannot really judge its virtues by its exterior. The most beautifully colored and formed peach may prove a mealy disappointment. The most humble exterior may have interior flavor beyond compare. Then there is the plum. Plums go far back into history. It was in the Near East and the Orient that the first gardens were planted, they say, and perhaps there was located the legendary Garden of Eden. Since the flowers of the plum tree burst forth from bare boughs, preceding its leaves, the plum blossom became to the Chinese the symbol of immortality, and it decorates many of their cloisonné pieces.

When Europe was settled, men brought plums with them for the first orchards. The Crusaders, who returned from their travels with many novel dishes, imported the damson plum to the Western World. The plums of Damascus were justly famous. They were so fine and tasty, their name became a corruption of Damascus. During the Fifth Crusade (thirteenth century), the Duke of Anjou spent the winter in Jerusalem. When he returned to France in the Spring, he brought with him the plum of Damascus. An early gourmet, the Duke's name still lives in the Anjou wine glass.

It was natural that Europeans should bring their favorite fruit trees to America. Spanish and French missionaries, in particular, were active in planting plum trees promptly. When Petrus Stuyvesant was Governor of New Amsterdam, stomping about on his peg leg, he maintained one of the finest orchards on Manhattan Island in the Bowery. The pear tree he planted on Twelfth Street and Third Avenue lived for almost three centuries—and bore fruit. The same is true of the pear tree planted by Governor John Winthrop, who arrived to govern Massachusetts in 1630.

Nobody will deny that fruits are nature's own desserts. The difficulty is to obtain fruits which look appetizing and have taste and flavor. To purchase them properly takes the instinct of an expert, preferably one who was born to fruits. The finest adornment for home or restaurant is a great bowl with artistically arranged fruits—the pineapple, symbol of hospitality of the South Seas, pears, peaches, apples, luscious clusters of grapes, with a lime here and there to contrast and set off their colors. A Paul Revere bowl in its austere and elegant simplicity is perfect for such an arrangement, with the presentation built high. All of it speaks an invitation to the guest of abundance, grace and hospitality.

Men who were once immune to sweets, being content with fruit and cheese, are succumbing (like their fair companions) to the temptation of desserts. Desserts are now accepted by both sexes, who enjoy the exquisite morsels. Fruitcake brandied is a "must" for Yuletide holidays. Many enjoy *baba au rum,* pears in *creme de menthe,* brandied apricots, peaches and dates, without even waiting for the approach of Christmas. Festive dishes sometimes go beyond the bounds of good taste as home and restaurant chefs insist on excessive decorations. The host who serves a gondolier made out of spun sugar, a

goddess carved out of raspberry ice, or layer cakes excessively decorated with trees, ships or volcanos in eruption, violates the spirit of
the true artist, who conceives in harmony and proportion. While it
may have been in order in the ancient courts of Vienna or Paris, in
keeping with the Gargantuan banquets, such profusely decorated
pieces seem out of place in our present times. This, however, casts no
reflection on the ingenuity of the pastry artist, who creates wondrous
decorations to accompany festive fare. It is only a plea for moderation.

The extreme lengths to which our ancestors once went in fashion-
ing elaborate desserts has been graphically described by Horace Walpole, who recalled a function celebrating the birth of the Duke of
Burgundy. Walpole told of how the Intendant of Gascony "treated
the noblesse of the province with a dinner and a dessert, the latter of
which concluded with a representation by wax figures moved by
clock-work of the whole labor of the dauphiness and the happy birth
of an heir to the monarch."

Americans of an earlier era have been treated to fantastic food
shows, both in our hotels and in such establishments as Delmonico's
and Sherry's, where the emphasis on desserts produced sensational
effects involving days of labor on the part of the confectioners. Some
remember ill-fated Stanford White's great dinner in the old Madison
Square Garden roof-top restaurant on Twenty-third Street, where the
nursery rhyme about the "four and twenty blackbirds baked in a pie"
was literally revived. Two dozen beautiful American show girls
danced out on the table from under a gigantic pie crust. The famous
architect had other ideas for delighting his guests, which were unfortunately precluded by the bullet fired by Harry Thaw in defence of
the honor of Evelyn Nesbitt.

It must not be thought that a simple dessert, in appearance, that is,
is simply prepared. Great skill and knowledge must be accorded such
a concoction. Dropping a few peaches into a bowl and pouring some
brandy over them does not produce brandied peaches. The choice of
the peach and of the brandy, or both, may have been wrong. The
brandy may be so potent that it kills the flavor of the peach. The fruit
may be too ripe or too firm, too sweet, or lacking in flavor. Such things
should be left to the skilled hands of the restaurant magicians. A

hostess entertaining at home may be more certain of success if she buys brandied peaches in a jar, slices them in a chafing dish, adds a little more brandy for general flaming, and spoons the warm peaches over ice cream.

More people are now enjoying versions of the regal desserts they have tasted in a fine restaurant. At home it is possible, for that special occasion, to select a good brand of native fruit flavors like cherry, apricot or blackberry as an accompaniment to holiday mince pie or fruitcake. On the other hand, there is no substitute for the elegant elixirs, like benedictine or chartreuse, available only in the original. To please a connoisseur of cognac with a flaming dessert, it would be a mistake of judgment not to use the imported product. American whiskeys have proven their worth, however, for enhancing desserts, and should not be neglected. Both bourbon and rye are delightful for flaming plum pudding, date and fig puddings.

Liquored desserts should be attempted with caution by home chefs. It is not possible to create exemplary dishes, merely by adding liquor. Tragic errors can be made by the purely imaginative in violation of basic rules. Some desserts may have a good appearance as to color, but the flavor would be a disappointment. *A creme de violette liqueur,* suggests food writer Thomas Mario, poured on cooked Bartlett pears, produces a beautiful contrast of deep purple and creamy white, but the mixture of flavors is not a happy one. On the other hand, plum pudding can hardly be more plebeian in appearance, and yet in its ingredients and flambeéd, it is superbly delicious.

The delight of the fire ritual is in using the proper ware for the purpose: a gleaming chafing dish or a properly proportioned pan of copper. The food to be flamed should be heated and kept hot before the liquor is added. When pouring cold liquor on a hot chafing dish or hot saucepan, at least a minute should be allowed before applying the flame. When the inside of the pan is flaming, it should be kept directly over the heat. When canned fruits are used, their syrup should be largely drained off before the alcohol is added, as it dilutes the alcoholic strength of the liquor. Some liquors have more strength than others: anisette liqueur is usually bottled at 54 proof, which will not give it the fire strength needed, whereas kirsch or mirabelle are both

100 proof brandies, and green chartreuse is 110 proof—both capable of making a brisk little bonfire.

The beauty of a flaming dessert served in a restaurant is the showmanship of the captain who knows the ritual. The host at home may resort to a match to set the pan ablaze. Not so the experts who perform at their serving tables before the expectant guests, quickly moving the pan, containing the food they are heating, over the potent flame of an alcohol lamp, rotating the pan back and forth in a rocking motion so that the small spray of alcohol vapors sets the inside of the pan on fire. This takes skill, which is developed only after long practice. The spirituous desserts—including the old favorite, crepes suzette, in its elaborate orange sauce, invariably invoke admiration and arouse the spirits of the guests.

What we call ice cream—the frozen delicacy made of milk, cream, sugar and flavoring—was enjoyed by the elite of Europe before 1600. They were called mousses, parfaits, frozen custards. Early restaurateurs of New York, who had French cooks, served them, but most historical references say that Dolly Madison made ice cream popular by serving it at a White House dinner in 1809. It was the American trade fairs which gave the impetus to food manufacture. At the St. Louis Exposition in 1904, the pastry cornucopia was displayed which became the ice cream cone. Before that the "sundae," ice cream covered with a sauce, fruit, nuts was displayed at an exposition in Ithaca, New York, in 1897. Even earlier, in 1874, at the Semi-Centennial Celebration at the Franklin Institute in Philadelphia, the soda was introduced—ice cream with syrups and soda water.

The French, in particular, have always been past masters at the art of the dessert. Gastronomically, a dinner cannot be elegant or complete without dessert. The bit of sweet at the end of the repast is part of proper planning. I think too much emphasis is placed on reducing in American life. Proper nutrition and a sense of well-being include fruits and sweets. The point is to *cut down* on foods not to *cut out* sugar, for sugar is the physical basis of all life. It is the first substance manufactured by all green-leaved plants which, in turn, support all human and animal life on this planet. Through sugar, the energy of the sun is made available to man. Sugar is the solar battery which combines the miracle of sunshine, air and water. Sugar is the first source for quick energy of any of our foods. Physiological chemists say the body begins to use sugar within five minutes after it is eaten. Minerals, proteins and vitamins will not suffice alone. We need more energy to maintain proper weight and vitality. It is an obsolete notion that one must eliminate sugar to reduce. This is substantiated by Dr. Frederick J. Stare of Harvard University. Dr. Stare holds that, even though sugar contains only calories (a level teaspoonful has but 16) it is not enough to make any difference. In fact, it is just the small amount necessary to reduce one's appetite a little.

In Europe, cuisine was based on the use of beet sugar. It grew out of the experiments of a German chemist, in 1747, and was finally put to use in 1802. The French lacked the technical knowledge to make their factories work and so tried to derive sugar from grapes, by finding a grape syrup which could be used in place of the very costly cane syrup. Involved in the Napoleonic Wars, the French were cut off from their sugar supplies from the West Indies. Prices went to more than a dollar a pound. Necessity brought success to the efforts to produce sugar from beets. Napoleon signed a decree at the Palace of the Tuileries to place 79,000 acres of land to the planting of the beets. From them came the sugar needed to energize Napoleon's armies.

For his part, Napoleon loved food, and especially desserts, as only Frenchmen can create them. He would often give directions to the kitchen as to just how he wanted his dishes prepared. Records contain passages vividly depicting Napoleon's increasing bulk. As a young man he was estimated to weigh between fifty-five and sixty kilograms (121-132 pounds). In middle age, after forty, he shot up to 75 to 80 kilograms (165-175 pounds). While this was a marked increase, it was not enough to make the Emperor truly obese. He was short and of a small frame and the extra weight was evident. Some writers have blamed this on Napoleon's sweet tooth. Now it seems that this was not the reason for the emperor's weight increase. In a rather recent book called "Napoleon Immortal" published November 22, 1959, Dr. James Kemble of London gives a diagnosis of Napoleon's condition. He states that Napoleon lost an empire because he gained too much weight. However, he exonerates the sugar interests which have long been held at fault for this.

"His pituitary gland failed him prematurely" writes Dr. Kemble. It was the failure of that tiny gland which changed the events of his future years. "The lean young soldier, subject to nervous rashes and fits of rage, had become obese. His hair had thinned and his skin was smoother. His mental activity was lower. He wanted to sleep more. He did not make decisions with the same imperiousness." Apparently Napoleon was not sluggish because he ate too much. "Napoleon," holds the English physician, "suffered from Frohlich's disease which Dr. Black's Medical Dictionary defines as 'bodily changes typified by the fat boy in *The Pickwick Papers* . . . results arising from disturbed pituitary function!'"

Napoleon was always interested in food and drink. On the eve of the Battle of Marengo, he directed his kitchen in the manner he wanted his dinner prepared. Down through the years, every cookbook worthy of the name contains this famous recipe. It is interesting, therefore, to find a doctor's conclusions of the emperor's physical condition affecting the course of history. At the height of the Russian campaign, in 1812, it is known that Napoleon suffered a "mysterious malady." Meanwhile, by decrees, he had encouraged France to erect 334 small beet sugar factories in 1812 and 1813 in order to produce quick-energy for his soldiers on the march. Dr. Kemble has probed all of this period and has hazarded a diagnosis of the "malady" as acute cystitis—inflammation of the bladder, which may or may not have resulted from the eating of sweets or rich foods. In Paris, those pouring out millions of francs to support the war, bitterly criticized Napoleon for his inactivity during the campaign. Apparently, his indecisiveness was forced upon him by the sudden onset of this painful organic disease.

Napoleon finally approached the finale of his meteoric career. Waterloo came on June 18, 1815. Before his heralded downfall, the English doctor pictures the commander as fat and flabby, slow in mind and movement and exhausted by yet another complaint. Writers of France have tried to solve the enigma of Waterloo. Dr. Kemble states "it really was no enigma at all . . . it was hemorrhoids" which undid both emperor and empire. Meanwhile the beet sugar industry, born of urgent necessity, experienced its own difficulties. Waterloo not only defeated Napoleon, it crushed the industry he had created. With his defeat, the blockade was lifted and ships from the West Indies hastened to dump their cargoes of accumulated sugar, produced by slave labor, into the ports of the Continent. Prices collapsed. Struggling with primitive processing methods and raw materials of inferior quality, the industry could not hold its own. One year after Waterloo, only a single beet sugar mill—at Arras—remained in operation in France. The industry retained its adherents and soon better beets—richer in sugar—were developed. Laws were passed to equalize the conditions of competition between the producers of the Indies and those at home, which brought about its restoration. The emancipation of slaves in the West Indies finally put the sugar industry of Europe in a competitive position with tropical sugars and, by 1854, the industry was operating on a large scale.

Now, a century or so later, beet sugar is produced from the United Kingdom to Russia, from Finland to Italy, in every European country but Norway and Portugal. Today it is raised in the Near East—Turkey, Syria, Afghanistan, Iran and in the Far East—Japan, Manchuria; in the Americas, Canada, Chile and in the United States. It was not until 1897, however, that sugar beet production became successful in California.

We are indebted to Mr. W. F. McCrea of the Amalgamated Sugar Company, Ogden, Utah, for some up to the minute comments on beet sugar. We learned that nearly one-fourth of all sugar consumed in the United States comes from beets. During the three-month period at the beginning of World War II, 40% of all sugar consumed in this country came from beets. Each year, the sugar beet industry pours some half-billion dollars of new wealth into the nation's economy. The availability of sugar was vital during World War II, writes Mr. McCrea, and no one knows how indispensable it may become in this atomic age.

And what is the difference between beet and cane sugar? Mr. McCrea states emphatically that "the sugar of commerce (sucrose) is in fact all chemically alike, whether cane or beet, whether from maple trees, sorghum, watermelons, or any other plant. After long testing,

68

the United States Department of Agriculture reported that 'by no chemical test can the pure crystallized sugar from these different sources be distinguished.' " He goes on to tell us that other government chemists, as well as physicians, home economists, dieticians, and large manufacturers of canned goods, candy, bakery products, and confections have long confirmed that pure beet and pure cane sugars are identical. The beet sugar industry has come a long way since Napoleon's time. It is now available in all forms—granulated, liquid, cubes, tablets, powdered, and brown. For generations, European cooking has been based on beet sugar and the finest creations of French chefs and the best English jams and biscuits call for its use.

While sugar derived from beets is of fairly recent origin, the sugar cane predates the Christian era, being known in India and the Orient, and mentioned in the Old Testament. In Jeremiah 6:20, the prophet asks, "To what purpose cometh there to me incense from Sheba, and the sweet cane from a far country?" In Isaiah 43:24 there is the complaint—"Thou has bought me no sweet cane with money." Europe did not discover the art of crystallizing sugar until the fourth century. It was the Elizabethan period before sugar became an article of household use, being previously limited to medicinal purposes. The Arabs learned about sugar cane when they swept over Persia, brought it to the northern coast of Africa, and thence into Spain. The Crusaders found cane plantations in Tripoli, Mesopotamia, Syria, Palestine and Antioch. As we know, the Crusaders brought many new food ideas home with them. A lively trade in sugar followed between northern Europe and the seaports of the Mediterranean. And even before the Crusades, Venetian merchants conducted a commerce in sugar, spices, silks, and other products of the East. In 1319, Tomaso Loredano, a Venetian merchant, sent a hundred thousand pounds of sugar to England to be exchanged for wool.

The Venetians increased prices as the demand grew and consumers complained. It was the Portuguese who were the first to take action against the monopoly the Venetians enjoyed. Prince Henry the Navigator, in 1419, discovered Madeira, and his countrymen there planted cuttings of cane they had obtained in Sicily. As further discoveries were made, cane was planted in the Azores, Cape Verde Islands and the Canary Islands, so that by 1472, sugar cane was being cultivated on virtually all of the islands as far south as St. Thomas. It may have been one of the factors which helped Lisbon to grow in power and wealth, surpassing Venice, whose glory began to decline. Christopher Columbus brought cane with him to the New World. In a letter to Ferdinand and Isabella, he expressed satisfaction at "the way a few small canes planted here have taken root." The Spaniards spread its cultivation in the islands of the West Indies and on the mainland of South America, where it was nourished by slave labor, and prospered for a century and a half.

Without a doubt, sugar is the jewel of cuisine, the prize, the ransom over which wars have been fought. It gives a lift not only to the palate, but to the body and the spirit as well. Like any other staple food, its virtue lies in its moderate use. To omit some kind of dessert is an error, whether it be a Fruit Compote, a piece of French Pastry, a Meringue Glacee, a Peach Melba, a Parfait aux Liqueurs, or one of the wonderful soufflés from the Patissier's deft hands. The flamed dessert remains very popular, combining a sweet with liqueur, which is most satisfying to the senses. Perhaps no other food has played such a fascinating role in the history of the world as sugar, which has retained its allure century after century.

CHAPTER

9

Coffee, the Elixir of Life

*"I think if I were a woman,
I'd wear coffee as a perfume."*
—JOHN VAN DRUTEN

SOME CRITICS WILL JUDGE A RESTAURANT solely upon its ability to serve a good cup of coffee. This is the acid test of its success. No matter whether it qualifies as first-class in every other respect, if it fails in this important ritual, it does not receive their approbation. Actually, coffee is not a difficult beverage to prepare properly. Constant supervision and meticulous attention to detail is all that's needed. The coffee urn must be scrupulously clean. Coffee oils cling and must be scrubbed from the inner surfaces of the urn as ordinary rinsing won't do the job right. Use freshly drawn cold water, as hot water from the faucet affects the flavor for hot water pipes contain minerals which can ruin the taste of the brew. The cold water should be heated until it is boiling hot.

Each gallon of water takes a half-pound of richly blended coffee to produce a full-bodied aroma. It has been said that a perfect cup of coffee depends almost as much on the person drinking it as on the coffee itself. Various coffee brands offer a number of blends to meet varied tastes. It is generally agreed that the perfect cup of coffee must be fragrant, sparkling clear without dregs, and have a rich, full flavor. The best coffee is freshly ground. Otherwise, coffee of maximum strength and flavor should be bought in vacuum-sealed cans to lock in its freshness.

The coffee is placed in a filter sack and the boiling water poured over it. The brew is drained out of the spicket of the urn and run back again. This is repeated five times, no less. Then the cover of the coffee urn is kept on five or ten minutes to keep the aroma of the coffee sealed in. Finally, the sack is removed with the grounds so that the brew will not turn bitter. At home, coffee should be made just before it is served. In a restaurant, it should first be made close to the peak business hour, and every fifteen or twenty minutes thereafter as needed. There are really only two basic ingredients in producing a perfect cup of coffee: coffee and fresh water. One must, however, follow the rules.

This formula produces a fantastic cup of coffee which cannot be equalled for aroma, body and quality. The use of a silex for making a small quantity is the finest method I know. As a matter of actual practice, it is difficult to achieve perfection in a restaurant's kitchen because the executive chef cannot give his attention to all details and, unless the owner himself or the manager does so, there is the risk of having a superbly prepared and elegantly served dinner ruined by a disappointing cup of coffee. There is always concern that failure in one detail will ruin a dinner. A salad may be poorly prepared, or a vegetable over or under done. While many restaurateurs concentrate on the entree, there are actually only three important factors comprising a good dinner, and each must be perfect: coffee . . . salad . . . vegetables.

Iced coffee is an American invention and an abomination to connoisseurs of the dark brew. It is now being promoted as "Coffee on the Rocks" as a euphemism. It is made with instant coffee and stirred with a cinnamon stick. Coffee, a favorite beverage for many years, grows ever more popular. However, many culinary sins are committed against it. On the West Coast, coffee is often served as soon as the patron is seated. It is taken on an empty stomach and throughout the meal. Invariably, it is a very thin brew. While coffee is sometimes taken with the entree in the East, custom here decrees that it be served at the end of the meal, even after the dessert, when one takes either coffee or espresso.

For five consecutive years, Mayor Robert Briscoe of Dublin, Ireland visited the United States to bless the St. Patrick's Day parade. He brought with him a delectable new drink—Irish Mist Coffee. It is made of Cream—"rich as an Irish brogue"; Coffee—"strong as a friendly hand"; sugar—"sweet as the tongue of a rogue"; IRISH MIST—"smooth as the wit of the land." Representatives of Munson G. Shaw Co. of New York, who import Irish Mist Liqueur, assured us that the following was the proper way to prepare Irish Mist Coffee: Heat a stemmed or regular-size Old Fashion glass. Pour in one jigger of Irish Mist, Ireland's Legendary Liqueur, and three or four times that amount of strong black coffee. Add sugar to taste, stir to dissolve. Fill up remaining inch or so of glass with whipped cream, letting cream float on top. Do not stir after adding cream. By drinking the hot coffee and Irish Mist *through* the whipped cream, you will discover the full, unique quality of Irish Mist Coffee.

Coffee has a long history. As long ago as 1470 the Arabians drank coffee. It was the Arabian dervishes who made it a secular drink and the chosen stimulant on nights devoted to religious rituals. They say the first known coffee houses were in Mecca and called Kaveh Kaanehs. It was sipped as a beverage by the inhabitants, who found out what made the dervishes whirl so energetically. Leisure was spent in drinking coffee, playing chess and other games, discussing the news of the day, and singing.

The existence of such a delight was spread by travelers. By 1530, the City of Damascus had two widely known coffee houses. The owners had lovingly named them "The Café of the Roses" and "The Café of the Gate of Salvation." Coffee houses appeared in Constantinople in 1554, where they were most luxuriously appointed. Late in the century, Persia had her coffee houses, and so great was the respect for their operation that elevated chairs were provided upon which sat poets and historians, who made speeches and told stories. It was only a step to Europe where, some authorities hold, the first coffee house was established in Italy. Some time in the sixteenth century, the delightful coffee beans were brought from Egypt to Constantinople.

73

The elegant cafés there were copied by the Venetians in the seventeenth century.

English scholars take exception to the Venetian claim of being the first to have a café. They say there is indisputable evidence that a man by the name of Jacob, from Lebanon, who was in London on business, lingered to open the earliest English coffee house. This was at Oxford and bore the name "At the Angel at the Parish of St. Peter in the East." The date is given as 1650. Only two years later, London succumbed to the aromatic temptation, and the first coffee house there appeared in St. Michael's Alley, the proprietor a Mr. Bowman. Soon others opened their doors and became famous as gathering places for the intellectuals of the day. Samuel Pepys, the tireless diarist, called The Rota—"The Coffee Club." It served as the meeting place for a debating society for political opinions. Ben Jonson's favorite coffee house, known as "Devil Tavern Club" on Bread Street, became the gathering place for the most brilliant men of the time. "The Mermaid Tavern Coffee House"—usually referred to simply as "The Mermaid" —was host to William Shakespeare, Sir Walter Raleigh, Francis Beaumont, John Fletcher, among other distinguished men.

Sometimes they amused themselves in exchanging versions of the stories travelers brought about the coffee beans. There was an Italian traveler, it was said, Pietro del Lavalle, who was most emphatic that the marvellous black brew was the nepenthe which Helen of Troy had at her disposal. The story is told in Homer's *Odyssey:* How Telemachus, in search of Odysseus his lost father, is seated at table with Menelaus; the whole company is in tears and cannot be comforted:

"Then Helen, daughter of Zeus, turned to new thoughts. Presently she cast a drug into the wine of which they drank, a drug to lull all pain and anger and bring forgetfulness of every sorrow. Whoso should drink a draught of it when it is mingled in the bowl, on that day he would let no tear fall down his cheeks, not though his mother and his father died, and though men slew his brother or dear son with the sword before his face, and his own eyes beheld it. Medicines of such virtue had the daughter of Zeus. . . ."

74

Coffee, the Elixir of Life

"It must have been coffee that Helen mixed with the wine," said this Pietro del Lavalle. But it could just as easily have been hashish. Yet this account of Helen's drug is not unlike the clinical effects of strong black coffee, since it is difficult, if not impossible, to shed tears after drinking a quantity of it. Of the many legends scholars amused themselves in relating, none was more colorful than the story of the dancing goats. It told how, in the arid desert adjacent to the Red Sea, known as the land of Yemen, there stood a monastery called Shehodet. As this name implies, the monastery "bore witness" to the all-powerful Allah to whose glory it had been built. Herds of goats belonging to the monastery, finding little food among the foothills of Yemen, were in the habit of wandering off to the volcanic mountain-tops, returning after many days even leaner than when they went away; for nothing grew in that barren region. As the goats provided the monks with milk and meat and their skins became the parchment leaves of the Koran, the monastery in return provided a goatherd to tend them. These fellows, living continuously with their herds, knew all of their peculiarities as a shepherd knows his sheep. Though they may wander away in search of salt, or nibble the bark of the palm trees, or indulge in the playful habit of butting each other, these were idiosyncrasies well known to any goatherd. When day was done the herd would come together and, with limbs outstretched, sleep through the night; and alongside would squat the faithful goatherd, head on breast, dozing undisturbed until dawn heralded the coming of another day.

The day once came, however, when certain of the goats, having returned at dusk, had no wish to sleep, and to the annoyance of the goatherd, they danced and jumped about as friskily as colts. All through the night they leaped and capered, chasing each other and bleating continuously, a performance they repeated on succeeding nights until the whole herd was affected. The goatherd concluded that they were victims of the goatsucker, a bird with the unpleasant habit of pecking at their teats and driving them crazy. Examination showed no signs of this, so the goatherd decided that, on the morrow, he would follow the herd to their remote grazing ground in the hope that he might find a clue to their strange behavior.

The next morning—the story goes—he came upon the herd among dense bushes in one of the wadis, eating from a shrub with leaves like a laurel and flowers like the jasmine. Where the flowers had died away, little berries had formed, and it was this fruit the goats were devouring with obvious relish. Tearing off a small branch laden with the berries, he made his way to the monastery to tell his story to the Imam, and to show him as proof the branch of the shrub. Now the Imam knew full well that goatherds were famous liars. The master had no knowledge of it growing in the land of Yemen, and he resolved to investigate in person the strange report. Nightfall came and the Imam watched the antics of the goats and in the morning he followed them to the hills where he saw them nibbling the fruit of the mysterious bush. He noticed the shrubs grew in neat rows as if planted by the hand of man, and having gathered a quantity of the purple-tinted berries, he returned to the monastery. There, in the privacy of his cell, he examined the berries carefully and found that within the outer casing was a kernel that was unaffected by immersion in cold water.

He experimented further and found that heating the kernels until they were burned a dark brown, having them pounded in a mortar into a fine powder, he could boil some water and cast a handful of the powder in, which produced exciting results. As he leaned over the steaming bowl, the Imam experienced a feeling akin to intoxication. It felt like wine going to his head. This was a forbidden pleasure to all Mohammedans, to whom the Prophet denied the solace of the fermented juice of the grape, having witnessed in Greece the extravagant worship of Bacchus. So the Imam who lingered over the steaming liquor experienced a curious exhilaration and enjoyed the intriguing aroma. Satisfied that it was not an intoxicant, he drank from the vessel and the bitter liquor was warm and comforting. He seemed to have new strength and great energy, and dispelled the heaviness of sleep for the hour was late. "This is no drink of Bacchus," he said to himself, "but of Apollo." Once more he sipped the steaming brew and instinctively he knew he had stumbled upon a rival to the magic of wine. He reflected on this magic potion and remembered how the shrubs grew in neat rows. Could the black Christians of Ethiopia have planted them? They had invaded the land of Yemen from the country known as *Kaffa* and had brought with them their own domesticated animals and perhaps the shrubs also. Perhaps these were Kaffa trees.

English travelers had seen for the first time coffee houses in Arabia, Turkey and Egypt as numerous as the taverns of their own country. Aytoun Ellis in his remarkable book "The Penny Universities: A history of the coffee houses" (Secker & Warburg, London, 1956) makes a penetrating study of the whole subject and we are indebted to him for the story of the monks and their prancing goats. In France, a coffee house was opened in Marseilles in 1671, near the Commercial Exchange. It immediately became popular with merchants and travelers, who spread its fame to other cities. Many imitations soon sprang up. It is said that about 1672, Pascal, an Armenian, opened a coffee drinking booth at the fair of St. Germain, marking the beginning of the Parisian coffee houses—the cafés. Before long the fad became immensely popular and spread to every part of France.

By the middle of the seventeenth century, coffee houses were numerous throughout London. People went there to enjoy coffee, tea and chocolate, which were the new drinks of the period. In addition to Paris, the large cities—the Hague, Marseilles, Hamburg and Vienna —established coffee drinking places. London continued to call them coffee houses, while Paris called them cafés, as did Vienna and Venice. They were patronized by fashionable, literary and political folk as a meeting place of inspiration, communication and enjoyment.

Vienna is well known for her cafés. The Vienna Prater belongs to all of the people. The most expensive restaurants were there, as well as modest places. An ice-cream in the Eisvogel, or a cup of coffee in the Sacher Pavilion, or a bite at the Lusthaus were within the reach of almost every purse. Wars have left their blight. Yet on the left-hand side of the main avenue of the Prater, coming from the city itself, you can still see one coffee house after another. More than a century ago (1844), the poet Adalbert Stifter wrote of them and, for the most part, it is still true that "from each of them comes the strains of music. Under the trees are many thousands of seats filled with people in their best clothes. There is a laughing, a talking, a clinking of glasses, and before the eyes of the crowds the elegant carriages roll along the avenue, which stretches away with no end as far as the eye can see—as far as the Vienna Woods."

The Viennese, in fact, claim that it was from Vienna, not Venice, that coffee began its conquest of the world. In 1683, the city was liberated from its captivity by the Turks. As the Turks were routed, it was found that they had left behind large sacks of coffee beans, which they were unable to take with them in their hurried retreat. The hero of the liberation of Vienna was Franz George Kolschitzky, a courageous Pole. As a reward for his valor, he was presented with the aromatic beans. The grateful Town Fathers also placed a house at his disposal for the public sale of the coffee. That is how Kolschitzky became a hero twice over, once as a warrior, and again as the hero of the palate. His place was called "Zur Blauen Flasche." To this day, Kolschitzky is honored in Vienna as the patron saint of the café. While the Viennese may not have given the café to the world, the typical Vienna café which they developed has become a model for most of the countries who love coffee. Café life sprang quickly into favor for artists, pensioners, and bohemians, for in the café lay illusion, and the smallest illusion, they say, is capable of making the Viennese happy.

Franz Schubert could not do without coffee, and often he liked to make it for himself. He called his small and humble hand-coffee grinder *the home of his Holy Spirit*. He swore that the best ideas and melodies were inspired by the monotonous grinding of coffee beans, from which process, he said, came his D Minor quartette. Beethoven's approved recipe for coffee was sixty beans to a cup!

America was not slow in adopting coffee. The Dutch who settled New York drank beer for breakfast and every meal thereafter, but by 1668 many began to substitute coffee as the morning drink. There was a reason for this change in habit. In the seventeenth century, the Dutch began coffee cultivation in Java and distributed the plant for cultivation to several tropical countries. The English took it to the Island of Jamaica. Thence it traveled to Central and South America, and soon coffee was very popular in Europe and the Americas. Mocha and Java originally referred to the places from which the coffee came, but now they are both grown in Brazil, where Santos is the greatest coffee port in the world. Today Mocha and Java designate a particular kind of coffee.

It was in Boston (rather than in New York) that the first coffee place appeared, in the late seventeenth century. It was called "The London Coffee House," and soon several others opened, including one known as "The King's Head," a rendezvous for colonial society. "The Green Dragon," which stood on Union Street for 135 years (from 1697-1832), was the most widely known of the Boston coffee houses. During its long career, it was host to earls, dukes, red-coated British soldiers, crown officers, colonial governors, citizens of means, conspirators in the Boston Tea Party, and revolutionists.

New York's first coffee house was "The King's Arms," a tavern on Broadway between Trinity churchyard and Cedar Street. It was founded in 1696 by John Hutchins, and for many years was the only one in town. The "Merchants Coffee House" was opened in 1757, and became popular with Army and Navy officers of both the American and British forces.

Coffee has been praised by poets, writers and statesmen. Benjamin Disraeli, famed English statesman and Prime Minister to Queen Victoria, had tremendous respect for the beverage itself, and for the coffee houses which served the delectable brew. In a moment of enthusiasm, he declared that "The history of coffee houses is that of the manners, the morals, and the politics of the people."

10

How to Rate a Restaurant

> *"It is impossible to reduce civil society to one dead level. All striving against nature is in vain...People differ in capacity, skill, health, strength; and unequal fortune is a necessary result of unequal condition. Such inequality is far from being disadvantageous either to the individuals or to the community."*
>
> Pope Leo XIII (1810-1903)

THE FRENCH HAVE LONG PROVIDED GUIDE-books to the ways and byways where their cuisine may be found. In one of the earliest of all restaurant guides, "Almanach des Gourmands," dated 1803, Grimod de la Reyniere wrote in his preface: "The author will regret neither the cares nor the indigestions his researches have caused him, if the alimentary art owes new progress to his efforts." Other authors delightedly followed in his footsteps, sampling their way to literary renown.

In an engaging article, *The Lure of the Cuisine* in the New York Herald Tribune, Herbert Kupferberg followed the starred routes of *Le Guide Michelin* and concluded that the way to a guidebook's heart is not through the historic sights pointed out, or even the evaluation of sleeping accommodations, but through the stomach. Michelin, a tire company, originally entered the guidebook business to encourage motor travel, and now issues a vast series of regional and sectional guides, maps and books, not only for France, but for other countries, as well. Its most well-known publication is the red-covered book of nearly 1,000 pages which lists almost every city, town and hamlet in France, its historical points of interest, and rates hotels, restaurants, and other eating places. This is meticulously revised annually and serves as a bible for the discriminating traveler.

Michelin grants one asterisk (*) for "a good meal for the district—a good place to break your journey,"

two (**) for "an excellent meal—worth a detour"

and three (***) for "one of the best tables in France—worth a special journey."

In 1960, the Socony Mobil Guide appeared, edited by Alden and Marion Stevens, and published by Simon and Schuster. This book introduced the star rating system of Europe to America. Using the symbol of stars (or asterisks) for hotels and restaurants in the United States was effective, but it should have been limited to Michelin's three classifications of first, second and third rate restaurants and hotels already familiar in Europe and America. The award of five stars as maximum recognition was ill-advised, I fear, and confusing to diners. The subject aroused great interest among people in the field upon publication of the Stevens' Guide to the American traveling public. A letter I addressed to the Editor of the Herald Tribune was published, in part, on July 4, 1960.

The complete original text explained how under a system of first, second and third class restaurants, *** would apply to a restaurant of the highest order, ** to second, * to third. To qualify for the highest category, an establishment, within the terms of the industry should meet with these specific requirements:

DINING ROOMS:

1) The establishment should have a seating capacity of not under 100 persons.

2) The décor of whatever country or region should be in good taste within the standards of the American Institute of Decorators, of the National Society of Interior Designers.

3) Silverware, china, stemware, tablecloths, setting of tables must be impeccable and proper to its kind.

4) Staff: A restaurant cannot be classified in the highest category unless fully staffed with maitre d' hotel, captains, waiters and busboys who are well trained for their posts to insure service with dignity.

5) A place to qualify for three stars (in my proposed category) the highest distinction, should have an atmosphere enhanced by a distinguished clientele.

6) It should be courteous to unknown patrons. A place may have all of the physical attributes and fail in its classification because of negligible or even discourteous treatment to unknown guests, unknown and unrecognizable as public figures. This is in violation of the basic principles of hospitality.

7) The exterior of the building should be staffed with doorman service from the opening hours and throughout the evening to assist guests.

Proper lighting of a restaurant would fall within its décor, even though it is part of the interior design subject to architecture and engineering. It is far more complex to achieve proper lighting than color schemes or ornamentation. In the construction of a new restaurant, it becomes a prime problem of installation.

The three pillars upon which a successful restaurant builds its reputation are: food, service and atmosphere. The interior designer and master electrician can do nothing about the province of the chef, but they can make a valuable contribution to service and atmosphere. Service reflects the spirit of management and ownership. Atmosphere affects employees as well as the clientele. The staff takes pride in working in a beautiful and well-ordered place. Lighting sets the mood of the dining room, which should suit the time and the place itself.

Lighting can be bright and vivid when the room is full and talking is animated, as is usual in many places at luncheon. When more leisurely hours arrive for enjoying dinner, patrons like to linger over their courses, their coffee or after-dinner liqueurs. Then the lights should be muted to match the mellowness of the mood. Such a lighting system is costly to install but, with its variations, is a wonderful instrument for a restaurateur. The lights (high hats) are nested within the ceiling itself and light spreads from a pattern of apertures.

Improper lighting can be irritating to diners, such as candles which flicker, and have the same effect as driving against the lights of an oncoming car. Just as irritating are rooms which are too dark. While some women may prefer this, men become bored with rooms so darkened that they find it difficult to see what they are eating. Just as irksome are lights in wall brackets, or the gigantic crystal chandeliers and other monstrosities of modern lighting which do not properly light the restaurant. To disseminate light over the entire room to the right degree, it must be controlled. This variety of control by buttons on a board is an advantage found in newer establishments. A change in lighting for later hour dining gives a new dimension to an interior. The classes of clients react to different gradations of light. A group of loudly conversing businessmen at the peak of the day want light on their food, or for making notes during their discussion. Pleasure diners prefer softer lights as the evening wears on.

In the same way, the acoustics of a restaurant require careful study by the architect. An excellent cuisine and faultless service can be defeated in its purpose if the ceiling does not absorb the bulk of the noise. It detracts from the comfort of dining, causes irritation. A restaurant which may qualify in every other respect, may fail in providing the desired atmosphere because it is far too noisy to be conducive to serenity. On the other hand, too great an emphasis by the engineer on noise absorption may reduce a lively, full room to almost dead silence, which is fatal. The best background accompaniment is the quiet hum of the diners in conversation. If diners are heard in whispers, the whole mood of the interior may be defeated.

We are indebted to William Pahlmann's article "Restaurants Achieve Personality Through Interior Design," in *Cooking for Profit* Magazine, for his pointed remarks on lighting and acoustics. Mr. Pahlmann, F.A.I.D. is recognized as a color and lighting expert in the field of interior and industrial design, and was in charge of the "Designs for Dining" exhibit at the National Hotel Exposition in New York City's Coliseum in the fall of 1960. Today the importance of proper décor is constantly being stressed in its relationship to the successful operation of an establishment, whether a restaurant or other eating place.

A restaurant is also defeated when space requirements have not been properly met. The distance between tables is important. If they are too far apart, diners feel isolated. If they are too close, it is not suitable to privacy. People dislike having their conversations overheard by diners seated nearby. Nor does a guest like to be brushed by waiters or passing guests, nor be fearful of being soiled by the service of soup in close quarters. The tops of tables should be generous enough for comfort. It is frustrating for a group to be seated around a circular table which is so wide in circumference that it is impossible to speak to the people opposite without raising one's voice.

Tables should be of proper height, and chairs and banquettes should be engineered to be compatible with that height. Sometimes banquettes are so low, the diner cannot eat comfortably, or the width of the banquette is too wide or too narrow. Chairs should have rounded backs without sharp corners which poke customers in the ribs or catch in the pockets of the waiters. They should not be so large, with arm rests, that service by waiters becomes a problem. There is also the consideration of weight. Restaurant furniture should be substantial and yet not too heavy to be mobile. A client does not want to fight a heavy mahogany chair when he desires to rise, nor do waiters want to move heavy furnishings in rearranging the dining room. It is very possible that clients do not return to a restaurant because they vaguely remember some discomfort, though they cannot put their finger on the source.

The subject of chair comfort has been thoroughly analyzed by manufacturers for the reason that people have changed. Growth statistics show Americans are increasing steadily in weight and stature. According to the Department of Agriculture, males are two inches taller than their fathers and from four to fourteen pounds heavier. Much of this additional weight centers in the hips for men as well as women. The practical side of the phenomenon is seating which can accommodate the additional spread. Seating engineers recognize the physical change in Americans must be provided for.

In his penetrating article for "This Week" (November 6, 1960), Leslie Lieber pointed out just how "We're getting too big for our britches." "In 1944," he wrote, "the Haywood-Wakefield Company petitioned Harvard University for a study on the changing shape of Americans so its seating factory standards could conform in providing seating for new railway-coaches. The University entrusted this assignment to the late Dr. Ernest Albert Hooton (author of "Up from the Ape") who for two years measured, in a special chair, the population which surged through given railroad stations. On the basis of this on-the-spot research, it was decided the definitive measurement suitable for a railway seat was 21.3 inches.

In a good position to comment are the people who since 1885 have been building about 90% of the public seats in this country. When the American Seating Company ("The future of America rests on our seats") were asked to quote on seating for the Metropolitan Opera House in 1951, they dispatched a representative to Italy to measure the seats of the La Scala Opera House in Milan. He found these seats measured thirteen inches in width. Those who have attended La Scala as well as the Folies Bergere in Paris know just how narrow those seats are. The increasing spread of Americans was recognized in 1938 when the eighteen-inch theater seat was outlawed in many states of the Union on the ground that it was a tight fit and would be difficult for the patron to rise quickly in event of panic. Since then, most seats have been twenty inches in theaters. According to Richard L. Nolan of the American Seating Company, the Lincoln Center will have seats built with a twenty-two inch width, and Mr. Nolan feels that within the next ten years, twenty-four inch theater seats may be standard.

Chairmasters, Inc. of New York, who formed their company in 1946 (in a father-and-son arrangement, Felice and Al Jehair) have contributed a style, tradition and drama in their designs for dining for leading decorators and architects. These seating engineers furnish the chairs, tables, banquettes and bars upon which the successful operation of a dining area depends, manufactured in their own factories. Most of their standard stock chairs run seventeen inches and more, and are a delight of engineered comfort.

Alert restaurateurs must provide chairs and stools which are properly proportioned and still esthetic, a chair in which a diminutive person will find comfort and dignity, and a large person will be adequately provided for. One of our well-built patrons, James Arness, the popular Marshal Dillon of Television's *Gunsmoke,* completely obliterates a dining room chair, and yet Chairmaster has designed it so it supports him firmly.

While over-indulgence at the table is often blamed for the tendency toward mid-ship spread, the truth is we are, for the most part, a sedentary people. More persons remain seated during their waking hours than ever before in history. The statistics say that 13½ million men hold posts for which they sit almost all of the time. The average business man—in the course of his working career—spends about 60,000 hours in the "executive position." This occurs after 15,000 hours of sitting from kindergarten through college. By the age of retirement, a man has already spent ten solid years sitting, and, after retirement, he is entitled to sit for the balance of his life, if he chooses.

KITCHENS

The kitchen should be properly staffed and also have its own pastry department on the premises. This is very important. How can a leading place be awarded *****, **** or even ***, when it is not equipped or staffed to fill any order? When a good client requests at the end of his dinner a luxurious dessert on an occasion for Bon Voyage, Birthday, Anniversary, etc. and a pastry chef is not on hand to comply, the place "loses face." I have often read of places being considered first-class restaurants, although they have never employed a pastry chef.

On the other hand, there are places in New York which do qualify as first class, such as: The "21" Club, Le Pavillon, the Colony Restaurant, Le Chateau Richelieu, and several others. These restaurants have the proper equipment and other requirements, and it is simply a matter of taste as to which place diners may prefer.

Once a party of guests discussed the merits of hotels such as the old Plaza, the Pierre and the St. Regis. One gentleman asked my opinion as to which I thought was the best. I answered that they are equally qualified as Number One hotels, and it would be unwise to vote one above the others. There is no best lawyer, actor, or doctor. Each has something individualistic to offer. No two human beings are alike. This holds true, as well, of a restaurant. The finest restaurants are kept in exquisite order and, although known for a certain basic décor

86

which becomes their trade-mark, the owners strive to make them ever more elegant. They are, let us say, like lovely women in brilliant attire. The Fall Season of 1960 saw the Colony in pale new brocades and glittering chandeliers of the old tradition. The Pavillon, the stage on which society plays out many of its comedies and dramas, presented astonishingly realistic murals of Paris by Bernard Lamotte. A large monetary investment goes into the maintenance of such lavish cafés which serve the public in lieu of private mansions staffed with many servants.

The editors of Mobil Guide, in bringing the subject of rating of restaurants to the fore, are to be congratulated for their efforts to achieve something concrete, not commercially but factually. It requires only that they go into more detail as to the standards of the industry. The top award of *** instead of ***** would have been in better taste, and less confusing to clients. In New York, it would have been better to indicate ten or twelve restaurants with ***, specify the qualifications necessary to attain that rating, and what is required to qualify for ** and for *. The restaurateurs themselves would then have felt less sensitive about being classified, and would be encouraged to increase their standards to qualify for a higher rating.

We have given the qualifications for a place to attain ***. Those who, in my category, would qualify for ** are restaurants which are equally as good in performance of service as the ***, but unfortunately they do not have a Pastry Department.

* is the designation for restaurants with few cooks who, in a modest way, produce very good dishes, an excellent, attentive service and cuisine. There are also well-known places with atmosphere and large seating capacity, popular with the public, which by the rigid standards of the restaurant industry star-system I propose, would not qualify for more than one star. The unstarred no longer qualifies as a restaurant, and yet one can obtain very well cooked food there, clean service and good attention. In Italy such a place is called a *trattoria,* in France a *bistro.* They specialize in their own cuisine as good eating places. The term *restaurant* and *eating place* are often used indiscriminately. To my knowledge, after many years in the field, the proper definitions are as follows:

87

A *restaurant* provides for the client anything he wishes on the market, in season, and within the cuisine advertised.

An *eating place* is limited to its own specialties. The choice is not within the province of the patron, but is subject to the limitations of what the kitchen can offer.

According to dictionary definitions, both French and English, no distinction is made between the two classifications. In France, the term *bistro* is used to designate a simple eating place, although even French dictionaries define it as a "restaurant or eating place keeper."

There are restaurants within nightclubs and cabarets which may also be graded, although the service of food is usually incidental to the entertainment and liquor departments. The terms for these establishments are often used interchangeably. According to my knowledge, the definitions are:

A *nightclub* serves food, drink, has music, and provides a floor-show.

A *cabaret* serves food, drink, has music for dancing, but no floor-show.

Upon his return from Europe, Mr. H. Gregory Thomas, one of New York's travelled and distinguished gourmets (engaged in the fragrant profession of perfumes as President of the House of Chanel) reminded me of *Le Guide Michelin* in France, where restaurants and "eating places" are listed and described. Crossed spoons from 1 to 5 are used as indications of the equipment, décor and creature comforts of restaurants, with 1, 2 or 3 stars being added, depending solely upon the gastronomic excellence of the restaurant.

In this way, Mr. Thomas pointed out, a very elaborate restaurant with somewhat routine international food, even though prepared by a large staff of cooks, and having a well staffed, fully equipped dining room, might be so devoid of gastronomic distinction as to earn no more than the five crossed spoons; whereas, a very simple bistro, or small country hotel, would deserve three stars and only one crossed spoon symbol.

As to the term *bistro,* so widely used to designate the family type of eating place—sawdust on the floor and café curtains at the window, with very well prepared food of the provincial variety, it came about during one of the wars of France when the invading Russian soldiers found themselves walking the streets of Paris, tired, hungry and thirsty. They flocked into the places crying *Bistro! Bistro!* "Quick! Quick!— something to eat and drink"—and so the name was born.

Since the time of Karl Baedeker, the making of guides for travelers has been an earnest undertaking. The pioneer guide maker, Baedeker was born in Essen, Germany, at the turn of the nineteenth century. His father had a printing place and bookshop, and as soon as Karl was old enough, he branched out for himself in Coblenz. It was there that he issued the first of the series of guide-books with which his name is associated. He used as a model the even earlier guide-book of England prepared by John Murray. Baedeker's books covered, in the course of years, the greater part of the civilized world. Karl's son, Fritz, transferred the business to Leipzig, in 1872, and continued to issue guidebooks. Karl used to travel incognito, making a record of the minutest details of cuisine and management of the various hotels he visited.

Duncan Hines followed in the footsteps of Baedecker as he traveled about and noted the places he could recommend to others as having true merit. When he died recently, he left the heritage of the Duncan Hines Institute at Ithaca, New York, and three books to guide travelers to places to spend the night, a vacation, or to procure good food. Thirty employees work all year around in the hundred-year-old house in Ithaca, which is Institute headquarters. Like Baedecker, Hines was a printing salesman, from Bowling Green, Kentucky. About twenty-five years ago, he sent out a few hundred Christmas cards listing restaurants around the country where he had found the food exceptional. When requests for additional copies of his list caused him to put it into a book, he discovered a new profession, though he was in his fifties at the time.

Hines did not use the star system. He simply told in a conversational manner the places he found worth visiting, gave road directions, the number of the nearest turnpike exit, the days and hours open, and price ranges. His guides list 4,425 places out of the 235,000 in the United States, 37,500 being in New York City. There is a 10% turnover as places are dropped and replaced with others. Roy Park, Editor of the Institute, reminds readers that restaurant food is not a standard manufactured product which is guaranteed to be the same every day in the year. Cooks are changed, ownership changes, places come and go. The three books thus go through regular re-issues. They are "Adventures in Good Eating," "Lodging for a Night" and "Vacation Guide."

Twenty-five inspectors, who are responsible for the reports, are recent graduates of schools of hotel management like those at Cornell, Michigan State, Denver University, Florida State University and Oklahoma State. They pay for their meals. Places do not pay for a listing in the guidebook and none accept advertising. When Mr. Hines first went into this business, he personally tested the places he liked, he knew good food and liquors, and most people agreed with him.

When Roy Park took over the Institute, he devised a system of writing to the fellow members of the Public Relations Society of America, to the Sales Executive Club, Advertising Club and other associations. He asked each member to fill out a simple form suggesting the places in his part of the country to which he would take an important guest. The first three would be "cost is no object"; the next three should fit the bill of "good food and pleasant surroundings at a reasonable price level." Then Mr. Park wrote for recommendations to top executives, newspaper editors, local columnists, food writers, and society editors.

As the recommendations rolled in, folders were made up, the restaurants contacted with requests for menus, wine lists, and other specialties. When a place received corporate endorsements of 20 or 30 or 40 votes, the Institute gave it an enthusiastic rating, following the inspector's confirming visit. If it doesn't stay on top, the rating is changed. It is the experience of the Institute that running a restaurant or eating place is so difficult that 80% of all new places fail in their first year. Therefore, Duncan Hines does not list a place until after the first year of operation.

"Adventures in Good Eating" has tried to select a good place in each section of the country. They found, however, that America is not yet fully colonized in this respect. In West Virginia, there are only 13 listings in the whole state. Gastronomically, this is the national low. But as anyone visiting there will tell you, private hospitality in

West Virginia is another matter. Their tables are justly famous, presided over by most charming hosts and hostesses.

The Institute has stated that there are places in the United States where a motorist can ride 150 miles without finding even a recommended cafeteria. The wise traveler, therefore, brings his portable ice-box and alcohol lamp with him when motoring cross country, and takes advantage of the wonderful bounty of the food fairs in shopping centers, thus enjoying a fine dinner in a cozy motel. A certain amount of picnic equipment is needed, dexterity comes with practice. We found in motoring to California and return, to Florida and return, through New England and deep into Canada, that this dependence on one's own resources greatly added to the fun of vacationing on wheels.

A restaurateur of experience can gauge the percentage into which his clientele falls, give or take a point. The Duncan Hines Institute has consequently gone on record to classify the professions gastronomically. Mr. Hines, who employed every means possible to assist him in ferreting out good places, with an eye to cleanliness, sought the help of doctors in the cities through which he passed. He assumed that if doctors recommended a place, it would be clean. He soon found out, however, that the doctors had only vague acquaintance with the restaurants of their area, though a closer knowledge of the eating places. As a group, he said, physicians are not gourmets. This is not through lack of culture, by any means, or inclination.

In an interesting article for *Today's Living* (August 21, 1960), Creighton Peet conceded: "Harassed and overworked, doctors snatch coffee, milk and sandwiches on the run, seldom settling down to a civilized meal. Lawyers, too, were found not to be good eaters, and bankers were soon dropped (as ones in the know) when they recommended economical lunch counters." While there are many exceptions to the rule, on the whole this seems to be true. In America, those who know fine food and wines travel back and forth to Europe. They are the corporation executives who entertain. They are advertising and public relations men and women. Since they have credit accounts, and their firms pay the expenses, they dine at the best places, mingle with people who are acquainted with the rules, and sometimes they even become gourmets themselves.

More and more people, aware of the delights of social dining, are concluding that the first-class places, for value received, are not as expensive as they had imagined. Timewise, they are dividing what used to be the rule of "dining-and-theater" into "dining-or-theater." Celebrants discover that in order to dine well and graciously, it is better to reserve the evening for this purpose alone, or to plan to arrive at their favorite restaurant around 6 P.M. in order to get to the theater by curtain time. More and more people are versed in restaurant classification, and know what to expect in the way of cuisine and service within the price structure, which is a most encouraging trend for the industry which has its set standards of operation.

11

London Re-Visited

*"I had an excellent repast—the best repast possible—
which consisted simply of boiled eggs and bread and
butter. It was the quality of these simple ingredients
that made the occasion memorable. The eggs were so
good that I am ashamed to say how many of them I
consumed ... it might seem that an egg which has
succeeded in being fresh has done all that can reason-
ably be expected of it. But there was a bloom of
punctuality, so to speak, about those eggs of Bourg, as
if it had been the intention of the very hens themselves that they should be promptly served."*
                          —HENRY JAMES (1843-1916)

THERE IS NOTHING STATIC ABOUT OUR INDUS-
try. The restaurant man who becomes satisfied with his place sooner
or later loses his perspective—and his patrons. He should visit, at least
once a year, the restaurants in his category in his own city to compare
the service and the quality of cuisine, watching out for any innova-
tions. His busman's holiday should also include restaurants in other
large cities, such as Chicago, San Francisco, Los Angeles, New Orleans and Washington, thus becoming familiar with the tastes and
customs of various regions of America.

In addition, the intelligent owner should make tours abroad to the
principal cities of the Continent, visiting Italy, France, Austria, Germany, Switzerland, England and other countries, if possible. In this
way, he can note trends of service, cuisines, and the effects upon places

by world changes. In 1931, I made an extended tour of the Continent and England, which proved of great interest and value. The time was between the two World Wars, and there was much of elegance remaining in the various capitals. In 1948, I returned and toured many nations. The effects of World War II were marked. We went abroad again in 1953, and in 1956, benefitting greatly from the opportunity to observe.

My trips abroad to study the service and cuisines of the world capitals and cities, large and small, always include London. After listening to and talking the languages of the Continent, it is like the first stop toward home-in-America to hear English spoken. Since they are precise and conscientious in service, I have always enjoyed dealing with the English. In the 30's, I found a very elegant London clientele dining at the splendid hotels. Yet the years prior to the First World War saw the height of cuisine and service, with London a training school for chefs, restaurateurs, captains, waiters. It was almost a must to have some London training to qualify for posts in the good restaurants of other European cities and New York.

To retreat a little in time. While we take for granted being able to eat away from home, such an idea was unknown in ancient days. Then there were inns where one could sleep, eat and get provisions for one's horse when travelling. There was no such a thing as a restaurant. History tells us they began in England in the Middle Ages, where two kinds of establishments became the forerunners of the modern restaurant: The Tavern and The Cookshop. Even in the twelfth century, there were cookshops in London. Their chief business was the preparation of cooked meats which customers took home to eat. Occasionally they served these cooked dishes on the premises, which is the basic idea of a restaurant. The true ancestor of the restaurant is the ancient tavern, which developed the custom of providing a daily repast. It was called an *ordinary*, and at a certain hour every day, a meal was served.

The word *restaurant* was unknown until about 1765. At that time a Frenchman, Monsieur Boulanger, opened such a place in Paris to serve light refreshments and meals. It became instantly popular and was quickly imitated by others. Many places opened in France and

94

called themselves restaurants. However, the word was not generally used in England until the end of the nineteenth century. In England the idea of restaurants spread more slowly than in France. England had her coffee houses, taverns, ordinaries and tea shops. Finally, in 1873, the first restaurant was opened in London.

From early years, the English were connoisseurs of food and drink, customs which they brought with them to America during colonial times. The first New Yorkers drank prodigious amounts of Madeira, claret and other wines, to say nothing of beers and ales . . . and rum. At naval and military dinners the variety of courses was exceeded by the number of toasts drunk. The Revolution might be said to have been launched on the fruit of the grape and hops. No official dinner after Independence was complete without drinking at least thirteen toasts, one for each state, followed by toasts to popular officers, and almost any abstraction, such as love, the beauty of women, and the bravery of men. While toasts were the order of the day in England and America, they were not drunk in France until the French Revolution.

The word *toast* comes from the English. When they drank anyone's health, a piece of toast was placed at the bottom of the common beer pot. Whoever drank last got the nicely soaked toast. There have been legends of baths in champagne and one, of course, comes out of Merrie Olde England. The story goes that Anne Boleyn, one of the most beautiful women in all England, was taking her champagne bath, a ritual witnessed by the lords of her suite. The gentlemen, very humanly courting her smiles and favor, each took a glass, dipped it in the tub, and drank to the beauty's good health. All but one—a dark and handsome lord who stood apart from the others. Asked why he did not follow their example, he is said to have replied: "I am waiting for the toast!"

At an English dinner, toasts were always drunk to the ladies, extolling their charms and beauty. Well known for his chivalry, Lord B . . . , a true gallant, proposed: "Gentlemen, I drink to the beautiful sex of both hemispheres."

"And I," responded the Marquis de la V . . . , in a flash of realism, "I drink to both hemispheres of the beautiful sex."

It is difficult to say what country excels in cuisine when each has contributed so much to the happiness of mankind. It would take volumes just to touch on subjects pertaining to food and drink. Perhaps the most popular titles of publishing houses are those relative to cookery and culinary arts. John Ruskin (1819-1900), London born, concerned himself mostly with moral and social problems, and yet he saw particular significance in the effect of food on well-being. His definition of cookery is a classic:

"Cookery means carefulness and inventiveness, willingness and readiness of appliances. It means the economy of your grandmother; the science of the modern chemist; it means much tasting and no wasting; it means English thoroughness and French art and Arabian hospitality."

In England, the reputable innkeeper was held in high esteem. Some of the old epitaphs reveal their life's story, such as the one of John Wigglesworth of Whalley (mentioned in Mr. Charles G. Harper's delightful two-volume work on old and historic English inns.)

HERE LIES THE BODY OF JOHN WIGGLESWORTH

More than fifty years he was the perpetual
innkeeper of this town.
Notwithstanding the temptations of that
dangerous calling,
He maintained good order in his House.
Kept the Sabbath Day holy, frequented
the Public Worship with his family;
Induced his guests to do the same, and
Regularly partook of the Holy Communion.
He was also bountiful to the poor, in private,
As well as in public, and by the blessings
Of Providence on a life so spent
Died possessed of competent wealth.

There is no doubt about it, as the inn reflects England and the English home, so does the dignified innkeeper truly reflect the Englishman. If you search your memory, you may recall Chaucer's description of the host of the fourteenth century Tabard Inn. With minor alterations, it is suitable to all efficient hosts, and a fair portrait of the

Englishman. Thomas Burke, in his book "The English Inn," maintains that if one wishes to isolate the typical Englishman for study, it would be possible to see him in the person of the master of a really good inn. I find this of pertinent interest because, in a sense, it aptly describes what, in general, is expected of the successful restaurateur.

In no profession (save, perhaps, medicine) is the tradition of courtesy, service and respect for the calling more closely observed. If the innkeeper or the modern restaurateur could fulfil his varied and incessant duties without the criticism of the public, he would be not man but an angel. In the first place, not only has he to know more than most business men: he has to *be* more. He must adapt himself to many types of people. He must be silent with the silent and talkative with the chatty. Not alone should he be able to converse with the sportsman, the merchant, the amateur politician, the great statesman, banker, industrialist, lawyer, stockbroker, the elegante, bon vivant, the publisher of legal treatises, the humorist, the disillusioned, the old man, the dashing youth, actor, singer, facetious man, gloomy man, pompous and arrogant man or woman, the loose man, the teetotaller and the tippler, but he must convince each one that he is intensely interested in their affairs to the exclusion of all others.

He must also be able to absorb a certain amount of spleen on the part of customers when they are out of sorts, at which times even the most delightful dishes will be found fault with. Criticism such as an out-of-humor patron can level at a hapless captain or host is well understood. If such a patron were to aim his remarks at one of his own staff, it would end in him being abandoned to his resources. If aimed at a spouse, there could be no retreat; at a relative, it would weaken the bonds of kinship. By paying for his dinner, the badgered individual feels safe in badgering in his own turn, which gives him a certain amount of satisfaction.

It is the personality of the owner or manager-host which makes or mars an establishment. He may have a delightful place, beautifully furnished and luxuriously appointed, an excellent chef and crew for the service; but if he himself is not a pleasant person whose emotions are well balanced, then all these accoutrements will count for nothing. People will simply not "take to" or "go for" the place. They will be

97

vaguely aware of something lacking in the atmosphere, whether they see the head man or not; and they will warn their friends against it. That is why the company-owned and managed establishment lacks personality, for the person of greatest importance, the owner, is not there. Trade comes and goes, constantly being renewed by the efforts of the drummers of trade, but the place does not become a home to patrons because of the lack of a congenial personality at its head.

Now to London Town in our own century. In 1909-10, the Claridge of London was at the height of its elegance. Attendants in the lobby and the doormen were attired in period costume with silk stockings and knee breeches, and powdered wigs. When I visited London in 1931 I found the attendants had elegant livery and the atmosphere and service of the hotel was the breath of opulence.

Times changed and so did the old institutions of hospitality. A visit in 1953 proved disappointing. My wife and I, returning from a summer in Italy, stayed for a while in Paris and reluctantly leaving the George V's comfortable quarters, crossed the Channel from Calais, France in the *Invicta*. It was something of an historic barge since it had served in the Royal Naval Auxiliary in 1942 at Dieppe for the Normandy Invasion. We went from Dover by train to London through the lovely County of Kent with its sheep, orchards and hop fields. England dearly loves its beer and ale. It has long been customary for workers from London to take "vacations" in Kent, where they can earn something extra by picking hops. We saw prefabricated homes which had been hurriedly erected after the war to house those who had been bombed out.

Eleven years after World War II, butter and meat were still being rationed; sugar had just been put on the free list. Powdered eggs were in use. At the Claridge, our first luncheon comprised a cup of boullion, two small lamb chops, braised celery, some cooked fruit and wine. The cost was £3 6s. At the time a £ was worth $2.50. I remember the French wine was a 1937 vintage called *Chateau La Rose*. The waiter had opened it elsewhere, and had decantered it, bringing the canter to the table and nesting the empty bottle in a wine basket. There was no way to determine whether the wine offered had come from that particular bottle. Ostensibly served in a canter to eliminate the sediment expected in an old wine, we found when the caraffe was empty that the bottom was covered with sediment. It seemed to us that every indignity possible had been visited on the wine, its mode of service, and the patron in an age-old ritual which should have been proper, full of grace, and a thing of joy.

When the wine steward was called to the table to give an account of himself as to why he had opened the wine without our permission and without first showing us the unopened bottle with its label for approval and determining if the selection was satisfactory, he said that "the wine had been opened three hours earlier to get it at room temperature." He could not answer our question as to how he would know that this particular bottle would be called for by anyone, or why he had decantered it away from the table and not in our presence. It was obvious that this man dressed in the uniform of a wine steward, with his insignia of the sommelier, was an incompetent who did not know wine from beer.

This particular wine suffers from exposure to air. When opened even ten minutes it undergoes chemical changes and was, of course, supposed to be opened before us, and served immediately or a few moments before the entree. The service of the luncheon was poor, and still further to destroy any pleasure one might experience in the beautiful old dining room I had remembered from earlier visits, in which so many historic people had been entertained, the waiters quarreled among themselves behind the screen near which we were seated. It was, indeed, a far different Claridge from its great old days.

Yet it was in London where the great luxury hotels entertained the wealthy and powerful. The sprawling metropolis of London joined by the River Thames to the City Westminster and its West End, and heading twenty-nine boroughs, still has its fine hotels in which great changes have transpired. On Oxford Street, which begins at the Bank of England, is the famed Ritz, queen of luxury hotels. At the Savoy, waiters still appeared in their long tails, but the elegance of service was missing, a waiter bringing a plate of soup across the room instead of serving it from a container bowl over a flame to keep it piping hot. Here where only those attired in full formal dress were previously admitted, now casually attired young people danced to an indifferent orchestra.

It was obvious that the war had done more than destroy buildings and churches. The great iron railings around Hyde Park had been taken for the war effort. Once called Millionaire's Row, there were not enough millionaires to people Park Lane. As for our waiter at the Claridge, we later discovered that his earnings were discouraging. He got £7 from the house, and the balance of £4 to £5 in tips averaged out to $30.00 a week. He bought his own full dress suit with tails, paid for his own laundry, and shouldered his heavy English taxes.

To get the feel of old London requires a visit to Fortnum & Mason at Piccadilly W. 1, the variety house which has been in the merchandising business since 1707. In its six stories are packed a great number of things. On the lower ground floor is hidden the gift department, china, glass, luggage, a travel bureau, clocks and watches, the ground floor has the grocery, prepared foods, tea and coffee, wines and spirits, fruit, flowers, a Spanish Bar and a soda fountain. Then follow clothes, household furnishings, men's tailoring, typewriters, and finally on the fourth floor a restaurant.

In 1788 this store sold boned portions of poultry and game in aspic jelly, decorated with lobsters and prawns; potted meats, hard-boiled eggs in forcemeats (Scotch eggs) eggs in brandy-soaked cake with whipped cream; mince pies, dried fruits. During the Napoleonic Wars, officers posted abroad called for clothing and trade boomed at the store for tailors and breeches-makers. The store was the source of many delicacies during the reign of Queen Victoria and its popularity carried into the Edwardian age. High society was having a splendid time, despite the fact the aging Queen was living in almost complete seclusion. She had some sharp things to say about goings-on from time to time. When she died, her son became Edward VII, and London under the inexhaustible guidance of His Majesty, became the gayest city in the world, outstripping all previous records in the way of balls, parties and picnics.

Fortnum's was there to supply the needs. At this time they undertook the provision of food, wines, flowers, table requisites and decorations, complete with chefs, butlers and footmen—a complete catering service, including if need be toastmasters, musicians, whole orchestras. In 1908 they set up a new department to provide camping equipment and necessities for safaris. In 1956 the fine new restaurant was installed on its top floor which appointed its own Groom of the Pastry. Under him and his assistants, a bakery was created in the old tradition.

Celebrating its 250th anniversary in 1957, the unique store published an unusual brochure entitled "The Delectable History of Fortnum & Mason." The Sherry Wine and Spirits Store on Sixty-first Street and Madison Avenue, New York, are the sole United States representatives of the London merchants, obtaining from them some very good ports and sherries among other things. We are indebted to them for the inside story of the landmark we visited in London's Piccadilly.

There is only one London where the culinary arts once reached their greatest flowering against an historic background without an equal in historic memories. Historic—not artistic—for great art one leaves behind in Italy and France. In the Kensington Gardens of Hyde Park is the Prince Albert Memorial which the English guide himself admitted is an "artistic horror," and Albert Hall, which can seat 10,000 people, and has one of the largest organs in the world. London itself is poor in monuments and fountains, and those which exist are strangely uninspired. In Chelsea, which used to be the artists' center in the old days, they will not deny it. Yet it is thrilling to hear the booming voice of Big Ben on the Parliamentary buildings on the Thames as you watch the slow progress of the coal barges coming from Newcastle, carrying 2,000 tons of coal a day to be used by the power station which generates electricity for the ancient city.

All the familiar names are here: Chelsea Bridge and London Bridge, which cross the River Thames; Lambeth Palace, the home of the Bishop of Canterbury, which was heavily bombed during the war. William Rufus built Westminster Hall some 900 years ago. And 600 years ago Richard II commissioned architects and engineers to raise, by some means, a roof which became the widest unsupported wooden roof in the world. It was in Westminster Hall that Richard II was feted in a magnificent banquet after his coronation in the Abbey. Here the English law courts presided up to 77 years ago, and Charles I was condemned to death. Weakening timbers are replaced from great oaks on the estate in Sussex whence came the original beams. This is the true heart of London. Westminster Hall leads into the Houses of Parliament, part of which was demolished by bombs and had to be rebuilt. At the time of this bombing, Big Ben was stopped. One can never forget this famous timepiece. It is the largest and most accurate clock in the world, with a minute hand fourteen feet long. Ben's tremendous voice commands attention and respect.

Hampton Court, a few miles outside London, was the scene of many great feasts and dinners whose culinary perfection became the basis of English cookery. Cardinal Wolsey built this mansion in 1510, intending it for himself, but Henry VIII found it eminently suitable for himself. As everyone knows, Henry had a Gargantuan appetite. His other propensities—wives, for instance—paled in comparison. At Hampton Court we were told that Big Henry was 6' 2" in height and 58" around his middle.

The dining rooms, especially, are magnificent. Here truly is an edifice worthy of a King of England. When Henry coveted the great and beautiful house, the disappointed Cardinal gave in and lied: "Ah! I built it for you, your Majesty." Cardinal Wolsey was a great gourmet and often entertained five hundred choice guests to whom six hundred servants administered. This retreat was a favorite place for royalty up to 1760. King George II lived here in 1732 and used to box the ears of his son George III when he failed to do his lessons. Young George (who, as you know became the King during the American Revolution period) came to hate Hampton Court and as soon as he could went off to Windsor Castle. It was William III who planted the lovely yew trees you see in the garden. Now over 250 years old, they have witnessed the arrival of many guests, have heard the laughter and joyousness of great festivals echo and re-echo from wall to wall and spill over into the gardens and orchards as men and women dined, wined and reveled in the palatial salons.

To see Old England is to understand its modern counterpart. It is interesting to note that the elegant Savoy Hotel of London is the source of the classic handbook of mixed drinks which has found its way to many well-known bars of New York and other American cities. Published by Messrs. Constable & Co. Ltd of London, "The Savoy Cocktail Book" first appeared in 1930. On its title page the popular drinks of the hotel were included in this fashion:

THE SAVOY
COCKTAIL BOOK

Being a compendium of

COCKTAILS

Sours	Flips
Toddies	Coolers
Smashes	Daisies
Highballs	Egg Noggs
Tom Collins	Sangarees
Punches	Cobblers
Rickeys	Juleps
Slings	Shrubs
Fizzes	Frappe

Fixes & Cups

Nicholas Bentley Drew the Pictures
Peter Coffin Designed the Cover

The volume includes as well "sundry notes of amusement and interest concerning the cocktails, together with subtle observations upon wines and their special occasions, being in particular an elucidation of the manners and customs of people of quality in a period of some inequality." This book sold rapidly during the 1930's and was reprinted eight times within eight years. Expensively produced, war conditions forced it out of print, and since then second-hand booksellers have found it difficult to meet requests for copies. In 1952, a new edition of the famous pre-war Savoy Cocktail Book was published in a less extravagant format, containing all essential information about cocktails and other drinks, and with a great deal of new material added.

It proved extremely popular and paved the way to the issue of the text in an inexpensive edition of 5,000 copies in November of 1954, which sold for ten shillings. A new specially designed edition followed, bringing the material up-to-date and meeting the continuing demand for the popular bar book. The author of the volume was Harry Craddock, who for so long headed the famous American Bar at the Savoy. He contributed his recipes and they were augmented by his successor at the Savoy, Johnny Johnson, who included some of his own discoveries, among them his appropriately named "The Comet."

It was in 1933 that the Wine and Food Society, under the presidency of the world's foremost wine authority, André L. Simon, was founded with headquarters at 30 Grosvenor Gardens, London, S.W. 1, and so great has been the public interest in the world of wines and food that branches have been established in many countries: Scotland, Wales and Eire, of course, then Australia, British East Africa, Canada, Ceylon, Far East, India, Japan, Malaya, New Zealand, Northern Rhodesia, South Africa, Southern Rhodesia. In the United States there are branches in several states: Ohio, California, Maryland, Massachusetts, Illinois, Indiana, Hawaii, Missouri, Connecticut, Minnesota, Louisiana, New York, Pennsylvania, and in Washington, D.C.

The objects of the Society are to bring together and to serve all who believe that a right understanding of wine and food is an essential part of personal contentment and health and that an intelligent approach to the pleasures and problems of the table offers far greater rewards than the mere satisfaction of appetite. To raise the standard of cookery by organizing periodical dinners and luncheons at different hotels, restaurants and clubs when the fare and the wines will be happily partnered and when deserving chefs will be accorded a fair measure of articulate appreciation.

To promote a wider knowledge of the wines of the world and a more discerning appreciation of their individual merits by means of periodical tastings and visits to various vineyards. To maintain a library of MSS, books and documents relating to the art of good living, which shall be accessible to members of the Society.

Mr. Simon has done a prodigious amount of writing in behalf of the culinary arts. His books, dating from 1905 to the present, number 112 volumes. Some can be found in the New York City Library, but most are out of print, and some have been superseded by current books. Certain titles by Mr. Simon as well as other authors are now available from Society headquarters in London. The Society has available culinary glossaries of pocket size in French, Spanish, Italian and German, as well as vintage charts which are revised yearly and printed in vest-pocket size on celluloid. The gastronomic organ of the Society is its "Wine and Food," a quarterly magazine obtainable by annual subscription.

VINTAGE CHART FROM WINE AND FOOD SOCIETY
of London, England

Every care is taken by the Society to make the chart an accurate factual index at the time of its publication. However, the list is not all-inclusive for there are always some very good wines made when a vintage is not deserving of the highest marks, just as there are some bad wines made in the best vintages. The chart grades the wines from zero to seven, the highest grade.

Year	Port	Claret	Burgundy	Rhone	Rhine and Moselle	Sauternes	White Burgundy	Champagne
1938	5	4	3	5	4	3	4	4
1939	3	2	2	3	3	2	2	2
1940	5	4	2	2	3	3	1	3
1941	4	1	1	3	2	0	1	4
1942	6	3	3	5	5	4	4	5
1943	5	5	5	6	5	6	6	5
1944	4	4	2	3	3	4	2	3
1945	6	6	7	6	6	7	6	6
1946	5	3	4	4	4	3	5	3
1947	7	7	7	7	6	7	7	7
1948	7	6	5	4	5	4	5	4
1949	4	7	7	6	7	5	6	6
1950	5	6	4	6	5	4	6	3
1951	3	3	3	4	2	3	3	2
1952	4	6	7	7	6	6	6	7
1953	5	7	6	6	7	7	7	7
1954	5	4	4	5	3	3	4	3
1955	7	6	6	7	5	6	6	7
1956	1	3	2	5	3	4	3	4
1957	4	4	5	4	5	3	5	2
1958	5	5	3	6	5	5	4	3
1959	–	7	7	5	7	7	7	7

England has always been known as a country which enjoyed its port and sherry. One company, in particular, devoted its efforts for many years to handling these two wines. When in London, one will be intrigued by 13 Sherborne Lane, which backs on 20 St. Swithins Lane, and is occupied by the offices and wine vaults of George G. Sandeman Sons & Co. Ltd. We learned that the origin of this family's connection with port and sherry began back in 1790 when George Sandeman, a member of an old Scottish clan, founded the House of Sandeman in London. His father had lent him £300 with which he purchased a modest wine vault, with no idea that the undertaking would eventually expand to world-wide proportions with vast port wine lodges in Oporto, Portugal, and extensive sherry bodegas at Jerez in Spain.

By the end of the eighteenth century, conditions essential to the production of fine port wine had been discovered, and by 1790 this knowledge was applied to Portuguese Douro wines so that they became favorites with the English, to whom they were exported. Also at this time, Vintage port was introduced, and George Sandeman shipped the 1790 vintage which was a sample of this wine at its best. Those familiar with the customs of the English coffee house know that it was used for the transaction of business both in England and in America, to which the coffee house tradition was brought. At first George Sandeman did not have an office at all, but simply used a portfolio for his papers, and did his business in Tom's Coffee House in Birchin Lane, Cornhill, in the City of London.

At Tom's he met other importers and merchants like himself. It was at Lloyd's Coffee House, in fact, that the Lloyds of London Insurance Company was founded in the late seventeenth century. His first office, a very small one, was at 24 Old Jewry. Later George Sandeman began to travel both in Portugal and Spain, enlarging his activities so that by 1805 he was able to secure the lease of 20 St. Swithins Lane together with the adjoining premises, where he lived with his family. Mr. Sandeman wore breeches and top boots. He had a white wig and people called him "Old Cauliflower." After his death in Brussels in 1841, his nephew, George Glas Sandeman, took charge of the company until his own death in 1868.

The company added linens, cotton goods, etc. and purchased their own clipper ship *Hoopoe* to run between Oporto and the east coast ports of England. On his father's death, his eldest son, Albert George Sandeman, succeeded and operated the company until 1923, bringing his three brothers into the firm as partners. Albert George mingled with aristocratic circles, and married the eldest daughter of the Visconde da Torre de Moncorvo, then Ambassador at the Court of St. James. While conducting the company, he also became Director of the Bank of England and was its Governor in 1896 and 1897.

His eldest son, Walter Albert Sandeman (1858-1937), succeeded him in 1923. At that time, new commercial practices were employed and extensive advertising used. It is the old story of family loyalty and devotion building a fine business enterprise. In 1928 the firm acquired the Company's now universally known Spanish trade-mark. The black-coated figure in silhouette with the Spanish hat and raised glass over the blocked letters of SANDEMAN PORT has been kept unchanged. From the first, the firm banked on one characteristic: by temperament the Briton is suitable to port because of the English climate. That simple premise became the foundation of a respected house which today features great ports and sherries: Three Star Ruby, Three Star Tawny, Picador, Partners, Imperial . . . its White Ports are Three Star White and Imperial White. Vintage Ports come from the vintage years of 1927, 1934, 1935, 1942, 1943, 1945, 1947, and 1950, with its famous Sherries, Three Star Dry Pale, Three Star Brown, Dry Don, Apitiv, Amontillado, Brown Bang and Royal Pemartin . . . wonderful wines with a wonderful history. While we corresponded in the past two years or so with Mr. Patrick Sandeman, the last letter was written by David Sandeman who told regretfully of his father's death in June, 1960. Here surely is a dynasty of wine merchants in the finest tradition.

The English have always had a basic instinct and appreciation of the comforts of life, a philosophy which is enduring. The oft-quoted prayer found in Chester Cathedral epitomizes the significance of man's short span on earth, during which good friends and humble enjoyment of food and drink should properly play an important role. The poet's name has long been forgotten, but his well-chosen words still inspire us.

> Give me a good digestion, Lord.
> And also something to digest.
> Give me a healthy body, Lord
> With sense to keep it at its best.
>
> Give me a healthy mind, good Lord,
> To keep the good and pure in sight
> Which, seeing sin, is not appalled
> But finds a way to set it right.
>
> Give me a mind that is not bored,
> That does not whimper, whine or sigh.
> Don't let me worry overmuch
> About the fussy thing called I.
>
> Give me a sense of humor, Lord.
> Give me the grace to see a joke;
> To get some happiness from life,
> And pass it on to other folk.

Escoffier, the Royal Chef

"Nothing is so contagious as enthusiasm. It is the real allegory of the tale of Orpheus; it moves stones and charms brutes. It is the genius of sincerity and truth accomplishes no victories without it."
—BULWER-LYTTON

THE NAME OF ESCOFFIER IS HELD IN REVERENCE by restaurateurs and gourmets alike. It connotes genius of a high order. To the knowing restaurateur it means even more. He realizes that here was a Frenchman divinely inspired in the creation of new dishes and the transformation of the old; additionally, he had the abilities and talents of an engineer which he applied to revolutionizing restaurateurship to such a degree he has become known as the "father of the modern restaurant." No work on the culinary arts would be complete without pausing to consider Escoffier. For a long period only those who knew the French language had access to the mysteries of Escoffier's secrets as revealed in *The Escoffier Cook Book*. However, in 1941 this hefty volume was issued in an English translation by Crown Publishers of New York, and since that time has gone through many printings.

This fascinating volume contains 2973 recipes and is the Bible of Culinary Art which every chef keeps in his desk for ready reference. The recipes are as given by Escoffier, with the weights, quantities and terms according to American usage. While it is known to be the treasure of connoisseurs, chefs and gourmets, it is also widely read by those who appreciate excellence in food preparation. Continually in demand, the book had its twenty-first printing in 1960. It contains 923 pages, and by some miracle sells for less than four dollars.

The proudest boast of any chef is that he served under and received training by Escoffier, whose name is now a legend. Born the son of a blacksmith, in 1846, he was at thirteen apprenticed to his uncle, who ran a restaurant on the Riviera. Diminutive in size, George Auguste Escoffier in his prime (with his handle-bar moustaches of snowy white) presented a distinguished appearance. He was to prove highly deserving of the title: "The King of Chefs and the Chef to Kings."

When Escoffier arrived in Paris in 1865, he was nineteen years of age, At that time he was already a chef of stature, having long been an apprentice and having absorbed intimate knowledge of the culinary arts. Word soon sped around Paris that here was a young man whose theories were revolutionary. For one thing, he made the pronouncement that "Food should look like food." At this time every effort was being made to disguise a dish so that it was anybody's guess as to what it might actually contain.

Furthermore, Escoffier was firm in his belief that food should be digestible. It had long been accepted that to dress in the height of fashion one must, of course, be uncomfortable. To dine on food which tasted fine enough for the gods, one must expect indigestion or some other ill effect. Escoffier said this was nonsense; cooking to be a great art must please the stomach as well as the palate—and many royal and noble stomachs were duly grateful. He quickly eliminated many of the elaborate garnishes and trimmings which formerly made food look artistic and colorful. Since a guest was obliged to eat these indigestible creations, it was detrimental to his health. Escoffier substituted attractive but less lethal garnishes.

It had been customary also to cover entrees with heavy flour-thickened sauces. Escoffier said this was absurd: an insult to the meats, fish and vegetables with their own delicate flavors. He introduced, instead, the technique he had developed of simmering foods in their own concentrated juices. However, Escoffier did not neglect presentation. A beautifully prepared dish served on an awkward platter was a lost cause to him, and he set about designing his own series of platters, sauceboats, servers, serving spoons, and other utensils to meet his exacting standards of service.

Quality not quantity was the banner which he hoisted over his originally created kingdom of culinary delights. Quite correctly, he held that it was impossible for a human being to plow through the usual twenty courses of a formal dinner. From Greek and Roman times, innumerable courses had always signified wealth and consequence. Henry VIII was the standard-bearer of the multi-coursed banquet. Escoffier trimmed menus down to seven courses in a sequence "carefully designed to create a symphony of flavors."

His experience was wide from his earliest years. During the Franco-Prussian War, as a young cook, Escoffier practiced his trade in the army. His immediate problem was to create food out of practically nothing. The troops had consumed just about everything edible in their ravaging marches. When his unit was faced with eating horse-meat, or going without this necessary strength-giving source of protein, Escoffier devised a way to make the meat more tasty. His recipe was to scald and cool it before cooking, thus killing the strongly bitter taste.

It is said that his military experience helped him to create delicacies which lent themselves to preservation in cans or glass. Some of his most famous sauces are available to restaurants and homemakers: *Sauce Diable* is a tangy blend of tomatoes, vinegar, sugar, tamarinds, dates, mangoes, raisins and spices, which goes extremely well in enhancing the flavor of fish, meats, eggs and all kinds of grilled foods; *Sauce Robert* is a combination of tomatoes, vinegar, sugar, pimentoes and spices for steaks, chops and poultry, described by an appreciative cook once as "the world's most elegant ketchup." Not to be overlooked is his *Sauce Melba,* delightful on ice cream. Escoffier sauces are made available by Julius Wile of New York. Himself the great magician of the sauce, Escoffier warned of the importance of avoiding excessive seasoning for he knew that many makers of inferior sauces thus camouflaged their insipidness, which he called "an absolutely deplorable practice."

It may be thought that Escoffier possessed the temperament and arrogance some artists believe their privilege. It is a false assumption for this truly great culinary artist realized early in his career that an irrascible temper or fits of anger were inexcusable, even in a genius. He had seen too much of tyrannical chefs who ruled over kitchens by fear and force. This was the order of his day, and these chefs, who operated more like custodians of serfs than sensible managers, rarely hesitated in loudly cursing their assistants when they were slow or forgetful. Nor did they hesitate to beat the young apprentices who made mistakes. Escoffier felt this established an atmosphere of resentment and unhappiness which went poorly with the creation of dishes meant to bring joy and elation. And yet, in our own time, some chefs, who claim to be his faithful followers, have felt they are entitled by their exalted position to displays of temperament and egoism. They still operate (as far as they are allowed) by the rule of the rod, and a hapless assistant may get a badly broiled steak thrust into his face, this supposedly teaching him how to broil it properly the next time. It is an ill-conceived attitude not in the spirit of Escoffier.

Escoffier was so short in stature he wore built-up shoes to keep his head away from the oven flames. He always worked hard, was alert to learning everything possible, and was swift in his movements. It is not surprising, therefore, that he was ready when his great opportunity appeared on the horizon. He was an unknown when he was hired by César Ritz, the great Swiss, to be the chef of the Grand Hotel in Monte Carlo. The two men were perfectionists. Fate brought them together and made them into a powerful team. They spent most of the balance of their careers working in perfect harmony. The name of Ritz has entered the language as a synonym of luxury. Like the Pied Piper of Hamlin, whose music was irresistible to the children who followed him into oblivion, these two were followed from hotel to hotel by the royalty of Europe. Russian grand dukes, England's Prince of Wales, the titled and wealthy of many countries, constituted their Court of Exquisite Tastes.

Together they operated the most aristocratic hotel in London—the fabulous Savoy—where for the first time, at the turn of the century, was served on the menu *Cuisses de Nymphes à L'Aurore*. The Prince of Wales, son of Queen Victoria, who later became Edward VII, was simply entranced. Translating the French, the guests read "the thighs of nymphs at dawn." The delectable little white thighs poached in a white-wine bouillon were steeped in a cream sauce, seasoned with paprika, tinted gold, and covered by a champagne aspic—served cold. But what fowl or flesh were they? It was a crucial moment. Would English society accept what they really were—frogs' legs, so divinely presented? The very thought of Frenchmen eating frogs' legs, to which they had long been devoted, was considered by the well-bred Englishman to be a form of barbarism. It was a magic and majestic feat. Escoffier watched the diners through the circular window of the door of his kitchen. He was gratified to see that acceptance was immediate. Opportunity then beckoned at the Ritz in Paris, from which Escoffier later returned to London to rule the kitchens of the majestic Carlton Hotel.

Escoffier insisted on absolute cleanliness of both kitchens and employees. He established an atmosphere of efficiency of which calmness was the potent ingredient. As a youngster, he had vowed that if he were ever fortunate enough to become a chef he would put an end to the indignities he suffered in his youth. He was often tempted by carelessness, stupidity and outrageous, inexcusable errors to lose his composure, and it took great strength of character, nerves of steel, to leave the kitchen at such times, saying "I can feel myself getting angry. I am going out." Small as he was, dignity was his trade-mark. During the week, he supervised his kitchen dressed in a black dress coat which had been severely tailored. On Sundays, he wore the traditional *Toque Blanche,* high white hat, and a white coat. For his evening meal he invariably had a bowl of soup with some rice, and some fresh fruit. He neither smoked nor drank to keep his senses of taste and smell at their peak of sensitivity. He supervised his cooking, not by taste, but by sniffing the odors.

When the Carlton Hotel was opened in London in 1899, Escoffier was in charge of the great kitchens. A revolutionary move was the introduction for the first time of a completely *à la carte* restaurant service. It was, indeed, a daring innovation which required much clever engineering to serve a turn-over of five hundred diners a day from a large selection of dishes on the menu. Perhaps this was Escoffier's greatest achievement. He perfected a system of specialization which comprised a division of the kitchen equivalent to what in a factory would be an assembly line. In order to produce dishes in time, he organized his workers into separate teams. One team worked on soups, another on fish, another on fowl and roasts, some made sauces only, still another was in charge of pastries, sweets and other desserts.

This is how it worked. A waiter brought the captain's order to *L'annonceur*. This worthy was chosen for the strength and enduring qualities of his lungs. He cried out the dish to be prepared in a loud voice. If it were a roast requiring a sauce, the teams of both those departments immediately set to work preparing it. This worked very well in Escoffier's time, and since then the same principle has become accepted practice in hotels and restaurants, as I have outlined in the chapter Kingdom of the Kitchen—with the exception of the vocal blasts. This for the most part is omitted. Nothing can be worse in a small kitchen adjoining the dining room, where the guests are made to understand that a French chef is going through his culinary gymnastics to produce for them an expensively priced dish. Such exhibitions of vocalism should be left to the yodelers of the Swiss Alps. They have no place in the well-ordered kitchen, and only result in a highly nervous staff who feel that they are being treated like galley slaves. A French chef who acts in this manner wanders far from Escoffier's original intention.

When a dish was ready to be taken to the dining room, it was brought to Escoffier, who gave it the blessing of his approval, or sent it back if it was not the epitome of perfection. The inspiration which prompted Escoffier to reorganize the old-fashioned system of the kitchen was most timely. This feat alone entitles him to be renowned as the "Father of Modern Restaurant Service." A specific example will show the efficiency introduced. Under the old regime, Eggs Mayerbeer took a cook at least fifteen minutes to prepare. But under the system of specialization, an *entremetier* baked the eggs in butter, a *rôtisseur* grilled the kidney, a *saucier* prepared the truffle sauce, and the diner quickly had his eggs on the table. That is the way a well-organized French kitchen is operated to this day. Nothing was too unimportant to receive careful attention. The successful chef and restaurateur today must adhere in essence to the same principles, for success is achieved by the efficient management of a myriad details.

Sarah Bernhardt was addicted to Escoffier's eggs. He always mixed them with a knife on whose point was a small clove of garlic, which gave the omelet a heavenly flavor, though the actress was unaware of its source, and always maintained that she could not bear the aromatic lily. It is a compliment to one's guests when a dish of eggs is properly prepared. It is necessary to cook Eggs Benedictine as they should be prepared, for many a reputation depends on doing it correctly. The insults which have been heaped on the egg are inexcusable. The cook of the eccentric Gertrude Stein certainly had the right idea when she declared that one's respect or disrespect could be shown in the method one used to prepare eggs for a guest. Said she one day: "Monsieur Matisse is staying for dinner this evening. In that case, I will not make an omelette but fry the eggs. It takes the same number of eggs and the same amount of butter, but it shows less respect and he will understand."

When the Ritz-Carlton hotel was conceived for New York as a direct descendant of the Ritz in Paris and the Carlton in London, it was to win the esteem of royalty and set the standard for an America eager to learn the ways of elegance. Robert W. Goelet, the real estate tycoon, persuaded César Ritz to manage and operate an American hotel on a grand scale. Robert Dana of the *N. Y. World Telegram & Sun* points out that "it is quite possible smart Madison Avenue and surroundings owe their modern chic affluence to Mr. Goelet and the astute César Ritz." Auguste Escoffier was brought to New York to impregnate his culinary standards of excellence and classical French cuisine. The grand manner was maintained for forty years by Chef Louis Diat, who gave a lifetime of devotion to the Ritz-Carlton, as he followed faithfully in the footsteps of the little master—Escoffier. Others have carried on his traditions. When the Ritz-Carlton at Forty-sixth Street and Madison was torn down, the profits from its sale built the new Carlton House at 680 Madison Avenue, sixteen blocks north.

With the move went many of the permanent residents of the old hotel, its restaurants and much of its staff. As the Ritz-Carlton Company celebrated its golden anniversary in 1960, there were seventy of the staff who had been with the original Ritz for half a century, and remembered Escoffier.

Today's executive chef who is justly famous and remembered for his long association with the old Hotel Lafayette on lower Fifth Avenue is Monsieur Gaston Martin. Gaston Lauryssen, president of the Ritz-Carlton Hotel Company and general manager of Carlton House, in turn, has stressed fine service with all captains required to study a book on French wines in order to make intelligent use of a good wine cellar. Maitre d' George Stich, formerly with the Colony Restaurant, is President of the Sommelier Society of America, and is one of the small band who strives to keep alive the tradition of the old masters of food and wine, whose patron saint is Auguste Escoffier.

Another great Frenchman who made a notable contribution to France as an exponent of the culinary arts, was Alexandre Dumas. In his happy collaboration with Auguste Maquet, he produced the famous "cloak and sword" romance *Les Troise Mousquetaires* in eight volumes. Based on reality, the material was discovered in the *Memoires de M. d'Artagnan* (Cologne 1701-02) of Courtils de Sandras. The many who are familiar with this classic feel that they are personally acquainted with the gigantically proportioned Porthos, the ingenuous and clever Aramis, the melancholy Athos, the glamorous and villainous Milady de Winter. The Musketeers it seems united their talents in defense of the honor of Anne of Austria against the machinations of the wily Cardinal Duc Armand Jean du Plessis de Richelieu (1585-1642) who really ran the country of France. Dumas brought the action of The Three Musketeers down to the murder of Buckingham in 1628. People loved the book and popular acclaim brought forth two sequels: *Vingt ans après,* in ten volumes, published in 1845, and *Dix ans plus tard ou le vicomte de Bragelonne,* which appeared three years later. The action of the latter opened in 1660. It shows us a mature d'Artagnan as a respectable captain of musketeers, and contains the magnificent narrative of the heroic death of Porthos.

The Three Musketeers became as famous in England as in France, as well as his *Le Comte de Monte-Cristo* in twelve volumes. For a long time these works were published in condensed very much abbreviated form to squeeze within the covers of single volumes. All of the voluminous original works of Alexandre Dumas abound with the joy of life and the delight of consuming food and drink. There are hundreds of references to food in great detail. Dumas himself considered the crowning work of his arduous life not one of the hundreds of volumes he wrote by longhand, but his enchanting Dictionary of Cuisine. It was an injustice to the world that this great work was always difficult to obtain. It was available in abbreviated form in French, but unobtainable to those who read another language. This culinary dictionary was the true expression of Dumas as a man and as a writer, with his wit, often ribald, his passionate attachment to France, his wide-ranging travels, his extensive general knowledge, his maturity and wisdom, and his own great personal vitality channeled from Mother Earth herself. Dumas firmly believed that man does not live on what he eats, but on what he actually digests, and which becomes part of his body. The Dictionary is a gold mine of fascinating legends, the history of foods, anecdotes, horticulture, and name-dropping, which has to be read to be believed.

Escoffier frequently referred to it. Many of his inspirations, and his courageous espousal of culinary revolution in the kitchens, can be traced directly to his possession of this unusual Dictionary of Cuisine by the brilliant French novelist. Here are a few excerpts as a sampling or *hors d'oeuvres:*

BOUILLON: There is no good cooking without good bouillon. French cooking, the first of all cuisines, owes its superiority to the excellence of French bouillon, which derives from a sort of intuition with which I shall not say our cooks, but our women of the people are endowed. Rivarol, leaving his soup plate three-quarters full, used to say to the gourmands of Lübeck and Hamburg: "Gentlemen, there isn't a sick nurse or a charwoman in France who cannot make a better bouillon than the best cook in the Hanseatic League."

PHEASANT: Croesus, seated on his diamond-encrusted throne,

crowned with his diadem, and clothed in purple and gold, asked Solon whether he had ever seen anything so fine: "Yes," the philosopher answered, "I have seen pheasants and peacocks." The flesh of the pheasant is perhaps the most delicate and savory there is . . . Braised, it may be served with a truffle sauce on a bed of olive ragout. The author of *The Henriade*—Voltaire—has written a poem far superior to his epic on the Bearnais King. It has only one line: The bird from the Phasis is a dish for the gods.

PORK: Pigs were the principal nourishment of the Gauls, who had great herds of them. The Romans cooked them whole, in two ways. One was to boil them on one side and roast them on the other. The second method was called the Trojan, an allusion to the famous horse. It was stuffed with fig-peckers, oysters and thrushes and basted with good wines and delicate juices. This dish became so extravagantly expensive that the senate enacted a sumptuary law forbidding it.

Humbert, Dauphin of Vienna, leaving for the Crusade in 1345 set up regulations for the management of his wife's house in his absence, limiting it to thirty persons. For these thirty persons, he allotted one pig a week, plus thirty salted pigs a year, which made it three pigs per person. The pig and the rabbit are the most prolific animals in the world. Vauban, an excellent mathematician, wrote a treatise on pigs that he called *La Cohonnerie*. He calculated the progeny of a single sow over twelve years: 6,434,838 pigs. (Probably with tongue in cheek.) (Of course Charles Lamb's famous Essay on *How to Roast a Pig* came along much later to tease the palate.)

QUAIL: This is the most darling and lovable of game. A fat quail gives equal pleasure by its flavor, color and form. It is an act of culinary ignorance to prepare quail in any way except roasted in buttered paper, for when they are in contact with a liquid their flavor is dissolved, evaporated and lost.

EEL: The Egyptians set eels among the gods and worshipped them. They raised them in ponds and special priests were charged with feeding them daily on cheese and entrails. They decorated them with jeweled collars. (Today the eel is favored by the Scandinavians, who punctuate their smorgasbord buffets with boiled eel.)

The entire Dumas Dictionary is delightful, if not always instructive on the actual means of food preparation, for it is not a recipe book, per se. That work was reserved for Chef Escoffier, but the Dumas book served as a firm foundation. Happily, a masterful translation was recently made by Louis Colman, and the Dictionary was published by Simon and Schuster, Inc. of New York City in 1958. I recommend it most heartily to all lovers of good food.

CHAPTER

 13

Great Chefs of New York

"Cookery has become an art, a noble science; cooks are gentlemen."
—Robert Burton, *Anatomy of Melancholy*

"Observation more than books, experience rather than persons, are the prime educators."
—A. B. Alcott, *Table Talk*

Even if a man received his training in France, it was customary to have service in England before coming to the United States. As mentioned, the Claridge of London was the last word in elegance. Built in 1845, it is still imposing with its white-walled rooms, white period furniture, and suite arrangements with large bedroom, dressing room, and private marble bath of enormous size. Its service naturally suffered as a result of war and post-war rationing and the general destruction of London under bombardment.

One of New York's fine chefs, Adam Wozniak, of Polish and French origin, now retired, served with Escoffier in England, as did many others while receiving training for a high post. Wozniak worked at the Claridge and at the Ritz in London before coming to New York where he became chef at the Alamac Hotel on 71st Street. This twenty-story building with 600 rooms was privately owned and managed. The dining rooms had an exclusive dinner trade, and Chef Wozniak had a staff of ninety under his supervision.

From our friend Wozniak we have reminiscences of olden days.

120

There was Scotto, another protege of Escoffier's who served under him at the Ritz in London before becoming executive chef of the Ambassador Hotel, on Park Avenue and Fifty-first Street, which is now the Sheraton East. Scotto made his reputation on the ship *Kaiserin*. His first post was in a small hotel in Cincinnati before coming to New York. Scotto, who died in the early Thirties, worked with Louis Diat at the Ritz in New York. The Ritz had been built in 1907, it has been dryly observed, to reward the rich for being wealthy. It was a wonderfully luxurious palace with soft rugs, great gilded mirrors, glittering chandeliers, its outsize bathtubs of truly Roman grandeur. Its hushed atmosphere of continental elegance was calculated to sooth the nerves of millionaires, and serve as the scene of memorable meetings and liaisons.

The food was superb. With all the many contributions he made to the culinary arts, Chef Louis Diat's greatest achievement is remembered as his invention of Vichyssoise around 1912. His "Primer for Gourmets" is full of interest and wisdom. For some time the *Gourmet Magazine* of New York City ran chapters of it for the enlightenment of its readers. Louis Diat was chef de cuisine of the Ritz Carlton, and its undisputed arbiter, for over forty years. Diat was most particular in his culinary terminology and patiently pointed out in his book the basic facts needed to understand French cuisine as it was developed against the background of France. He loved his native land and her traditional customs devotedly.

"It would take a tremendous social upheaval," wrote Diat, "and generations of living to remove *pâtés* from the French scene." He averred that this might seem strange to Americans who regard *pâtés* as just "extras" in an already bountiful array of French dishes. To a Frenchman, *pâtés* are a favorite for every important social occasion and, of course, an indispensable part of *la haute cuisine. Pâté de foi gras* opens a fine dinner in elegant style. French restaurants have their own *pâté maison* which *spécialité* reflects the chef's skill in blending meat mixtures and seasonings.

Diat was aware that it had become customary to describe as a *pâté* any of the finely ground mixtures made of pork, veal, fowl, game and liver. Technically speaking, most of these mixtures are not *pâtés* at all, but *terrines*. While the basic meat mixture remains exactly the same for both, when the meat is baked in a casserole lined with fat pork, it is a *terrine*. When it is baked in a crust—or, as the French say, *en croûte*—it becomes a *pâté*. Further, if the mixture is made from a fowl or game bird, and steamed instead of baked, then it is called a *galantine*. Louis Diat admitted that such precise information had little value in America, but it was helpful to anyone traveling in France. Sometimes, through lack of knowledge of French terms, people have ordered a *terrine* of game, expecting a kind of *fricassee* or stew prepared in a casserole, and were surprised and disappointed when slices of what they would have called *pâté* appeared on the table. People in France do not make their own *pâtés* because they can buy very good ones from the scores of charcuteries: shops which specialize in making *pâté, terrines, galantines,* and all the other *hors-d'oeuvre* specialties.

Diat showed his appreciation to the Ritz Carlton in his own way. As a chef he made hundreds of *terrines, pâtés* and *galantines* every Christmas during his forty years of service, and sent them to "the wonderful people who put their money, thought and skill into organizing the hotel and maintaining its standards. They were all gourmets, and most of them either had a continental background, or had spent much time in France, so that they really appreciated such a characteristically French gift."

The Ritz Carlton was operated with opulence and to it Diat contributed markedly. Today it seems like a dream of Scheherezade's *Thousand and One Nights*. Two waiters stood by day and night, on every floor of the hotel, to take care of the in-between-hunger of its fortunate guests. It is little wonder that the princes, premiers, the wealthy wanderers of the world flocked to the Ritz, which was the luxurious background for endless balls, receptions, cotillions and debutante presentations. When Barbara Hutton of Woolworth fame made her bow to society in 1930, it was in the massive golden ballroom of the Ritz, which was decorated with $10,000 worth of eucalyptus trees. For the coming-out party of another gilded deb, the same room was transformed into a tropical jungle with live monkeys jumping and squealing from tree to tree, causing great merriment among the guests.

Louis Diat rose and fell with his hotel, of which he was an integral part. His association spanned all of the years from opening until closing in 1951. Known as Monsieur Louis, he won many culinary honors including the *Order of Chevalier du Merité Agricole*. (He died in August of 1957 at the age of seventy-two.)

After four decades of dazzling prominence in the hotel world, the swank Ritz reached the termination of its career. When the management announced that the end had come, and the hotel would be demolished to make way for a twenty-five story office building, a chorus of protest arose. Guests began to bid for favorite pieces of furniture and decoration of what had been their hotel home. New York merchants snapped up doorknobs and keyplates for resale as souvenirs. In the first week of May 1951, the Ritz closed its doors forever. The owners decided to auction off the rugs, mirrors, fireplaces, dishes, stemware and silver which bore the Ritz crest. A wealthy Texan, Amon Carter, a publisher, bought the famous Men's Bar as a memento for his son, and two of the elevator cages, which he transformed into Powder Rooms in his Fort Worth home. After that, the Ritz and its wonders became part of New York legend, along with Café Martin, Holland House, Hoffman House, Delmonico's, Sherry's and their predecessors.

Another noted chef of New York was Louis Sheres, who died about five years ago. He made an envious reputation at Holland House (Fifth Avenue and Thirty-second Street) and at the Biltmore, where I was serving in the dining room. His last name was Gourmajyezat, and he lives in my memory as a very fine looking man, over six feet in height, and a true gentleman in every respect. Then there was Chef Cretautero who was with the Savoy Plaza, built in 1904. He served with the Delmonico Hotel and is now in California, I understand, with the Hilton Hotel in Beverly Hills.

While not a chef, London born Claude Philippe of the Waldorf, the son of a chef, made a great reputation as a maitre d' and general manager. Later, it was he who went west to organize the Beverly Hilton Hotel in California, taking with him a crew of six well-trained men as the nucleus of the staff for the great kitchens. Philippe, it is said, was at his very best in managing a banquet for two thousand people. He did not skimp on the arrangements, but made a great show of beautiful stemware, trimmed with gold, and thus secured a higher price per cover from the client. This also took care of the breakage, of even a hundred pieces, which was gladly absorbed by the host, who was, for his part, immensely gratified by the accoutrement of beautiful linens, china and stemware elegantly displayed for his chosen guests.

Philippe was extravagant with china and floral displays, and his salesmanship has often been noted with admiration. When arranging for a debutante party, he would quote a price, then produce an elegant show-plate, and the host would inquire: "How much more for the use of these?" and Philippe would reply: "These, sir, will cost $2 more per dozen." He would also charge $2 more per dozen for the use of especially decorative stemware and silverware, thus covering losses from breakage or souvenir-taking, and also making a comfortable profit for the house.

As Vice President of the Waldorf-Astoria, Philippe displayed the imagination and energy required for catering and sales promotion. In 1958, as head of the Banquet Department, he had the misfortune (at the height of his glowing career at forty-seven) to have a misunderstanding with the Internal Revenue Service. They felt he had not declared everything he should have, which led to an indictment of some proportions. Philippe resigned his post, and went to serve the Astor Hotel in Times Square, where somehow he got on the wrong side of the press. They went so far as to call the Paris in April Ball he had made famous at the Waldorf "as French as St. Patrick's at the Astor."

Philippe has received many awards throughout the world for his artistry as a gourmet and for his charitable works. At the Waldorf, he supervised the activities of an army of 600 men, and was responsible for purchasing more than three million dollars in food and two million in beverages annually. A man of much talent, he was, on July 1, 1960, named Executive Vice President and General Manager of the Hotel Commodore, and will very likely remain in the higher echelons of management where he belongs.

The Voison Restaurant was opened at 375 Park Avenue by Otto Baumgarten, who had been with the Ritz Hotel in Paris. The Voison was in its glory from the time of World War I. Adam Wozniak began work there as chef in 1917 when the capacity of the dining room was ninety people, and there was only one seating. The Voison was well-staffed and equipped for the finest service with maitre d', four captains, and many waiters. People often sat on the carpeted stairs waiting to be served. Patrons included Mrs. Harriman, Mrs. Jay Gould, Baron de Meyer, who was a Delmonico patron, and other notable persons. Voison now holds court at 575 Park Avenue.

At the beginning of the War in Europe, the Voison was hardly known, having been opened only a little over a year. Suddenly it became a popular place, with delegations from England, France and Italy in military uniform. Mr. Wozniak recalls four officers of the military came in and asked if the place was the Voison which they had heard so much about in Paris. Being assured that it was, they expressed interest in the fine food. Soon after there began an influx of military men from all over the world, and their colorful outfits gave the dining room a magnificent appearance. Prince Poniatowski and the great Paderewski dined there, too.

For a time, Max Herring, whose father had a restaurant in Switzerland and who had received very good training there, was manager of the Gotham Hotel, one of the elegant hostelries designed and built by the architect Stanford White. Mr. White also built the University Club, which used to be strictly man's province, with ladies invited for Ladies Day only once or twice a year. Now the ladies are permitted their weekly invasions. At one time, it had a reputation for very fine cuisine. There was a clique of gourmets at the University Club which met weekly in a party of ten or twelve, with a special menu, and who took possession of the dining room for themselves. This went on fifty-two weeks in the year; but the band of gourmets have wandered off, and there is nothing resembling the old times with the fine cuisine. Mr. Herring was with the Elysee which he opened. Baumgarten was President and Herring Vice President. Opening in 1918-19, the Elysee was prominent for about twelve years and showed good profits. Then it was closed and the building demolished. Mr. Herring died about five years ago. He is remembered as a fine host. Chef Wozniak served the Richelieu from 1943-1947, when he retired.

Before World War I, it was customary to train in Switzerland for the kitchens of the world. There were several distinct stages during which a man was taught the intricacies of the Sauce Department, Roast and Fish Department, Pastry and Bakery Department. Each required months of training, so that the courses extended over three or four years. Not until its satisfactory completion was the pupil admitted to the actual cookery. There were also the Butcher's Department and the Chemistry Department. Training was given as well in the conduct of service in the dining rooms, the reception of guests, and office procedure, including details of cost accounting and bookkeeping.

Coverage of all the essential studies often took ten or twelve years before receiving a basic education in the field of hotels and restaurants. The procedure was to pay tuition for the first year or two. After that, the student received his food and lodging, with the parents of the young hopeful supplying clothing and pocket-money. The custom was to work in this way for hotels and restaurants in an apprenticeship which extended for a year or a year and a half before the novice's name went on the payroll. This method of training also prevailed in Germany and in France before the first World War. Schools are still maintained in these countries, as well as in Switzerland, but they have had to change to conform to the revolution in world conditions pertaining to the culinary arts.

The Hotel Pierre in New York City has always maintained an aura of elegance in its favorable position overlooking Central Park at Sixty-first Street and Fifth Avenue. It opened on September 18, 1930, a year before the new Waldorf-Astoria. The mansion owned by the Robert Livingston Gerry family was torn down and the stately hotel erected on the site. The original sponsors were: Robert Livingston Gerry, W. P. Chrysler, Edward F. Hutton, Otto H. Kahn, Charles H. Sabin, James J. Bush, Vincent Bendix, Finley J. Shepard, Herbert L. Pratt, LeRoy W. Baldwin and C. K. G. Billings. It is presently owned by Mr. J. Paul Getty.

The elegantly appointed hotel was named in honor of Mr. Charles

Pierre, the famous restaurateur, who operated a well-known restaurant in New York City. A gathering place for the elite, the Pierre is forty-two stories high, has more than 600 rooms and suites, and is staffed by approximately 700 employees. The motto of the hotel used in its crest is "Hinc Spes Affulget," which translates into the encouraging legend: "From this place hope beams." Perhaps that is the true meaning of hospitality.

The Pierre Grill was opened on February 13, 1946, by the late Frank A. Paget, who unveiled a striking new restaurant for the public which, like the Savoy Grill in London, has become the favorite of society and literary and theatrical people. The Edgar Miller murals take man through a sweeping panoramic history of gastronomy. The prevailing motif is the atmosphere and color of India. Maitre d' Emil Pape was brought east by the late Oscar to the Waldorf-Astoria from the Palace Hotel in San Francisco, before which he was with the Mark Hopkins in that city. To classic French dishes are added East Indian curries. The preparation of the rice is as important as the curry itself and takes over an hour of steaming with constant stirring. This is the province of Riag Ali, who was with the Calcutta Club, the popular rendezvous for British officers and civil service agents in Calcutta, India. Curries are served on veal, lamb, beef, chicken, shrimp, lobster, scallops and swordfish. The service is on hot wagons supervised by two young Indian men in native attire.

Colonel John Jacob Astor began building the St. Regis in 1904. A frequent traveler to Europe, he was familiar with the splendors and comforts of the famed hostelries of England, France, Italy and Germany. An expansive longing for creating magnificence (and the wealth to indulge it) impelled Astor to add still another great Astor hotel to New York which was already blessed with the Waldorf-Astoria at Fifth Avenue and Thirty-fourth Street, and the Astor Hotel which opened September 1, 1904 on Broadway in Times Square.

Colonel Astor was on hand to thrust the first shovel into the ground and ceremoniously commence excavation. While it may be thought that the name is associated with *regal*, it has a humble origin, though bearing a close connection. Whoever has traveled in Switzerland and breathed its marvelous air has felt as if on a plateau close to heaven.

Regis was a monk attached to a mountain hospice in the Swiss Alps. So great was his devotion to aiding and comforting travelers that he was canonized for his hospitality, and thereafter was known as St. Regis. Little did he realize that his name would live on in a great hotel across the seas devoted to the ultimate in hospitality.

Luxuriously appointed, all of the original furniture for the St. Regis was imported from France. The corridors were of marble and the doors of solid bronze. At the time of construction, it was the tallest hotel in New York, being eighteen stories high. Two more levels were added in 1928. It is said to be the only hotel now in the city with room-service waiters on every floor. There was available a $50,000 suite with a $10,000 bed. The St. Regis soon gained a reputation for excellent service and quiet elegance, which it richly deserved.

The friendship of Prince Serge Obolensky and Vincent Astor went back many years. It was Astor who secured a position for Obolensky in a security house: Chase Harris Forbes, where he was in the foreign department under Mr. Rovensky. He remained there for three years, from shortly before the stock market crash to the beginning of the Depression. In 1932, Obolensky went to work for Astor in his real estate company, with Gerry Chadwick and Jack Gates, and became well acquainted with Astor's holdings. Two suggestions of value were made by Obolensky. One was either to rebuild or offer the City of New York, Astor's downtown tenement buildings, which were in deplorable condition. This Astor agreed to, and the city tore them down and built a housing project on the site. The other was Obolensky's contribution to the rebuilding of the St. Regis.

When the St. Regis Hotel opened in 1906, it was declared palatial. The prices in the restaurant were no higher than those of any other high-class hotel or restaurant, but it was rumored that the menus showed the choice of dishes without prices, which was untrue. The St. Regis found favor with many of the old guard, as well as with celebrities who swam in New York's gay social life. Among them were Mr. and Mrs. Bernard Baruch, Mr. and Mrs. Daniel Guggenheim, Mr. and Mrs. William K. Vanderbilt, Mrs. Herman Oelrichs, Mr. and Mrs. Ogden Mills, Colonel and Mrs. William Jay, Mr. and Mrs.

128

George Westinghouse, and that lovely lady of the theater, Miss Ethel Barrymore.

The roof garden had wide windows which overlooked the city and kept the room cool in the absence of air-conditioning. However, the architects introduced a system of filtering air believed to be unique. Air was circulated by means of powerful electric motors through cheesecloth screens or filters. It was warmed to the desired temperature by passing over steam coils. Thermostats in each room regulated it to a comfortable degree. The air entered through a register near the ceiling, which formed a part of the frieze decoration.

Vincent Astor inherited the luxurious St. Regis at Fifth Avenue and Fifty-fifth Street from his father, J. J. Astor. Later Astor sold it to the Duke interests, who were not interested in the hotel business, and it was returned to him for default on the mortgage which he held. It was a good property and the Dukes were wealthy enough to have handled it successfully if they had been sufficiently interested. They had added a whole wing to the hotel, and now all of the fabulous house was free and clear for Astor. While financially not a problem, the trade of the St. Regis dropped. Originally a perfectly managed hotel, back in the days of Otto Kahn, it fell into difficulties.

The Peacock Room designed by Joseph Urban was doing very little business. While expensively traditional, the Oak Room was depressingly funereal. The lobbies were dark and uninviting. There were no wine cellars; the food was ordinary. But there was much in the hotel's favor. The building itself was sound, architecturally attractive, and well situated near Fifth Avenue. Astor undertook its alteration and redecoration in 1935, and gave Obolensky the responsibility to revitalize the whole place with a new spirit. The choice of making him General Consultant was a wise one. Born to the luxuries of nobility, he had lived in the finest hotels of Europe and was attuned to elegance. And that is how a prince made his debut in the hotel business.

Mrs. Cameron Tiffany was engaged as Interior Designer and, together with Obolensky, planned a complete redecoration of the St. Regis, including the bar, restaurant, kitchens, roof and basement. Mr. Astor was pleased with their suggestions as the plans unfolded.

The bar was designed around the famed painting of Old King Cole by Maxfield Parrish. It was family-owned as Vincent's father, John Jacob Astor, had originally commissioned it for the renowned bar at the old Knickerbocker Hotel. Brought from the Racquet and Tennis Club at Fifty-second Street and Park Avenue—where it was on loan— the striking painting greatly enhanced the St. Regis bar.

Out of the basement room known as "The Seaglades" was fashioned the intimate boîte called the Maisonette Russe. Obolensky took particular pleasure in this creation, whose new motif was close to his heart. The small room was transformed into an imperially draped retreat in the White Russian grand manner. On opening night, it was blessed and sprinkled with holy water by the Rev. Vasily Kurdiumoff of the Russian Orthodox Church. A Slavic orchestra provided the music and Russian specialties were served. Cossacks served shaslik Caucasian on flaming swords. Borsch Russe and Saumon Poché gave the cuisine further authentic flavor. For the kitchen of the Maisonette Russe, Obolensky engaged a man who had been chef to the Czar at Livadia, one of the best chefs in the world.

The Iridium Room was completely redone and enjoyed Emil Coleman's music with its suppers. Yasha Nazarenko and an ensemble of Russian singers were introduced into the Maisonette. A nostalgic touch was achieved by the addition of a gypsy orchestra of Cadolban. It was Vincent Astor's idea to have an ice show. A skating rink was rolled out on the dance floor, an innovation which met with an enthusiastic reception.

A new ceiling was put into the Oak Room and a restaurant constructed. The roof garden was done in baroque to represent a Viennese *fete champetre*. This was conceived by Obolensky and Vava Adlerberg to resemble the temporary structures which Catherine the Great of Russia had Ludwig of Bavaria construct for their parties. On one side was a little pavillon and garden. The Viennese Roof became the place to dance and is still a delightful and favored room with a fine view of the city. Little wonder that the St. Regis, under the combined magic of Vincent Astor and Serge Obolensky, became the sensation of New York society.

When Vincent Astor died on February 3, 1959, his individual

President John Fitzgerald Kennedy, during his Senatorial days, exchanges a word with the Hon. Oran Eralp, Turkish Ambassador to Sweden. In the background, Mr. Walter Shirley, Mr. Robert Sweeney and Mrs. Igor Cassini. It was a proud evening for host Robotti.

Governor Thomas E. Dewey, on a festive evening is photographed between Peter Robotti and his wife, Frances Diane.

Vincent Price, popular screen and TV star, renowned for his knowledge of painting and the arts, exchanging views with TV's beloved Arlene Francis, witty panelist on "What's My Line?" and author of "That Certain Something: The Magic of Charm," as their host listens with amusement.

Photo by Standard Flashlight Co.

Charles Collingwood of Columbia Broadcasting System, described as "the most distinguished man of letters in his profession," and his friend Peter Robotti display the miniature menu Fountainhead Publishers designed to introduce "Much Depends on Dinner" for which Mr. Collingwood wrote a brilliant and glowing introduction, from his fount of knowledge as a recognized gourmet.

Photo by Standard Flashlight Co.

General and Mrs. Omar Nelson Bradley are feted at Richelieu. The general is chairman of the board of the Bulova Watch Company.

"Fredric March is my favorite actor." A long standing patron from the early 30's, he visited the Richelieu with his father, his wife, actress Florence Eldridge, and his brother, John M. Bickel. (A distinguished industrialist, who resembles his famous brother, John pioneered in the air conditioning industry and since his retirement has become a brilliant public speaker.)

Mrs. Drury W. Cooper III and Mrs.
John Blair Richardson discussing one
of their charities.

Photo by Edward Ozern

Mr. Robotti welcomes the Hon. Abe Stark, President
of the New York City Council, and, for an interval,
Acting Mayor during Mayor Wagner's absence
from City Hall.

Mr. and Mrs. Fritz Kreisler celebrate their fifty-sixth wedding anniversary at Le Chateau Richelieu. Mrs. Kreisler presents the beloved Maestro with a special cake fashioned into a reproduction of his celebrated violin. With them is Italian writer Luciana Pevrelli, and the smiling hosts—Mr. and Mrs. Peter Robotti.

Photo by Raimondo Borea

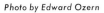

Actress Tina Louise sells a batch of tickets for a Boys Town of Italy benefit to Mr. Robotti. The Statue of Liberty was sculptured out of a solid block of sugar, an art of the Patissier.

New York socialites Mrs. Robert A. Hendrickson and Mrs. Pamela D. Law dining at Chateau Richelieu.

Photo by Edward Ozern

Mr. and Mrs. Rudy Vallee exchange toasts with their host Peter Robotti.

Stubby Kaye and Peter Palmer of the Broadway hit, "Li'l Abner" take a recess from Dogpatch.

Actor Edward Everett Horton anticipates a pleasant dinner with actress Lila Lee.

Photo by Richard Hochman

Executive Chef Raymond Richez gets admiring glances for a platter of delectables. Peter Robotti, William (Billy) Gaxton, president of the Lambs Club, and Walter Pidgeon.

Photo by Edward Ozern

Mallard Duck l'orange of Executive Chef Raymond
Richez is complimented by the propriétaire. Harmony
is the keynote of Richez's Kingdom of the Kitchen.

Owner-host Peter Robotti presides over the dessert course for a party which
includes Oscar-winning screen star Ginger Rogers and other celebrities. The
dessert was brought to the dining room embedded in the back of a great swan
carved from a solid block of ice, flanked by pineapples (covered with gossa-
mer spun sugar) the traditional emblem of hospitality.

ownership of the hotel created a problem requiring fast action to keep the St. Regis from closing its doors. Since the bank accounts of the hotel were in Mr. Astor's name, the money for salaries and immediate obligations could have been tied up while his will was being probated. To preclude this, his executors, Luke B. Lockwood and Allen W. Betts, filed the will the day before Mr. Astor's funeral. By this quick move, the executors were promptly granted authority to keep the hotel running without interruption.

About a year later (February 11, 1960) when the St. Regis was bought from the executors of the estate by the Zeckendorf chain for some $14,000,000, it joined other hotels in the group: the Astor, the Chatham, the Commodore, the Drake, the Manhattan, and the Taft.

At this time, Colonel Serge Obolensky was Vice-Chairman of the Board of the Zeckendorf Corporation. When he was elected President of the St. Regis Hotel, it brought his twenty-five-year career in the hotel business full circle. His first association was as a member of the Executive Board of Mr. Astor's St. Regis in 1935. Obolensky hastened to assure the press that the hotel would retain its "old world flavor under the new management." "The operating policies of the St. Regis," he said, "and the individual characteristics of this great hotel will be preserved."

Accustomed, it was said, to wave his "democratic magic wand with aristocratic taste," Obolensky was born a prince in Tsarkoe Selo, the summer residence of the Russian Czars near St. Petersburg. His father was one of the ten most wealthy of the two hundred princely families of old Imperial Russia, and Serge's family owned seven large houses in St. Petersburg, along with estates covering more than 50,000 acres of farms, forests and game preserves. The prince was educated and groomed to take over his father's vast holdings, and the training molded his character. Wounded in 1915 during World War I, he married his nurse, the noblewoman, Princess Catherine Yourievsky, the morganatic daughter of Czar Alexander II. Narrowly escaping imprisonment by the Communists, they fled to England. Circumstances changed and their love was over. After a divorce in 1924 in London, Serge married Alice Muriel Astor, daughter of John Jacob

Astor and Lady Ribblesdale; Alice, who died in 1956, was Vincent Astor's sister.

To his association with his brother-in-law, the Prince brought generations of culture, a fine intellect, and a combination of old-world charm together with wide experience in the vicissitudes of life. These qualities added up to the making of a perfect host and a highly successful hotel-keeper, which require a multitude of abilities. His title of Colonel comes from service in the American army in Africa, Italy, England and France. He made two combat jumps while on a special mission for General Eisenhower and General Castelano of the Italian Army. The newspaper files cover the story of the mission, which yielded Obolensky the Bronze Star from America and the coveted *Croix de Guerre* from the French Government.

Following the war, Colonel Obolensky became associated with the Hilton Corporation and began to revitalize the old Plaza. After his magic touch, the elite of New York crowded into the refurbished Persian Room and the young generation took over the RendezVous. Then Obolensky turned his attention to the Sherry Netherland, whose Carnival Room was designed by Count Adlerberg. There the Russian sword dance was performed, and flaming swords of shaslik were served by red-coated waiters. There was created an exciting atmosphere of Old Russia. The next challenge to Obolensky's talents was the Ambassador Hotel on Park Avenue. With his love of life and gayety, he vitalized this staid institution. The Ambassador originally opened in 1922 under the management of Theodore Kroll, a European of wide reputation, who had managed the Savoy in London. During his tenure, many famous people came to the hotel—Queen Marie of Rumania being perhaps the most publicised.

Obolensky redid the Embassy Club into a replica of one of the select salons of the royal European palaces. The Trianon ballroom emerged as a memory of eighteenth century France. To each assignment, Obolensky brings consummate artistry, and he sees to it that the highest standards obtain in service, the preparation of food, and in the wine cellars. In 1958, the Ambassador was sold to the Sheraton chain and re-named the Sheraton-East, but some people still think of it as the Ambassador. At one of its last functions, Obolensky performed his famous Russian dagger dance, which he does on Russian New Year's Eve. The dance, so well-known in Russia, is executed with five flaming daggers. At the exciting finale, the Prince stood up on a table, and below him, on a board on the parquet floor, were placed crisp dollar bills. With practised skill, he pinned the bills to the board with the point of the daggers, thrown one at a time from his mouth. Before the performance, he guaranteed his audience he would hit three out of five. When successful, the money on the board went to the Tolstoy Foundation. If not, the bills were returned to their owners. Before the dance, Obolensky drank dry a horn of plenty filled with champagne. In this colorful ritual there was kept alive the traditions of ancient Russia.

The Astor Hotel is one of New York's oldest, and the undisputed capitol of Times Square, the cross-roads of the world, where somehow the hotel seems strangely out of place. Before the Civil War, in 1854, Times Square was farmland and a farmhouse on the site of the Astor hostelry was owned by the family of Margaret Elizabeth Koch, who became Mrs. Margaret E. Berrian. She lived to be ninety-five and resided happily far off in the Bronx.

A ten-story French Renaissance style in red brick with white lime-stone trim, the Astor was always owned by the English branch of the family, whose name it bears. It was at the Astor in 1916 that Charles Evans Hughes went to bed in Suite 170 on election night, believing he was the next President of the United States. The following morning he learned that California's votes had re-elected Woodrow Wilson who, they thought, would keep the United States out of war.

Fifty-six years for a hotel is a long life. When the old Waldorf at Thirty-fourth Street was demolished in 1929, it was considered archaic, yet it was only seven years older than the Astor. Of course, it was then too far downtown for people conveniently to attend its dinners and balls. The Astor Hotel was the dream of a hotel genius, William C. Muschenheim, a German chef, who came to New York in 1872, when he was seventeen. Muschenheim became steward of the mess at West Point Military Academy, and didn't build the hotel until twenty years after he left the Point, but cadets and graduates have always considered the Astor their New York headquarters. General Douglas MacArthur, as a cadet, used to borrow a dollar or so from Muschenheim when he was short of date funds in New York.

It is said that Muschenheim conceived the Astor as the city's first great hotel devoted particularly to dining. Its 700 guest rooms took up only half of the space, the rest being used for dining rooms. He gathered together the finest kitchen crews available, who operated under departmental assistant chefs, all responsible to a supreme executive chef. The cuisine became famous across the land. At the time the Astor was built, theatrical Broadway ended at Rector's Restaurant. In Longacre Square there was a block of brownstone boarding houses for theater people called "old Soubrette Row," which were owned by the estate of William Waldorf Astor. The estate agreed to erect the eight-million-dollar hotel on this property. Longacre Square became Times Square when the Times newspaper built its tower there. Muschenheim took the responsibility of furnishing the large hotel, and paid half a million rental a year. The kitchen, 231 feet by 150 feet, is still one of the largest in the world—and according to modern standards of restaurateurship most inconvenient when concentration and kitchen engineering have become great labor savers. It is located in the basement and moving chains carry the food to the ballroom above, which seats 2,500 people. This is a great handicap to fine service but was the mode of kitchen location half a century and more ago. At one time the lobby of the Astor was elegantly decorated with a gold-leaf ceiling supported by marble columns, a mosaic floor and Persian rugs, all of which have now disappeared.

Robert Keaton Christenberry was responsible for streamlining the lobby and making the roof into a night club. It was there that Rudy Vallee and Harry James performed and Frank Sinatra began to achieve fame. Rudy's *Stein Song* of dear old Maine certainly made the rafters ring, and how many couples courted each other on the way to the altar to the tune of his band? The extensive renovation of the Astor was the first among the old hotels, the Commodore and Roosevelt later following suit.

The Astor, under the Zeckendorf Hotel Corporation, and with Obolensky in charge, was returned to splendor with its beautiful ballroom decorated by Valerian Rybar, and the architectural changes in the lobby under Diego Suarez, and Mme. Claude Alphand re-decorating the suites. A steel canopy was erected around the entire block from Forty-fourth to Forty-fifth Streets and from Broadway to Eighth Avenue. Eleven theaters are in the vicinity of the Astor, which still reigns supreme over the theatrical world.

The interesting, colorful story of the hotels, restaurants, and the unusual man who moved in the social circles for which they are the showcase, is revealingly told in Obolensky's book, "One Man in His Time," published by McDowell, Obolensky, New York City. Perhaps the whole significance of his life and times is capsuled in Obolensky's concluding remarks: "As for me, I remain one man in his time, simply an ex-Russian of a particular background and family, the foundations of whose existence were destroyed. I believe that for myself and for millions of Russians who once lived under communism, the terror and the hardship of those days did not for an instant destroy our faith, our interest in the world, and our love of life."

Mention of Rector's (built in 1899 at Forty-third Street) recalls an era of its own. Wilson Mizner, who was responsible for building exclusive Palm Beach, Florida, out of swampland, lived at Rector's in its hey-day on Broadway. Wilson Mizner arrived in New York early in 1905 from California with Klondike and Nevada credentials which led him directly to the theatrical, newspaper and gambling world. This unusual personality was explored in Edward Dean Sullivan's book *The Fabulous Wilson Mizner* published in 1935 (Henkle Company, New York). Mizner regarded himself as a drifter and ne-er-do-well, attracting to himself all sorts of unconventional people. At the height of his theatrical earnings in New York, he took over the Strand Hotel and invited fifty characters who depended on him for "flop money" to make their homes there. He coined the warning, "Never give a sucker an even break," but was known as the easiest touch on Broadway. "I never worry about money," he explained once, "unless a rich man comes anywhere near me. Then I can't sleep until I find a way to get in on the take." It was really the showman Phineas T. Barnum who declared that "there's a sucker born every minute." To this Mizner added—"and two to take him." As far back as his days on the Barbary Coast in San Francisco, Mizner had used the unusual

135

greeting, "Hello, Sucker," which, during the prohibition era in New York, was the well-known greeting of Texas Guinan in Manhattan's undercover places. "Everyone in the world is a fall guy for nearly anything outside of his own racket . . . the first dawn of smartness is to stop trying things you don't know anything about—especially if they run to anything over a dollar."

Mizner lived with other playwrights at the Rector Hotel which George Rector and his father had made one of the great hostelries of the world. It had a marvelous restaurant renowned for cuisine and service. And yet this million-dollar enterprise was ruined by an odd development. It appears that at the time Mizner lived there, another playwright Paul Potter was a guest. He had completed the translation of a French farce for Al Woods and the title was undecided. One day Woods arrived at the hotel to see Potter in regard to the forthcoming production. It was raining and as Woods stepped out of his cab, a beautiful young girl leaped out of a hansom cab and ran for the door of the restaurant. To protect her ankle-length dress, she raised it above the dripping sidewalk almost to her knees, revealing gorgeous legs encased in beautiful silk stockings. The dazzling creature was followed by her own rippling laughter as she made the safety of the restaurant door. It made a great impression on the producer Al Woods, and when he entered the room of Paul Potter he announced the title of the new play, *The Girl from Rector's.*

As it happened, it was one of the first of the saucy, naughty French type of plays on Broadway and it aided Rector's to the pinnacle of success in a wideswept publicity across the entire country and in Europe. Some wiser heads shook from side to side and warned of the prairie-fire. The association of the name of the play gradually gave the impression to the outlying districts that Rector's was the most daring and emotionally dangerous place in New York, as Mr. B. A. Botkin points out in his *New York City Folklore* (Random House, Inc. New York). Wives from a distance began to forbid husbands to stop there and the transient trade fell off. It was the beginning of the end of a splendid institution.

The early years of the twentieth century saw the appearance of sumptuous hotels to accommodate the wealthy of New York and the

visitors it attracted. In 1907 plans and work were begun for the construction of the elegant Vanderbilt Hotel, on which Alfred Vanderbilt
was to spend $3,500,000. Opened to the public in 1912, it is situated
on the southwest corner of Park Avenue and 34th Street and now
operates as Vanderbilt-Manger Hotel. Alfred Vanderbilt, who married Mrs. Margaret Emerson of the Bromo Seltzer fortune, was very
proud of his hostelry which competed with the Astors' holdings. But,
unfortunately, he was not to enjoy it for long. The advent of World
War I darkened the hopes of many.

In the Spring of 1915, the Vanderbilts were enroute to Europe for
a long holiday, but never reached their destination. The *S.S. Lusitania*
had given a good account of herself and had almost completed the
voyage when disaster struck. On May 17, 1915, a German submarine
loosed a ruthless attack on the *Lusitania* off the Old Head of Kinsale
at the southeast tip of Ireland. The ship had no means of defending
herself. She sank in eighteen minutes with a terrible loss of life—1,198
passengers, among them the owner of the Vanderbilt, Alfred Vanderbilt.

The Crypt Room of the Vanderbilt was built by Cornelius Gwynne
Vanderbilt more than forty years ago, yet its appearance remains unchanged. It has been the rendezvous for notables of society, the
theatre, the worlds of finance and sport. Few remember now that the
former Mayor William O'Dwyer was a bartender there and met his
wife, who was a telephone operator in the hotel. Theodore Roosevelt
liked the Crypt Room, and it was also frequented by Lillian Russell,
Irene Castle, John Barrymore, Maude Adams, Enrico Caruso and
Rudolph Valentino, who loved hotel dining. (He used to have a special table at the Biltmore, and I was happy to be assigned to serve
him in the days of his glory and in my early days of service.)

Diamond Jim Brady lived at the Vanderbilt Hotel, and the tales of
his tremendous appetite have become something of an American
legend. He began his meal with two dozen large oysters garnished with
crabs, just as an appetizer. He loved seafood especially. Maitre d'
Hugo Balza, well-known to the Della Robbia Room, who served at
the Vanderbilt for four and a half decades, recalls the parade of celebrities over the years. The menu of Diamond Jim was incredible. He did

not drink intoxicating beverages and his favorite drink was orange juice. The most enormous carafe in the hotel was filled to the brim with orange juice and cracked ice and he could drink it down without stopping. His consumption of food gave him a great thirst and he took perhaps four carafes before his dinner was over. He loved sweets, Balza further recalls, and had the capacity to consume six French pastries at a time, followed by a box of chocolate bon bons.

Mr. Brady was one of the first successful salesmen who utilized the Broadway beat to promote the sale of his commodities. He loved to be surrounded by handsome men and beautiful women at the table, and it was no unusual thing to lay covers for eight or ten guests of Mr. Brady, shrewdly selected to do him the most financial good, although he was the soul of hospitality itself. Diamond Jim was a gentleman in his generosity and his feelings even though he did wear his napkin around his neck. This was not due to the lack of etiquette but because his famous stomach began at his neck and swelled in a majestic curve toward his knees where there was too little lap. He wore great diamonds on his hands and in his shirt front, diamond buttons on cuffs and vest, all multi-carated stones, and some said he had diamond bridgework. When someone reproached him for his ostentation, he casually replied: "Well, them's that has 'em, wears em."

Over the many years of service, moved the great of society and characters from many stages of life. Balza's memories include the joyous and the sad. The news of the sinking of the *Lusitania* and the loss of the hotel's owner cast a shadow over the Vanderbilt hotel. By one of those odd quirks of fate, the Astors, too, were visited by a marine disaster: John Jacob Astor lost his life in the sinking of the *Titanic* while his pregnant wife Madeleine Force Astor survived to give birth to the present John Jacob Astor, scion of the old New York family.

The sumptuous hotels and private restaurants were the meeting place of the social and the wealthy. The chefs and their litle armies of assistants provided the cuisines for their enjoyment, which they have continued to do in an unbroken chain to our own times, and as they will into the bright culinary paths of the future. The secret of continuity is the pride of profession expressed in membership in the various culinary organizations and in their publications. The Vatel

138

Club, under the able leadership of Monsieur Chardenet, has its house magazine *Toque Blanche;* while the chefs' national house organ is the elegant little magazine *Culinary Review* of New York, ably master-minded by Editor George Serra. For some time now, the magazine has given deserved recognition to outstanding magicians of the range in its intriguing column: *Chef of the Month.* Loyalty and devotion to the culinary arts help to supply the narrowing ranks of chefdom.

CHAPTER

The Old Waldorf-Astoria

PEAK OF TRADITIONAL ELEGANCE

"Elegance is something more than ease—more than a freedom from awkwardness and restraint. It implies a precision, a polish and a sparkling which is spirited yet delicate."

—WILLIAM HAZLITT (1778-1830)

As a youngster, I spent lazy days in Fubine, my native village tucked away among the hills, slopes and green valleys of Piedmont. Miles of acres in the Monferrato wine region there are covered with God's beautiful green vineyards. In the little medieval suburb of the railroad-town of Alessandria, I can remember hearing of a magnificent palace in the distant city of New York which was operated for the pleasures of the public, that is, the fortunate wealthy segment who were outstanding business and social leaders. Stories circulated of this hotel until some believed the wondrous tales to be legends of a fairyland across the sea. I wondered vaguely if, some day, I would be privileged to see its famed grandeur.

I did not realize then that my education as a restaurateur would begin with another fine hotel, the splendid Biltmore, under the management of Mr. Nino Malnati, who was to become my idol and patron saint. As there isn't space for the story in detail of all of New York's "Palaces of Hospitality," I have chosen the Waldorf, which was the

140

epitome of magnificence and also a highly successful commercial venture.

At the time the old Waldorf was erected, the best hotels of the period were the Cambridge, the Albemarle, the Fifth Avenue, the Victoria, the Holland House, the Brunswick, the Buckingham, the Windsor. These places were not social centers at all, but glorified inns in which travelers or residents (uncertain of a prolonged stay) could eat and sleep, and where businessmen could lunch and meet other business people to discuss their mutual interests in the manner of tavern-day life.

In 1881 William Waldorf Astor (the great-grandson of the original John Jacob Astor, who came from Bavaria to win a fortune by trading in furs and in real estate) ran for Congress. Astor fully expected that his wealthy contemporaries, who were his Fifth Avenue neighbors, would vote for him and he would go to Washington in triumph. But the ways of politics are uncertain; the neighbors were very indifferent, he lost the election and was greatly disappointed. He was also so angered that he renounced his American citizenship in a country which had said by its votes that it did not want him to serve in public office.

Before transferring his allegiance to England, where he became the first Viscount Astor of Hever Castle, and eventually father-in-law of the present Lady (Nancy) Astor, the vociferous member of Parliament —Astor did quite a strange thing. He hired wreckers to tear down his lovely mansion at Fifth Avenue and Thirty-third Street, and his neighbors were outraged to learn that he planned to erect a hotel there. His cousin John Jacob Astor IV, who lived next door to the projected hotel and with whom he constantly quarreled, was most astonished of all. He would not live next to a hotel, he declared, and so sold his mansion also; and his land became a part of the site on which the Waldorf-Astoria of Fifth Avenue was built.

There were then some 60,000,000 people in all of the United States who enjoyed themselves after their own fashion, without automobiles, golf courses, motion pictures, or night clubs. But they had equally stimulating pleasures, such as carriage rides, the theater, horse racing, sleigh parties in winter, visiting road houses, the appreciation of art, the administration of many servants, and the luxury of beautiful homes and clothes, as well as travel abroad. At this time Park Avenue was a noisy, treeless street with the shanties and shacks of the poor in its upper stretches, who eked out a bare living keeping goats.

Smart parties were then private parties, given at considerable expense in one's mansion, where couples danced the Cotillion, the Lancers and the Quadrille. Society did not entertain at hotels. Astor's plan to build a hotel which would provide for public entertainment was regarded as a mad venture which would surely fail.

Astor did not think so. He hired George Boldt, who had successfully managed the Bellevue in Philadelphia which later became the Bellevue-Stratford. Newspapers began calling the project "Boldt's Folly." And a collosal error it surely seemed, for it opened on March 13, 1893, just as the country was gripped in a financial panic. The evening of the opening, New York was pelted with sleet and drenched in an all-night rain. Yet the hotel ignored the elements and proceeded with the opening festivities. The press was, by design, well represented and covered the auspicious occasion as the hotel was officially presented to the world. Boldt had wisely arranged to present a benefit concert for St. Mary's Free Hospital for Children, a favorite charity of Mrs. William K. Vanderbilt, who was then the leader of New York society. She approved of the idea, and was delighted when 1,500 tickets were sold at five dollars each.

Fashionable people came from Philadelphia, Boston, and even Chicago, which sent Mrs. Potter Palmer. Other famous families were represented: the Peppers, the Lippincotts, the Lowells, the Sargeants, the Averys, the Vanderbilts, the Stuyvesant Fishes, the Ogden Mills, the Goelets. These were the elite of American society, and for their entertainment Mrs. Vanderbilt had hired the New York Symphony Orchestra, which played classical numbers under the baton of a young conductor named Walter Damrosch. The menu included oysters, terrapin, *cotellettes de ris de veau, glacé a l'orange and glacé fantasie.*

The hotel had cost an estimated $5,000,000. It had 450 rooms and 350 baths. Luxurious furnishings had been brought from Europe. There were many fine public dining rooms. Success was immediate, thanks to the favorable reviews of the press and the unanimous approval of the guests. The New York Sun, in particular, was enthusiastic: "Louis XIV could not have got the likes of the first suite of apartments set apart for the most distinguished guests of the hotel." This was an exaggeration, of course, as the palaces of Europe in their golden splendor could be but palely imitated. The papers aroused further interest by printing long lists of the guests and describing the clothes they wore. The New York Herald was approving though flippant, calling the elite "swelldom" and saying "they ate a fine supper." However, even that caustic comment helped to publicize the hotel.

George Boldt was the guiding genius of the first Waldorf. He had come to America from the German isle of Ruegen in the Baltic Sea, was compactly built and of medium height, and looked like a physician from Vienna with his mustache and spade beard. Boldt provided a fortuitous opportunity to many in his selection of the executive staff at the new hotel. Among those who rose to fame and fortune was Oscar Tschirsky. He is the classic example of rising to prominence by being provided the perfect setting, rather than by talent forcing its way to success.

Oscar came from Switzerland to New York in 1883. His first job was as busboy in the Hoffman House hotel at Madison Square, then the center for celebrities in sports, the professional and business circles. Later he became a waiter there. Oscar himself never claimed to be a chef, or to have had chef's training. He was touched on the shoulder for stardom when Edward (Ned) Stokes employed him as a steward on his yacht. Nothing could have been more opportune for the young Swiss. Stokes was the owner of the Hoffman House. A scion of a social family, Stokes is chiefly remembered because of his passion for Josie Mansfield, the actress who was the mistress of Jim Fiske, the railroad tycoon, and for whom Fiske had built the opera house on Twenty-third Street and Eighth Avenue. New York was shocked when Stokes entered the Grand Central Hotel as Fiske came down the marble stairs, resplendent in evening clothes, and shot him to death.

After serving on Stokes' yacht, Oscar went to Delmonico's, where he worked for six years. His service was pleasing to the celebrities who dined there, and he became on excellent terms with them, to such an extent that when he asked for references, Lillian Russell, Diamond Jim Brady, and the Chief Justice of the Supreme Court, among others, readily accommodated him with letters of endorsement. He also had the wisdom to build a general client list. Thus armed, he risked asking Mr. Boldt for the chief position in the main dining room, when they began building the Waldorf. Mr. Boldt felt that Oscar would be an asset, and he was engaged as maitre d'. When the hotel opened, Boldt stood at the door with Oscar, flanked by a line of bellboys in shining outfits. It was the perfect opportunity, his courtesies were lavishly rewarded by the tycoons who made the Waldorf the center of their social and business life; and Oscar was soon on the road to riches and fame.

The Chicago World's Fair proved that the age of steel, coal and oil had arrived, which would create vast changes in American life. "Big Business" with its giant corporations was established; and the Waldorf met the needs of the *nouveau riche,* and the flourishing social families who benefited by the industrial revolution.

Boldt introduced Room Service, was the first to station assistant managers in the lobby to greet guests and to take care of them, and the first to send gifts to prominent guests with the compliments of the hotel. Under Boldt, men were permitted to smoke in the dining rooms, and women to smoke in public. Boldt abolished the ladies' entrance and women arrived on the arms of their escorts. Boldt hired expensive orchestras whose leaders were well-known. The Waldorf initiated the idea of a room with a private bath.

The old aristocracy were invited to entertain at the hotel, and the barons of coal, iron, steel and oil, from the wilds of the Midwest, were introduced to the beauties of elegant cuisine. The wealthy from the West came to spend their money lavishly. All of their lives their hunger had been appeased by ham and eggs, buckwheat cakes, boiled beef, liver, onions and potatoes. To make out of eating a luxurious social function was something new and exciting which Europeans had long enjoyed. Money was no object, and the Americans on the rise became willing pupils under the gracious instruction of Boldt and Oscar. Many forebears of present wealthy families took their first lessons in *joie de vivre* from the Waldorf school, where the succulent mysteries of *filet de boeuf, pate de fois gras, coquille de bass a la Virchow,* and other dishes long familiar to travelers to the Continent, were revealed to them. Since the menus were printed in French, head-waiters and captains interpreted their meaning to rustic guests and the dishes spoke eloquently for themselves.

Instead of a large inn, the Waldorf became a clubhouse for the elite, and important people dining there spread its fame throughout the world. Its success socially was assured when Mrs. John Jacob Astor, Mrs. William K. Vanderbilt, Mrs. Ogden Mills and Mrs. Stuyvesant Fish began giving elaborate dinners for long lists of guests at the hotel. Hostesses who had no ballrooms of their own began to hold their Cotillions at the Waldorf; and many were attracted to the new hotel who had previously patronized Delmonico's or the old Madison Square Garden. Peacock Alley, which ran from the Palm Room to the Empire Room, with gilt furniture and red plush carpet, became the promenade of the fashionable.

Meanwhile, John Jacob Astor IV lived in his mansion next door and observed all of the activity at the hotel. It was no longer possible for him to live in privacy, and he was soon induced to tear down his mansion and emulate his cousin by building a hotel on his property. This he did and, in 1896, it was merged with the Waldorf, the com-bined buildings having a thousand rooms. Ward McAllister, who was the arbiter of society, had already coined the term "Four Hundred" for New York's *creme de la creme.* Mr. McAllister's daughter is cred-ited with having conceived the name for the twin hotels—The Waldorf-Astoria. The original fur trader, John Jacob Astor, had once estab-lished a fur-trapping station in Oregon which he called Astoria, about which Washington Irving wrote a tale, so this name was part of the family's history.

The idea of joining two names by a hyphen in the British manner was new in the United States. Someone wrote a song which became popular and spread the hotel's fame still further. In addition, young people had a habit of saying: "Meet me at the Hyphen," just as other generations were to say "Meet me under the clock" which, of course, meant the famous clock in the lobby of the Biltmore. The Song ran like this: "At the Waldorf Hyphen Astoria / No matter who or what you are, / Be sure to nod to Oscar as you enter / Just speak to him by name. / And for Ten he'll do the same . . ."

The Astoria Hotel had a special barroom decorated with tiles, mosaics, mooseheads, a display of choice liquors, and a truly magnificent four-sided mahogany bar. In the custom of the times, drinks entitled the patrons to partake of marvelous food at no charge beyond the price of the drink. The "free lunch" it was called. This applied to the 5¢ beer at the corner saloon as well as to the barrooms of the fine hotels. Oscar sent letters to Wall Street people he had known since his days at Hoffman House, telling them privately of the merger and the advantages of the great barroom, where they would meet others with similar interests. From 3 P.M. on—when the New York Stock Exchange closed—the bar at the Waldorf was crowded with men making bets, handing out tips on stocks and horses, and making million-dollar deals. It was a man's paradise and all the tycoons patronized the place. These were the heroes of the day, before motion pictures, who made "big deals" under the sculptured mahogany symbols over the bar of the Wall Street Bear and Bull. Crowds sometimes followed them when they left to get their autographs.

Just before World War I, the famed Waldorf-Astoria began to decline. Homes were being built on Fifth Avenue in the Sixties, Seventies and Eighties, and it was a long ride to Thirty-fourth Street. Many men patronized the very elegant Plaza at Fifty-ninth Street, which had been erected in 1904. And the heart-beat of the Waldorf stopped with the death at his post of its guiding genius, George Boldt, in 1916. The income tax law passed in 1913 put the squeeze on the fat bankrolls of the old crowd. And, too, they were growing older and losing their youthful zest. It was then that Lucius Boomer came to head the Waldorf and under him emerged a new regime.

Boomer had been in charge of the main dining room of the Hotel Claridge when it was the great restaurant of Times Square. He had held important posts in the Willard Hotel in Washington, D.C. and the Windsor in Montreal. He became director of Louis Sherry's, president of the Sherry-Netherlands Hotel and at the same time president of the Savarins, the restaurant chain. Boomer was the man of the hour in restaurant and hotel life. The days of Sherry's, Delmonico's, Jack's, Mouquin's were numbered with the arrival of Prohibition. When eventually Sherry's left Forty-fourth Street and Fifth Avenue, it was Mr. Boomer who reorganized it and helped to build a new home for this old institution when it covered the block on Park Avenue between Forty-ninth and Fiftieth Streets in an eighteen-story building.

At Sherry's was developed the new idea in luxurious apartment living. Later the Sherry-Netherlands Hotel was to take up this idea on a more pronounced scale. The old Sherry's and the new one at 300 Park Avenue paved the way for a new way of life in New York City which combined the best features of modern hotel life with modern apartment house life, providing freedom from care as to procuring food, supplies, hiring and supervision of servants. It gave seclusion and privacy.

Lucius Boomer was associated with General T. Coleman Du Pont and together they had formed the Boomer-Du Pont Properties in 1918. This corporation purchased from the Boldt estate the lease and contents of the Waldorf-Astoria Hotel. Boldt had never been the owner but the lessee of the hotel. The grounds and buildings were owned by William Waldorf Astor and the estate of John Jacob Astor, who had lost his life in the Titanic disaster. Du Pont's wealth and Boomer's talents inspired the hotel once more to a revival of smoothness and elegance of operation, though lacking the Renaissance extravagance of its first lush period. With the coming of Boomer to the Waldorf, many patrons returned, the spirit of the massive inn was revived, it became the center for news and great events as it had been in Boldt's day. Prohibition, finance, social values, movement of the population uptown were all part of the problems and part of New York's progress in the restless decade from 1919-29.

Lucius Boomer was a perfectionist and a severe disciplinarian, meticulously supervising every detail. He worked hard and expected proper performance as well from his staff. He faced each day of the hotel's activities as if it were opening day. Furthermore, he was something of a Beau Brummel with his trim build and black hair, his

147

confident and handsome presence. He introduced many ideas for new methods of service. The War brought prosperity and largesse, but it was followed in 1919 by Prohibition. The famous Bull and Bear bar was padlocked, and gaiety fled from the sumptuous dining rooms.

The *New York Times*, in the early 1920's, noted that the gift of hospitality which the Waldorf had given to the city had disappeared. "The art of dining out is almost lost," wrote one columnist regretfully. "Most of those who eat in New York hotels do so because they are away from home and must eat somewhere. But the happy dinner parties of other days are gone, and as far as the gay suppers which once lent a certain fame to Fifth Avenue and Broadway—they are a memory."

Hotel managers could not buck Prohibition. Boomer actually bolted the doors of the Claridge Dining Room. "People simply will not eat where they are unable to get a drink," he said. Manager Albert Keller at the Ritz-Carlton likewise closed the famous Crystal Room. "Our patrons," he pointed out, "do not want a dry supper and a dry dance afterward. This is altogether too dry a time. A change has come over America since Prohibition. Every public assemblage seems to be merely a place where people go to get bored."

Prohibition was the last blow. Most of the hotels became indebted to the banks, and the managers had to be friends with the bankers, who put in their own men at good salaries. These officials went into the kitchens and supervised costs and purchases. They wanted profit percentage and took any means to obtain it. They substituted margarine for butter in Hollandaise sauce in all the hotel restaurants with the exception of the Ambassador. Reductions in staff, and the hiring of cheap help, further reduced the customary high standards. Commercial hotels had their kitchens staffed with many Puerto Ricans, whom they did not have to pay much. A chef could not produce fine dishes with assistants who watched the clock. The taste and appearance of food was of no interest to the newcomers who became mechanical cooks. Soon only a few key men of the old school were left. The unions came into power, and their supervisors and delegates now appeared in hotel kitchens.

148

The Old Waldorf-Astoria

Mr. Trevor, who used to be chef at the Waldorf-Astoria, left about five years ago. He admitted it is a pity when one has to work with incompetent assistants who have no knowledge of culinary artistry. "It is just like bricklaying," he said, "so many per hour." The reduction of immigration quotas excluded many well-trained people, who would have been a great asset to the hotels and restaurants of America.

With the Eighteenth Amendment to the American Constitution in effect, every hotel in the country faced a crisis. The bar had been their most important source of revenue. The nation saw the "noble experiment" invade personal liberties and crush a great industry. The sale of liquors was transferred to illegal hands as restaurants and hotels obeyed the command of the government. Mr. Boomer, for his part, proceeded in his own way to replace the lost revenue. He rebuilt the roof garden. Originally the old Waldorf had two main entrances, the one on Thirty-fourth Street flanked the original carriageway. There were less important entrances opposite the elevators and at the Astor Court end of Peacock Alley. Boomer closed the doorway to the east of the carriageway and in its place a street doorway was cut into the Italian Room which became popular.

The famous old four-sided bar in the Men's Café sold its last drink on the night of June 30, 1919. What happened to this great mass of mahogany and rosewood? It was cut down and parts distributed as souvenirs. The brass rail which supported the feet of so many famous personalities for twenty-two years was sold for metal. The entire room was dismantled and replaced by a men's reading room as a lounge and café. Many mourned the demise of the Santo Domingo mahogany bar and its whereabouts—after parts were hacked away—became something of a mystery. Some say it became a theatre ticket counter in a hotel, others that it went for firewood.

At the McAlpin Hotel, Boomer had set up an attractive candy shop and the hotel had established its own candy factory to supply it. At the Waldorf, Boomer used this idea. He created a de luxe candy boutique in the Italian Room which was most appealing, in the manner of the lovely candy shops of Milan, Torino and Rome. Many other hotels adapted the candy shop and soft-drink fountain idea. Afternoon tea in the Italian Room was soon so popular, it became impossible properly to serve the crush of guests. There was a limit to what one could charge for tea and cakes, so the service had to be discontinued. Boomer's idea of the roof garden was also a success. Boldt originally was against it, but it proved financially rewarding. In the winter, it was flooded and frozen over for ice skating. John J. Petit, who conceived the beautiful dining room of the Claridge Hotel, later reconstructed Boomer's roof garden on top of the old Waldorf, so that it was enclosed and suitable for a series of restaurants in keeping with the seasons. Each season it bore decorations in harmony with the months, in New York's first version of the Four Seasons.

In 1924 it was rumored that the Waldorf-Astoria would be closed. The property was acquired by the Waldorf-Astoria Realty Corporation in which important principals were involved: General Coleman du Pont and Mr. Boomer, industrialists W. W. Atterbury, Leroy W. Baldwin, M. C. Brush, Robert K. Cassatt, L. L. Dunham, Percy H. Honston, William C. Sproul, E. T. Stotesbury, John R. Todd. Taxation forced the valuable Thirty-fourth Street frontage to be converted into handsome shops for rental revenue. The corporation spent more than a million dollars to bring the hotel facilities up-to-date. The famous Bradley-Martin ballroom changed its name several times. It was known as the South Café, then renovated into the Jade Room, and became one of the popular hotel restaurants of New York. Offers came to lease the Fifth Avenue side of the hotel. This would mean the elimination of the two vast dining rooms—the Rose and Empire Room. The rental offered was $300,000 a year. The papers rested on Boomer's desk. The decision would be his. The offer was tempting enough but from a hotel man's point of view, the Waldorf-Astoria without these two great rooms would not be the same. They were the two largest and most magnificent dining rooms left on Fifth Avenue. Boomer was now closer than ever to his decision to abandon the hotel.

It was the Volstead Act that eventually killed the Waldorf. On December 20, 1928, Lucius Boomer announced he was throwing in the sponge. He sold the site on Fifth Avenue to the new corporation for $13,500,000, and the Waldorf's Board of Directors sold to Boomer for $1.00 the use of the magic name of Waldorf-Astoria. The final day of operation was May 3, 1929. It was called Employees' Day and every dollar taken in by the hotel for rooms and meals went into a special fund for the benefit of those who were to leave the service of the hotel for what they thought would be forever.

On May 1, 1929 a great dinner was tendered in the grand ballroom by thirty-eight organizations of the city. The New York Evening World called "The Final Dinner"—"The most glorious testimonial to a journeying friend New York City has ever witnessed." Every phase of New York life was represented. Dr. Nicholas Murray Butler, President of Columbia University, headed the committee on arrangements and on the dais were seated: Mr. George T. Wilson, toastmaster, Mr. H. Dykes, President of the Rotary Club, Mr. George Zabriskie, President of the Sons of the American Revolution, Colonel Franklin Q. Brown, President of the Army and Navy Club, Colonel Michael Friedman, President of the Fifth Avenue Association, Mr. Thomas Ewing, President of the New York Patent Law Association. There were members of the Church Club, the League for Industrial Rights, the Oil Trades Association, the New York Society of St. Andrews, the St. Patrick's Society. Mr. Adolph S. Ochs of the *New York Times* was also on the dais with Royal S. Copeland, United States Senator, and on his right the Rev. William T. Manning, the gentle Bishop of the Episcopal Diocese of New York. In attendance were guests who had for years lived at the Waldorf. Among them were Colonel E. H. R. Green, the son of Hetty Green, the eccentric Wall Street tycoon.

A large red flag fluttered from the mast of the Waldorf announcing SALE THIS DAY and auctioneers sold one by one the mahogany furniture which Mrs. Boldt had carefully bought, the canopied beds, the equipment and parts of the great four-sided bar, which had served such well-known personalities as Bet-a-Million Gates, Andrew Carnegie, J. P. Morgan, Diamond Jim Brady and Henry Frick, multi-millionaires all. The auction is said to have yielded about $500,000. Mr. Boomer and his wife Jorgine took a train to Florida for a rest. On October 1, 1929, which used to be moving day for New Yorkers, the house wreckers came with axe, hammer and dynamite. They destroyed the beautiful old mansion-hotel, leveling all of its fabled beauty to the ground. It was the end of an era, but the wreckers could not kill the vision of a new Waldorf which would rise Phoenix-like out of the rubble. The opening, two years later, of the shining new white-walled Waldorf-Astoria on Park Avenue, with the brilliant Boomer at its head, was the auspicious beginning of a new life for a grand old institution.

CHAPTER

The New Waldorf-Astoria

MISTRESS OF PARK AVENUE

> *"If cities were built by the sound of music, then some edifices would appear to be constructed by graceful, solemn tones, and others to have danced forth to light fantastic airs."*
>
> —NATHANIEL HAWTHORNE (1804-64)

WHILE LUCIUS BOOMER WAS IN FLORIDA VACA-tioning, Louis J. Horowitz, an old friend, telephoned him from New York. Horowitz was chairman of the board of Thompson-Starrett and Company. He made Boomer an offer: a banking firm on the board, he said, would provide finances for a new Waldorf, if Boomer would operate it, and allow the new corporation to use the name Waldorf-Astoria. In 1916, Du Pont had made a similar offer to Boldt.

The New York Central and the New Haven Railways owned the site extending from Forty-ninth to Fiftieth Streets and from Park to Lexington Avenues, which they agreed to lease to the hotel. At the time, some fairly new buildings were on the property. The American Express Company fronted on Lexington Avenue, with a loading platform adjoining the railroad tracks which ran under the basement. On the corner of Park Avenue and Fiftieth Street was a powerhouse. It cost one million dollars to move the powerhouse to a new location under the Commodore Hotel, 100 feet below the level of the street in solid rock.

153

The same pattern seemed to form for Boomer as for Boldt. When Boldt opened the old Waldorf in 1893, the nation was in the depths of a financial panic. The final papers for the new hotel were signed on October 3, 1929. Two days later was Black Thursday, the day the Stock Market crashed with a roar heard around the world. Depression wrapped its shroud over the whole country. Nevertheless, Boomer sent Nora Foley (who had worked with him at the old Waldorf and the McAlpin) to Europe to buy linens in Ireland and to make a survey of hotels such as the Mayfair in London, the Maurice in Paris, the Excelsior in Rome. Oscar went west to check on California hotels and to promote the new Waldorf. Boomer and his wife sailed to Europe to buy antique marble fireplaces in England, and choice pieces of furniture in various countries. They checked the sliding roof of the new roof garden at the Eden Hotel in Berlin, and in Paris their architects studied the gallery shops at the Ritz to get ideas for the stores in the lobbies of the new Waldorf. The Boomers wanted to import the best ideas available in the splendors of Europe's hotels for the new inn.

José Sert was engaged to paint murals for the dining rooms based on Cervantes' Don Quixote. This classic Spanish room bears the name of the artist. In the Park Avenue side lobby, Louis Rigal executed in marble-mosaic tesseraex the wonderful Wheel of Life in the floor of the great foyer. It is revealed in summer when the carpeting is removed. The design comprises six groups of life-size figures, united by floral fonds, depicting the whole story of human existence, from birth to old age and death, told in dramatic form. The exquisite shading is achieved by an unusual collection of marble from many parts of the world: Italy, France, Belgium, Africa, Ireland, Greece, and Turkey.

The Basildon Room was furnished from a salon which Boomer bought in England, when he learned that Basildon Park Berkshire was to be demolished. The paneled walls with carved moldings and recessed mirrors go back to 1776, when the old English castle was built. The touches of artistry from the Old World brought distinction and charm to the new Waldorf, into which many new American ideas were incorporated as well. Boomer obtained a new type of push-button elevator with automatic doors, never before used in a hotel. Joseph Carney, the engineer of the old Waldorf, worked on the design of the kitchens. The building itself which housed all this was 625 feet high, 47 stories, costing $40,000,000. When the New York Central approved the project, it advanced $10,000,000. On the Board of Directors of the Waldorf Corporation were Charles Hayden, Gen. W. W. Atterbury, President of the Pennsylvania Railroad, E. W. Beatty, President of the Canadian Pacific Railway, L. I. Horowitz, Richard F. Hoyt, Hayden Stone & Co., Condé Nast, John W. Prentiss of Hornblower & Weeks, Alfred P. Sloan, Jr., President of General Motors.

The idea of designing twin towers was originated by Schultze and Weaver, the architects who had built the Sherry-Netherland Hotel, Park Lane, and the imposing Breakers of Palm Beach, Florida. A private driveway was provided ninety feet wide and two hundred feet long. George C. Boldt had sacrificed 7,000 feet of ground space at the Thirty-fourth Street entrance to build a carriageway for the Fifth Avenue Waldorf. Boomer, too, thought a private entrance was important.

Boomer chose Frank Ready as resident manager. Ready had been with him at the McAlpin and had opened the Roosevelt Hotel, later serving at the Park Lane and the Barclay. There was also Augustus Nulle and Eugene Voit, able men. Joseph P. Hoenig, from the Bellevue-Stratford in Philadelphia, became convention and entertainment manager, J. A. Klugherz was chief clerk and Ted Saucier public relations director. Mr. Saucier performed a miracle of national and international promotion which spread the fame of the new hotel around the globe. His wide friendships included royalty, artists, writers, and the greats of business and professional life. His service encompassed over two decades of devotion to the dream of the Waldorf and he, above all, is responsible for much of its fabulous rise to pre-eminence in the history of hostelries. A devoted gourmet with a sensitive appreciation of culinary excellence, Saucier also embraced the creative role of a chef, often preparing dishes from his own original recipes, and even a complete menu with which he enticed the great Escoffier to be his guest.

The men Nino Malnati of the Biltmore recommended for the

important posts of headwaiters for the dining rooms were Ambrose Brogi for the Empire Room, Frank Ronga for the Sert Room, Ralph Schulder for the Lounge Café, and Robert James Hanson for the Norse Grille. I knew them all and they were excellent choices.

The Waldorf opened its doors on September 30, 1931, and 25,000 people attended the reception in its honor. Just as he had stood at the door thirty-eight years before with Mr. Boldt, when the Fifth Avenue building was opened, Oscar now received guests as the hotel's official greeter. Over the newly installed radio system came the voice of President Herbert Hoover from the White House. With his characteristic directness, he declared that "our hotels have become community institutions, the central points of civic hospitality, to be conducted in far larger vision than mere profit earning." Built in the depths of the Depression, the new venture was an act of faith in the future of America. Many years later, the Waldorf was to become Herbert Hoover's home and a comfort in his old age. There he now happily keeps eight secretaries busy at a very active eighty-six.

Lucius Boomer believed in the idea of "town house" living in hotels as the preferred way of residence in New York. This to him represented the final stage of gracious New York living, which was the fourth plateau of development:

1. Private detached houses and practically nothing else
2. Brownstone front, sometimes a two-family
3. Flats modelled after those of Paris which went up the social scale and became apartments
4. Hotel living, with facilities less of a hotel and more of an apartment

People were to think of the hotel as home so rooms had to be equipped with furniture and facilities not of an institution in monotonous sameness but individually. So the Waldorf had furnishings which were distinct, interior decoration, comforts, artistry only found in private homes.

The Waldorf had 2,000 rooms plus 300 residential suites, numerous ballrooms, dining rooms, restaurants, kitchens, foyers, lounges, corridors, club rooms. They represented the best work of the early American period, eighteenth-century England when such master designers and craftsmen flourished as the Adam Brothers, Chippendale, Sheraton and Hepplewhite, and the fine Louis XV and Louis XVI periods of France. The result was the absence of stuffiness, ample ventilation, air and lighting, with comfortable upholstery and attractive color schemes.

With every possible facility for luxurious living, the Waldorf could not compete with the Depression which tolled the death knell of the good life. One day in the summer of 1932, there were 1,600 people on the payroll and only 260 guests in the 2,000 rooms. The hotel was like a ghost town, but Saucier's promotion continued unabated. Distinguished Americans and foreign visitors were enticed to attend a parade of luncheons, dinners, breakfasts and buffet cocktail parties. Curiosity brought many to the Waldorf and found it not wanting in fulfilling its promises.

Repeal came on December 2, 1933. The great hotels of New York once more turned their attention to the art of dining, and to stocking cellars, but the scars of the drought were to remain for many years. The mahogany heads of the Bull and the Bear were again in evidence, as in the golden age of the famous four-sided bar of the old Waldorf. Now they preside in the Bull and Bear Restaurant, where women are not permitted to enter until after 3 P.M. Irvin Cobb said that the former Men's Bar at the Waldorf was the symbol of the male's occasional emancipation from the emancipated female.

The Gargantuan dinners of the Gay Nineties ran to nine or ten courses with three kinds of meat, five wines, cognacs, liqueurs at the end. Even this was streamlined from the twenty courses to which Escoffier mercifully put an end. Banquets now run to four or five courses because people's appetites have become smaller. In 1899, when Rudolph Guggenheim hosted a dinner at the old Waldorf, the menu, which was printed in French, comprised: oyster cocktail, turtle soup, lobster, chicken, lamb, sherbet, diamond back terrapin, duck, orange and grapefruit salad, fresh strawberries and raspberries, vanilla mousse, bonbons, fruits and coffee. These courses were punctuated by: Sherry, Rauenthaler, Berg, Champagne, Burgundy, Port and Liqueurs. The cost was $250 per person.

In 1937, the Waldorf celebrated the Golden Wedding Anniversary of Oscar in appreciation of his long service. There was a lavish menu reminiscent of the olden days: clear green turtle soup, olives, pecan, celery; brook trout, cucumbers and sour cream; mignon of beef, Bearnais sauce, new peas and lettuce; kirsch sherbet, gray-legged partridge with wild rice and currant jelly, Waldorf salad, golden anniversary dessert, wedding cake, fruit, coffee. First came the Sherries— London Club Amontillado Fino and Tio Pepe, then Imperial Amontillado, Wurzberger Sulvaner Riesling, 1935; a champagne, Chateau Latour 1925, then Musigny, Comte de Vogue 1930, and then a fifty-year-old Courvoisier brandy.

In spite of the heroic efforts of all concerned with the fate of the Waldorf, business did not pick up until 1939. By 1942, it was in full swing—as many other places were—as a result of the impetus of World War II. By 1944, the hotel's balance ledger was finally written in black ink.

Better times were ahead and, in October of 1945, the Waldorf had a great stroke of luck. The hotel and restaurant industry boomed as the war brought an influx of visitors to the city. The streets were alive with uniformed men from our own forces and the allied nations. Under these circumstances, Metro-Goldwyn-Mayer released "Weekend at the Waldorf" in a widely advertised and well-prepared opening night at the Music Hall in Rockefeller Center.

What few people realized, as they watched the actors playing their parts with the world's greatest hotel as their stage, was that behind this promotional bonanza was the astute Ted Saucier, Publicity Director of the Waldorf. The picture had, in fact, been conceived by Ted Saucier, who also collaborated on the story plot and synopsis. The shooting script, or final story, written from the synopsis, was by Sam and Bella Spewack. Anyone who knows Mr. Saucier personally is aware of his valiant courage, his devotion to cuisine, his lively imagination, his ready humor, and his booming, authoritative voice. He was, therefore, "right at home" when he went to Hollywood for the production of the picture "Weekend at the Waldorf," of which he was Technical Director. With him went his beautiful and social wife,

Ruth Saucier. The Sauciers are known for their hospitality, which has become a legend.

Everyone agreed that the studio had cast the show brilliantly. In New York, Joseph Homler at MGM (via our friend Fred Bullock, head of the Still Department at Twentieth Century Fox) gave us a run-down from his record sheet of the leading players: Ginger Rogers, Lana Turner, Walter Pidgeon, Van Johnson, Edward Arnold, Phyllis Thaxter, Keenan Wynn, Leon Ames, Lina Romay, Constance Collier, Robert Benchley, Samuel H. Hinds, and Xavier Cugat with his orchestra. Metro-Goldwyn-Mayer had been induced to gamble four million dollars on the premise that the American public would be curious to know what life was really like in New York's luxury hotel on famed Park Avenue. Audiences everywhere lived vicariously at the Waldorf, enjoying its exquisite Starlight Roof, its Peacock Alley, and elegant Empire Room. Young couples stretched their exchequer to spend their honeymoon weekend at the Waldorf. It became the modern Niagara Falls.

While the studio's investment was staggering, it proved eventually sound. And henceforth, the Waldorf-Astoria became a household word in every town, city, hamlet and village which had a projector and a screen. As for Ted Saucier, its creator, no one thereafter could doubt that he was the most daring and inspired publicist of restaurants and hotels in "Bagdad on the Hudson."

Two years earlier, Oscar of the Waldorf had gone into retirement, signifying the end of an earlier era. In 1943, after half a century of devoted service as the Waldorf's official host, he was tendered a banquet, sponsored by sixteen organizations, to do him honor. When he died in 1950, at the age of eighty-four, his name had become a synonym of hospitality in the grand manner. Claude Philippe, a young Frenchman, succeeded to the post of maitre d'hotel.

After many years of service to the Waldorf, Lucius Boomer passed away in 1947. He was succeeded in the presidency of the Waldorf Corporation by Frank Ready, his long-time assistant and understudy. In 1949, Conrad Hilton bought the Waldorf-Astoria. The closing of title to the famous institution came after several hectic years of negotiations. Hilton, the outsized Texan, had an outsized ambition to own the greatest hotel in the world. More than any other, he wanted to include the Waldorf in his corral of hotels scattered around the globe.

Hilton was not born in Texas, but in San Antonio, New Mexico, in 1887. During the Depression, he managed to hold on to his chain of eight hotels when 81% of the nation's hotels were in bankruptcy. Economy has been said to be the key to his success. During the financial debacle he had no income and a debt of half a million. From this precarious situation, Hilton raised himself to his present eminent position in the hotel world. To the Hilton chain, he added the Statler chain in 1954. Hotels bearing his name began to appear in San Juan, Puerto Rico; in Madrid, in Istanbul, in Mexico City, Acapulco, in Panama, in Cairo and West Berlin; also in Rome, Tokyo and London. There is no telling where they will spring up next, or if the chain will ever end. His was a conception of tavern-keeping beyond the wildest imagination of his predecessors. A recent addition is the Hilton at Tel Aviv, Israel.

Hilton is a legend in his own time, an Atlas holding on his shoulders an immense hotel world. Six feet two inches in height, weighing some 195 pounds, he has the drive of a man of thirty. He enjoys life to the full, is affable, frank, unaffected, a good pianist and dancer, with a keen zest for living. In classical times, he would be the god of hospitality. To him an ideal came within his grasp by becoming a deal, yet nobody can deny his genius.

Hilton gave the romanticists something to dream about when his May-December marriage with international glamour girl, Zsa Zsa Gabor was announced. The gay Hungarian's first husband was Burhan Belge, the middle-aged press director of the Turkish government, whom she wed when she was in her teens. A failure from the start, the marriage provided the already ambitious beauty with the first opportunity to move in fashionable circles, which in time led to Hilton's doorstep. From this union came a daughter, and the lifetime privilege of occupying a comfortable suite at the Plaza Hotel. In her own spirited way, the tantalizing blonde tells in her recent book of her new husband beginning their life together by his almost complete absorption in the details of a deal to buy the Blackstone Hotel in Chicago. They have long since been divorced.

As far as the Waldorf is concerned, hospitality on so large a scale had to be recognized as an institution of commerce to which must be applied modern business and accounting methods, as well as modern industrial methods applicable to the hotel business. It is a moot question whether it is possible to combine the old-time art of innkeeping in dispensing hospitality with current American business procedures. It is an actual fact though that the Waldorf has been turned into a profitable operation for the stockholders. If one must question the Hilton methods, consider that an institution which employs some 2,500 people, adding 500 part-time employees for special functions, with an annual payroll of nearly ten million, has no alternative but to treat hospitality as big business. And Hilton has made it profitable for it is said that the hotel earns over a million annually after taxes.

Presently the top executive positions are held by Frank Wangeman, who is General Manager, Carl G. Thurston, who is Manager; Miss Mary McCloud is Director of Publicity, and Clyde Harris is Director of Catering and in charge of banquets.

When royalty comes to New York, it is invariably entertained at the city's unofficial palace on Park Avenue. To catalogue these high functions of state completely would constitute a long assignment in itself. Menus are carefully devised to please the guests being honored and to present their hosts in the best light. The City of New York was the host for the gala luncheon extended to the young and lovely Queen of England, Elizabeth II, by Mayor Robert F. Wagner on Monday, October 16, 1957. There were more than seventeen hundred invited guests, including former President Herbert Hoover, Governor Averell Harriman and Mrs. Eleanor Roosevelt. This was one of the largest official luncheons ever given by the City. Richard C. Patterson, Jr., City Commissioner of Commerce and Public Events, fulfilled his responsibility well by arranging to seat sixty-two guests of honor on a four-tiered dais, all tiers decorated with a continuous hedge of pink and red carnations.

Pink tablecloths were decorated with the hotel's finest china, silverware and stemware, with carnations and candles in silver candelabra accentuating the service. In the hotel's west foyer, the guests were served at a pre-luncheon reception with dry sherry and New York State champagne. At the reception itself, Mayor Wagner sat in the center of the first row of the dais, with the young Queen at his right and Herbert Hoover on his left, with Governor Harriman next to him, according to strictest protocol. The only women on the great dais were the Queen, Mrs. Roosevelt, Mrs. Wagner and Mrs. Harriman. To ease the minds of worried taxpayers, Mr. Patterson explained to reporters that the cost of the royal luncheon was "being underwritten by a group of public-spirited citizens."

THE MENU

LOBSTER BISQUE WALDORF

WITH BRANDY

JOHANNISBERG RIESLING

ALMADEN

SQUAB CHICKEN MANHATTAN

WITH WILD RICE

TINY GREEN PEAS

BEAULIEU VINEYARD

GEORGES DE LATOUR CABERNET

1948

DÉLICES OF RASPBERRIES

À LA ROYALE

The wines were carefully chosen from the areas East and West of the Rockies. While the Declaration of Independence was not displayed, the young monarch could draw her own conclusions as to the ability of the former Colonies to stand, as it were, on their own feet gastronomically.

Wines Around the World

If on my theme I rightly think,
These are five reasons why men drink—
Good wine, a friend, because I'm dry,
Or lest I should be by and by,
Or any other reason why.
—HENRY ALDRIDGE, Dean of Christchurch,
1647-1710

A SINGLE GRAPE SPECIES, VITIS VINIFERA, is said to have originated most of the hundreds of varieties of the fruit of the vine. Historians tell us that the grape first began to grow around the Caspian Sea, and was thence carried to all continents. While its birthplace is not precisely known, we do know that wine was produced in Egypt around 2400 B.C., and in China before 2000 B.C. Wine culture in Asia Minor, which is described in the Old and New Testaments of the Bible, spread from that region to the shores of the Mediterranean where the country was sheltered, sunny, and perfect for grape growing.

In the eighth century B.C., Hesiod, writing in Greece, gave instructions for the care of the vine, and eventually Greek scholars wrote handbooks on wine. It was the progressive Phoenicians, merchants and traders, who took the vine into Italy about 600 B.C. The Romans adapted Dionysus, the Greek god of vines and vintages, and called him Bacchus. Horace, the Roman poet, wrote glowingly of *ardena falernum* of the vintage year 121 B.C. Pliny, who has revealed

163

so much of history, recorded fifty different kinds of wine during the time of Christ.

The Romans established wine production as an important agricultural pursuit in western Europe after Julius Caesar conquered Gaul, now France. In his day, every country along the Mediterranean produced wine for table use. Among the Greek and Latin nations, wine was then, as it is today, the customary mealtime beverage. At times it was their medium of exchange. Debts and taxes were often paid, at least in part, with wine. Minstrels sang of it and authors wrote in its praise. It has been said that wine is a living thing with stages like humans. It is brash and bold in its youth, full-blossoming in its maturity, and if not consumed in time, subject to senility, decay and death. Wine is at its best when in the company of food, and gregarious in the society of men and women who appreciate and love it, priming their wit, faithful in the rituals of worship, and serving as a medicine for both body and spirit. The naturally fermented juice of fresh, ripe grapes, wine is what André L. Simon has well termed it: "the living blood of the grape."

There are many countries in the world which produce wine to a greater or lesser degree. France is first and foremost; Italy is second, and also second in wine consumption; Spain has its heaviest production areas along the Mediterranean coast, in the southern interior, and in the Canary Islands. Spain is chiefly known for its Sherry, from the region around Jerez de la Frontera near Cadiz, and the dessert wine shipped from Malaga.

Wars certainly affect the wines. Rumania in World War II lost Bessarabia to the Russians and the regions of its white wines—Riesling, Leanyka and Furmint, grape varieties grown in Transylvania. Portugal sends its Port everywhere, and especially to British concerns; Argentina ranks first in the Americas for wine production and consumption. In the high plateau region backed by the Andes are produced the red table wines of Mendoza and San Juan. The Soviet Union under the tsars had many vineyards, which were expanded by the U.S.S.R. in the 1930's. The German invasion of 1941 retarded these efforts. There was considerable wine production in Armenia, Georgia and Azerbaijan in the Caucasus. Also in the north and in the Crimea,

Greece produces thick, sweet wines and some demand exists for its table wines, including the *Marco* and *Tegea,* a pink wine from the mythical land of Arcadia. Yugoslavia has wine production as has Hungary. There is a small high region in the northeast among the Carpathians which produces the superlatively sweet wine called *Tokay.* This wine comes from Furmint grapes left on the vine until almost dried. It takes years to develop the best, and it is said that this wine is almost immortal. It can live and improve in the bottle for centuries. Bulgaria produces mostly for its own use.

The Union of South Africa is a wine producer. Viticulture was pioneered in 1653 upon the arrival of the first Dutch Governor, Jan Van Riebeek. After 1688, it was considerably advanced by the Huguenots familiar with wines from France. Until the nineteenth century, the most famous wine was the dessert wine of South Africa from the Muscatel grapes in Constantia near Capetown. Later, European grape varieties were planted in several regions for white and red table wines. Turkey produces dry and sweet wines on the island of Tenedos, near the entrance to the Dardanelles; white wine in Smyrna; wines from the Black Sea and around Lake Van, formerly part of Armenia. Austria suffered vivisection in its many wars. Especially after World War I, Austria's territory was left with few of its famous vineyards intact. Many good red and white table wines of local repute were produced, with the chief areas in Styria and Lower Austria.

Brazil takes its grape varieties from North America, and seven of its states produce wines. Rio Grande del Sole leads, with Brazilians favoring sweet wines, especially Port and Muscatel. Australia's production is in the south, with New South Wales, Victoria, West Australia and Queensland in the order of their production. European cuttings started the industry at the beginning of the nineteenth century.

Who would think of Great Britain as a wine country? Actually it does produce a small amount of British wine, although its climate is not suitable for vineyards. The previously British-held Island of Cyprus produced, in 1939, more than all of the United Kingdom. Britain holds a peculiar place in the wine field. It produces nothing to speak of, it consumes little, yet it serves importantly as importer and distributor. Since the fifteenth century, it has regularly imported wines, and its tastes have influenced wine-growing practices in exporting countries.

Britain maintains huge cellars where it blends and bottles imported wines for its export trade, which reaches around the world. The Port wine of Portugal was developed to British taste and largely by Britons. It was Britain who bottled Port and carried it abroad to world markets in British bottoms.

It would be difficult to include every spot where wine is produced. Switzerland, Czechoslovakia and Albania grow grapes for local wines. North Africa produces, as does Morocco; Algeria and Tunisia contribute heavy wines. Wine is produced in Palestine, Syria, Iran, and even in parts of India, China and Japan. Canada has a wine production of about three million gallons annually. Mexico produces in a limited way from European varieties. In South America, every country participates to some extent. The fruit of the vine has devotees whose languages are as many as the Tower of Babel.

Harvest time in Portugal comes at mid-September when the slate-blue grapes hang in heavy clusters among the red vine leaves. Teams of pale-brown oxen draw wooden-wheeled carts, laden with the beautiful grapes on the way to the crushing, along roads with sparse clumps of umbrella pines and olive trees dotting the sunny valleys. Port wine, which is only 3% of wine production in this country, is named for Oporto in the north of Portugal. From Oporto one can visit the Pais do Vinho, the lovely port-wine country which lies around the River Douro, a region of wide-flowing valleys and deep river gorges. Outdoor cafés are in the European tradition, with a very pleasant one at the Palacio de Crystal. Monsieur Eiffel, who built his famous tower in Paris, fashioned the high double iron bridge over the deep river channel here. When enjoying their Port, it brings back pleasant memories of the old town with its goldsmiths' shops, its Portuguese silver and green porcelain. The great wine of Portugal is Lancers, in its familiar crock, imported by Vintage Wines Co.

The officially demarcated area of the famed Douro district extends some sixty miles up river from Oporto, roughly between the village of Mezao Frio in the west to Barca d'Alva on the Spanish frontier in the East, a total of some 1,250 square miles. The soil is impregnated with a soft foliated stone known as schist, from which much of the wine's uniqueness is derived. The hillsides are cut into walled terraces to ensure that the torrential rains which frequent this area do not uproot the vines which are planted on the great steps in rows from 2½ to 4 feet apart. Visitors to the Douro district remark with wonder on the Herculean task of building these terraces on the hillsides, and which it has taken centuries to complete.

Vintage time is towards the end of September. Bands of vintagers, many from far distant villages, trek to the vineyards equipped with small hooked knives with which they cut off the bunches of grapes. From smaller baskets, the bunches are emptied into larger ones carrying a hundredweight of fruit, which are brought to the press-houses by men moving in single file. The grapes are placed in *lagars* (stone tanks) which hold sufficient fruit for the production, after pressing, of ten to twenty pipes of wine, a pipe being the ancient measurement of 115 gallons. Then occurs the ancient method of extracting the juice as the grapes are trodden under foot. With periods of rest, this continues for several days to the accompaniment of music and high-spirited laughter and banter. Authorities claim that this antiquated procedure is actually superior to any other. The richness and colour of the must (freshly pressed juice of grapes) are retained without the pips of the fruit being crushed, thus avoiding excess astringency. After being tread, the must is left in the tanks to ferment.

While Sherry is made in many parts of the world, it is well to remember that the only true Sherry comes from Spain, where it enjoys a unique history and prestige. Juan I called the town of Jerez—Jerez-de-la-Frontera, in 1380, because it was a focal point of battle. The people pronounce the name of the town *Herreth*. Since 1264, when Alfonso X led his army into Jerez to establish a frontier between the Christians and the Moslems, the town was encouraged by the king to make wine and to extend the vineyards around Jerez. Here, then, were the modest beginnings of the export of Spanish wines. For those who enjoy following the Ariadne thread to its source, it may be noted that the ancient town was founded by the traveling Phoenicians around 1100 B.C. They called it Shera. Later it came under the rule of the Greeks, who perpetuated the name. In 206 B.C., however, the Romans took it over and called it Cerit or Ceritium. Pursuing the history of viticulture, we found that Columella, a citizen of Gades (Cadiz), who wrote about agriculture in the first century A.D., recorded enough about Jerez to conclude that even at that time it was a grape-growing and wine-making center. Archeological findings support this conclusion.

The Vandals, a tribe of Barbarians, invaded Spain in 409 A.D., leaving behind the beginnings of the town Vandalusia, now Andalusia. In the wake of the invaders came the Moors, who called the town Xerez. The Arabs pronounced it Scheris. By 1608, the name Sherry had been established, blossoming in the course of history from the roots imbedded in the past. The name of the wine became, therefore, a true geographical appellation.

The soil, compounded of 80% chalk with magnesia and clay, forms the first group for sherry known as *albariza*. The second grade of soil is known as *barro*, i.e. clay; and the third group is *arenas*—sandy soil. One cannot see the vineyards from the road or rail for they are situated away from the dusty high-roads and smoky railways of the hilly country. In the Carrascal and Macharnudo districts (some five miles north and north-west of Jerez) one finds the Albariza district whence the finest Sherries come. The House of Sandeman of London, England, maintain here their wonderful vineyards known as "El Corregidor" and "Cerro Viejo" where the vines are planted in rows five feet apart to form squares providing a coverage of some 2000 vines to the acre. From this area comes a yield of 7500 lbs. of grapes, which make 500 gallons of sherry. The crop from the other two sections of *barro* and *arenas* soil is even greater, but the quality is not so fine.

There are many ways in which vines grow and are supported. I will mention specifically the sherry-bearing grapes because the procedure is somewhat unusual. The vines are cultivated on a low trunk only 16 inches in height and having four branches which are supported by forked props to keep the fruit off the ground. Only two of the four branches are allowed to produce fruit in alternate years. The grapes are in themselves so delicious that the cultivators have to erect tower-like elevated structures in the vineyards, manned by armed guards at harvest time, to prevent theft. The towers are called *Bien-te-veo,* meaning "I can see you all right."

The importance of geological conditions, more than climate, is primary with regard to Sherry. It is from the nature of the soil in the Jerez vineyards that this wine of infinite variety absorbs its distinctive and exclusive characteristics. True Sherry (ranging from the very light and the very driest of wine through a diversity of styles, to wines that are dark, rich and sweet) can come only from that particular area in Spain where the requisite geological conditions pertain. If a Jerez vine, for instance, were transplanted in another part of the world, it would not grow Sherry. Another interesting point about Sherry is that this vine derives much of its exclusive character from a yeast known as *flor del vino* (flower of wine) which grows naturally on the wine itself. The casks are left open to the air as the wine absorbs a great deal of oxygen. They are purposely left only seven-eighths filled to leave space for the development of the flower. Twice a year, in Spring and Autumn, after periods of activity, the "flower of wine" falls to the bottom of the casks where it forms a crust known as "Mother of the Wine," which markedly influences both the style and character of the Sherry, and great care is taken not to break this beneficial deposit. This is similar, of course, to the "mother" used in the making of vinegar.

Sherry is a wordly sprite, experiencing many marriages. Under the skilled hands of a blender match-maker, perfect unions of various wines are attained by "marrying." Sherry is also fashion conscious. It changes its "robe" or color with the passage of time. One may purchase a very pale sherry only to find it has deepened in color before being consumed.

There is a general misconception about the use of sherry for cooking. I have often heard reference to "Cooking Sherry" as if it were an inferior wine good enough to embellish foods and sauces. This is in error. Wines selected for use in the preparation and improvement of foods must harmonize with the other ingredients to achieve a pleasing result. If one uses a dry, medium or sweet Sherry, it should be a quality which will enhance the flavor of the dish. Wine should not be used in cooking merely to add alcohol. The test is this: if a wine is not worthy of a place in a glass, it is not worthy of a place in cuisine.

Consommé is certainly greatly improved by the addition of either dry or rich Sherry, according to taste. The addition of Sandeman's 'Three Star Brown' or 'Brown Bang' Sherry in the preparation of ham, gives the meat a flavor which elevates it to a gourmet's delight. 'Brown Bang' Sherry goes well with fruit cake; 'Three Star Brown' Sherry added to a thick cream sauce for use with chicken crowns a simple dish with glory. The Englishman has been reared on Port and Sherry and needs no indoctrination. William Makepeace Thackeray, England's well-travelled author, who also sampled from the tables of New York City, capsuled the right attitude in a few words: "Grudge myself good wine? As soon grudge my horse corn . . .".

Other Sherries also serve nobly in the kitchen. Nothing could be better than Almadén Cream Sherry from California in preparing a ham for the oven. Here again is a dish which is almost timeless. The Romans, according to Apicius, boiled ham with figs and honey, adding wine and serving with it a sweet wine cake made with cheese, flour, bay leaf and sweet wine. Through the centuries, gourmet James A. Beard reminds us, every country has produced a ham of some distinction. At one time a ham found its way to the *Foire aux Jambons* in Paris from every civilized country in the world. Here one found pepper-cured hams, the hams of Westphalia, of Bayonne, the Jamón Serrano from Spain (and the Spaniards treated theirs to a union with Sherry), hams called *Lachschinken* from Central Europe, the ham of Parma which we know now as *Prosciutto,* recently arriving from Italy boneless, the exquisite hams from Milan and Paris, not to overlook those robust, rich-flavored hams from our own State of Virginia. A small restaurant in Paris, the *Chope Danton* in the *Carrefour de l'Odéon,* has gained fame with its recipe for *Jambon à la crème.* You will find it in many restaurants in France and especially throughout Burgundy.

The table habits of countries of South America often parallel those of Europe. In Chile, for instance, wine is served daily in all classes of homes and appears on every restaurant menu, a table necessity as much as a knife or fork. It is usually conceded that Chile produces the best wines of South America. Some are so fine that they have been accepted in Europe and the United States. Since the Spanish colonized this narrow country in the sixteenth century, grapes were harvested from the plantings of the missionaries, who needed wine for the sacraments. European cuttings were the original source and, in recent years, California. In all these many years the vines have grown strong in a sunny climate blessed by the Lord in escaping the diseases which plague vineyards, such as mildew or the dreaded phylloxera.

I cannot help being aware of phylloxera for its visitation to the Italian vineyards changed the course of my life. For generations, my family had been viticulturists and vintners. When the disease struck in 1914, it ruined many small landholders. Our ancestral vineyards were not exempt from harm. And the consequent decrease in family income spurred our migration to the New World. When my sisters and brother went to New York, it was furthest from my mind to follow them. My friends, my plans for the future, rooted me at home on the estate. However, I decided that I would pay a visit to New York, taking the voyage not as an immigrant, but as a traveler in first-class accommodations. When I arrived in New York, I was poorly impressed by its bustling comparison with the gracious, quiet life I had known and enjoyed in Italy. But soon I decided to stay and learn something about this great metropolis. And that was the beginning of my life as an American.

To return to the vineyards of Chile, it is interesting to learn that Chilean wines have no vintage years because the weather is unvarying and the production almost unvaried. The Andes rise on one side of the length of this ribbon of a country, and on its other side is the Pacific Ocean with its cold Humboldt Current. The combination of breezes from the sea striking against the mountain wall produces an ideal climate for fruit growing—grapes, peaches, pears, melons. Perhaps the finest quality wines come from the region near Santiago called Llano del Maipo. Lontué also produces wines of good repute. The wine regions begin at 30 degrees latitude around Coquimbo, and continue south to Temuco, which is 40 degrees. This area divides into three regions: Huasco and Elqui in the North; Aconcaque, Maipo in the central sections; and Itala and Cauquenes in the Southland. Summer comes in January, February and March, and winter in June. The eucalyptus and red pepper trees are like those of California.

As in Europe, the picking of the grapes is a social ceremony. In the tradition of my home in Piedmont, the well-dressed entrepreneurs visit their vineyards, mingle with the workers, pick and eat grapes during the height of the harvest season. Communal singing and ceremony are the high points anticipated all summer. This is the festival time. In many sections, the carts which carry the grapes are colorfully decorated with festoons of vines and grapes, boys and girls in costumes of their region dance and sing in the streets. Much good food is prepared, which is naturally accompanied by much good wine.

In Piedmont, a great deal of fine food and fruit are eaten in the autumn. It is always my aim to visit Italy at the harvesting of the grapes, as this is the most enjoyable time of the entire year. At this peak of joyousness of the earth's yielding, strangers can begin to understand why poets like Keats, Byron, Shelley and Browning were willing to give their hearts to Italy. It is one of the few countries where one may face exile with composure. One afternoon, as we walked toward the Ponte Vecchio in Firenze where Dante is said to have beheld his Beatrice, we remarked once more on the shining cleanliness of the streets, and my wife turned to me and said: "If you must be called away to duty or sojourn elsewhere, I can think of no place in the world I would rather be left to my own resources than Florence."

In Chile, the special day is marked by singing, drinking Chica, sharing a barbecue, and dancing the Cueca, the national dance. The countryman wears a native costume of tight black trousers, short jacket with ten buttons on each sleeve, boots spurred with silver, while the women wear colorful skirts and peasant blouses. Chile consumes most of its wine, with the red and white table wines selling in largest volume . . . called Tinto or Bianco. There are other wines. Reisling and Rhine wines are light, delicate, and somewhat dry. Harold J. Grossman (author of "Guide to Wines and Spirits"—Scribners 1943), who lived in Buenos Aires as an importer and exporter of spirits, knows the wines of Chile as well as those of Argentina. Grossman describes the sauternes and haut sauternes as "sweet, luscious, fragrant, full-bodied, the only wine made outside the Sauternais district of

Bordeaux which is made in the identical manner." This means, of course, made of the same grape varieties—Sauvignon, Semillon and Muscadette, the latter remaining on the vine until "pourri-noble" develops, meaning that its rich sweetness is a natural consequence. Mr. Grossman feels these are the best sauternes produced outside of France.

Chilean Burgundy, obtained primarily from the Pinot Noir, is a great red wine, soft, well rounded, full flavored. They have a Cabernet lighter in body than the Burgundy, and a good Vin Rosé. Chile ships some sparkling Burgundy to the United States. Most of the wines bear the name of The House of Undurraga, whose first vineyards yielded in 1888, and which is still owned and operated by this family. Vina Undurraga is packaged in a green bottle, almost round in shape, with the name pressed into the glass. This is one of the best Chile has to offer.

We are becoming increasingly aware of the presence of German wines in the world markets. Back in 1957, the press carried reports of the boom in the United States of these wines. Announcement was made by the *Herald Tribune* (July 23, 1957) that Germany would soon "challenge the leadership of France and Italy as the major wine suppliers of the United States market." The year 1956 figured large in exportation, when Germany's exports ranked fourth in volume, only 7,000 gallons behind Spain.

A recognized authority on German wines, Frank Schoonmaker, made twenty-one extended trips through the German wine country in the past twenty-four years and tested 17,000 different German wines, of which he kept a written record of over half. A valuable report was given to the wine world in his "Wines of Germany," published in 1956 by Hastings House. In Schoonmaker's opinion, the people of the vineyards belong to the timeless fraternity which has united people of good will in all centuries and all countries. What makes German wines unique is they are lightest in alcohol of the fine wines of the world, always refreshing, and easy to drink. Lord Byron loved the wines of the Rhineland and recommended drinking them with spritzer—soda water. The few truly elite great wines of this country are simply astonishing, from Hessia or Pfalz, from Moselle or Rhein. In the great years, says Schoonmaker fervently, they are almost in the nature of "bottled poetry." Moselles and Rhine wines are pale in the nature of cold country wines, and very light in alcohol. One hundred days are needed between May and October to produce good wines; they get this quota almost every year.

Actually Germany is not a wine-producing country in the same sense as Italy, France and Spain. Germany produces less wines than Chile, for example, yet attains a higher average of excellence than the wines of any other country in the world. Rhineland is wine-land. The Rhine Valley and the valleys surrounding the tributaries of the Rhone River have their wines. The Moselle waters meet those of the Rhine at Coblenz. A little farther south there is the Nahe River, whence comes admirable wines, not known outside of Germany.

As one might guess, Riesling in Germany is King. To this grape the wines of Moselle, Saar and Ruwer owe the floweriness of their bouquet. The Riesling grows grapes of yellow green in tight little bunches. The vines were transplanted to California with much success, where the wines are known as White Riesling or Johannisberg Riesling, of excellent quality, from the region around San Francisco Bay. The Riesling grape went to Chile to produce the best of white wine in South America, called Johannisberg. Riesling is also grown in the vineyards of Soave, perhaps the best of the Italian white wines, and flourishes also in Alsace overlooking the Rhine. Riesling is best, of course, in its native soil in Germany, creating Scharzhofberger, Marco Brunner, Forster Kirchensttick, where success is largely a matter of climate and soil.

As with the vineyards of other European countries, those of Germany are very ancient. Many of them of Moselle, Hessia and the Pfalz, date back to the dawn of the Christian era, a century or so after Caesar conquered Gaul. Ausonius, the Latin poet, who gave his name to Château Ausone in France, published a poem about the Moselle and its wines in 200 A.D. The Emperor Charlemagne (from the great palace he built at Ingelheim on the Rhine near Mainz) saw the slope across the river, now called Rheingau, where snow melted earlier than elsewhere. Charlemagne ordered the area planted in vines, and it is now the steep vineyard of Schloss Johannisberg. Many vineyards, as elsewhere, were created by the monks. The Cathedral of Trier still sells its wines.

Inquiries we made in Mainz, on our last trip there in 1956, elicited the response that Pfalz or Palatinate is the largest wine-growing district of Germany, with some 35,000 acres of vines, and an annual production of fifteen million gallons. This vast area is controlled by forty-two vineyard owners grouped in an association of quality wine producers. There are some fifty separate holdings, of which the estate of Dr. Basserman-Jordan is the most famous. Of the major vineyards of Moselle-Saar-Suwer comprising 20,000 acres, less than one-third produce wines of superior quality in the yield of ten million gallons.

Since Germany is now an important wine producer, it is pertinent to describe her regions in some detail. Rheingau has 5,500 acres (only 4,200 of which are in full production). Two-thirds of the results can be called good, with an average yield of 2,250,000 gallons; Hessia has 31,000 acres under cultivation, only 4,000 being in the eight townships. These produce wines of top quality, with a total yield of 13,000,000 gallons; Nahe has 4,500 acres, one-fourth of which is above average, and yields 2,000,000 gallons; Pfalz has 35,000 acres, not over 1/10th of which produces superior wine, and has a yield of about 15,000,000 gallons; Franconia has some 7,000 acres, less than 10% of which produces superior wines, and has a yield of 2,000,000 gallons; Baden-Württemberg has 33,000 acres, less than 2% producing superior wines, with a total yield of about 14,000 gallons.

With the national characteristic of thoroughness, the German wine cellars appeared to us to be of better physical quality than those of any other wine-producing country we visited. They are operated as co-operatives, and the government has good viticulture schools for training in this prominent industry. The plants have good presses, filters, special fermenting tanks, and insecticides for the vines. Since World War II, there is a noticeable trend toward the presentation of younger wines with an age of eighteen months or two years, rather than five or ten years. This also is the trend in France and America. Since less time is involved in handling, such wines are less expensive.

Germans are past masters in filtration processes. They have the great Seitz plant in Bad Kreuznach on the Nahe, which has been completely rebuilt since the war. German scientists have made great contributions to this exact science, introducing revolutionary methods which make possible early bottling and early marketing of white wines with a gain in quality. They have found a way of removing by filter the yeast cells which might produce a later fermentation. Bottles and corks are sterilized without pasteurization, which involves heating the wines and thus is highly detrimental to the quality. The wine growers who resisted any change from the tradition of centuries have had to concede that wines can be made with care, intelligence, and love with the aid of modern science's achievements of the past fifty years as applied to wineries.

The points to remember about German wines are:

1. Better wines carry the name of a specific town, plus the name of the vineyard;
2. Better wines are natural wines without the addition of sugar;
3. Better wines are estate bottled and clearly marked;
4. Higher grades carry special legally defined marks as to their quality and class.

Germany uses two basic bottles, which are easily recognizable. There is the slender long-necked Flasche, traditional for the Moselle and Rhine wines; the other bottle is the gaily designed Bocksheutel, a round-bellied flacon used for the wines of Franconia and occasionally for certain of those of Baden. Both of these shapes have been imitated by Italy and also used by Chile and California. The standard bottles are green for Moselle, brown for Rheingau and Hessia, green again for Pfalz and Alsace. Germany invariably uses corks from Spain and Portugal, which are generally shorter than those in France. Most are branded with the name, and sometimes with the coat of arms, of the producer.

Mr. Schoonmaker makes the interesting comment that the most renowned wines of some countries do not necessarily go with the cuisine of those countries. Portuguese certainly do not consume Port with their meals; Spain exports its sherry, and produces 45 gallons of table wine to every gallon of sherry. However, French wine goes with French food, and Italian wine is a good companion to Italian cuisine. Our experience confirmed Mr. Schoonmaker's point, for while it is possible to eat well in Germany, once one becomes reconciled to the large portions of potatoes, sauerkraut, pork, and pickled dishes, very few wines go well with such food. Native dishes are happier with beer, or some of the common wines of Württemberg and Baden. In Germany, many of their best wines are enjoyed between meals, as a treat in the evening after dinner, or on the terraces. Exceptions are made when special dishes appear, such as trout from the Black Forest, the Eifel crayfish, or salmon from the Rhine.

German wines, asserts Mr. Schoonmaker, belong to the world like German music. There is a sequence in the service of wines which should be observed. Just as a sweet wine should not be served before a red wine like burgundy, nor Château d'Yquem before Château Latour, the great German wines should appear with desserts or with no food at all. When German wines come from the cellar at 60°, they are just right. In America they seem better a few degrees colder. Since our ice buckets are so short, a German wine with its long neck has to be chilled neck down. Moselles and Rhines should be served in clear, thin-stemmed glasses.

I have just recently received a report from Mr. Schoonmaker concerning Germany's statistical standing in the wine race. His totals do not include Champagne or Vermouth, etc. They are simply for still table wines and fortified wines, such as sherry. Total importations for 1958:

Italy	1,739,000	gallons
France	1,459,000	"
Germany	661,000	"
Spain	564,000	"

"As you will see," writes Mr. Schoonmaker, "Germany has now passed Spain, and it is very likely, I think, to remain in third place. Since practically no red wines are exported from Germany, it is improbable, in my opinion, that Germany could ever come close to the figures of France and Italy."

The history of food and wine is replete with items which shed light on the precious culinary arts. It is known that Queen Elizabeth, the

Virgin Queen of England, loved Sherry. Her subjects, Sir Walter Raleigh, Ben Jonson, William Shakespeare, often drank Sherry in the Mermaid Tavern, and Sherry, as we have seen, was the English mispronunciation of the Spanish town-name Jerez.

In South America they call the before-dinner hour the *Vermouth*. Port has been called the gentleman's wine. It received this title because menfolk would remain at the dinner table, swapping stories and enjoying cigars while passing the Port bottle around until someone conscientiously remembered: "Shall we join the ladies?"

CHAPTER

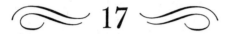

The Wines of France

*"When I demanded of my friend what viands he pre-
ferred, he quoth: 'A large cold bottle and a small hot
bird.'"*

—EUGENE FIELD

ALL OF THE COUNTRIES SURROUNDING THE
Mediterranean have made wine for thousands of years. In France,
wine-making has been considered an art for more than 2,000 years, and
the growing of the vines and the appreciation of the wine have become part of its civilization and culture. Latin scholars state that the
cultivation of the grape vines was developed in Gaul (in Marseille)
at the beginning of the sixth century B.C. The people of Marseille
were familiar with cultivation and pruning of the vines. It is the
pruning which makes the difference between wild vines and wine-
producing grapes. Up until 1869, the whole science of vine growing
depended on pruning of the vines. After that year, new improvements
were made through grafting, which has been practiced in France
ever since.

During the first century B.C., wine making took place all over
Gaul, and it was at that early period that vines which could resist
weather were "invented." One grown in the Rhone Valley was resistant to cold, and another in the Bordeaux region was resistant to
rain and storm. The Roman historian Tacitus writes of the commerce
of wine between Gaul and Ireland. By the end of the century, Gaul

179

exported wine to Greece and Italy and to all of the then known world. In the fourth century, the wines of Gaul were famed far beyond its own borders. Ausonius, a Latin poet, owned a vineyard in Bordeaux, and tells of his travels to see his customers in Germany. In Bordeaux, there was a "negotiator Brittanicus," who had a central buying agency for the British Isles.

The yield of the harvest and the aging of the wines were often fraught with the threat of failure. But science eventually corrected the varying conditions which brought damage. The long history of wine making in France proves that the French knew how to treat their vines and how to produce wine from the harvest, but it is more than this which makes French wines so unique. The difference lies in the fact that in France all of the conditions, geographical, geological and climatic necessary to the vineyards happen to be ideal.

It is the nature of the vine that it is dependent on the conditions of the soil, climate, and exposure to the sun. Thus the wines of one region or district cannot be duplicated in another. Therefore, the exact place of origin is the most important thing to know when buying a bottle, for it provides an idea of the probable qualities of the wine. That is why the name of the producer, or shipper, or importer on the label tells the exact story of what the wine represents.

Since origin is a decisive factor in the type and degree of greatness of the wine, the French law regulates the naming of wines very strictly. These regulations are called "Appellations d'Origine" and "Appellations Controlées." Each of the "Appellations" or names describes the permissible types of vines, method of planting and pruning, maximum yield per acre, and the process of wine-making. When you see V.D.Q.S. ("Vins Délimités de Qualité Supérieure") on the label, it means that although the wine is not the greatest, it is still of an excellent quality.

The key to understanding the wines of France is to have some knowledge of the regions of origin, there being only six or seven which divide the entire country.

The Wines of France

BORDEAUX

The range of wines from this section are truly wonderful. Production has been continuous for two thousand years, pre-dating Christianity. There are a great many varieties from this region which spreads along both banks of the Garonne River in the southern part of the country Caesar called Gaul, and which he "divided into three parts." From here comes the famous Clarets: rosé wines; dry, medium-dry, sweet and very sweet white wines.

The wines are known by the districts which produce them. Here are the principal ones:

MEDOC: Some of the famous parishes of Medoc are St. Estèphe, Pauillac, St. Julien, Moulis and Margaux. The wines of Médoc are red, light bodied, and unique for their elegant fragrance, mellowness and delicate and lasting taste.

ST. EMILION: The wines of this district are red, full-bodied, robust, having a strong bouquet and a distinctive taste.

POMEROL: This is a very small district, yet its red wines are elegant—a little lighter than the St. Emilions, with which they share most of the same characteristics in bouquet and taste.

GRAVES: Graves produces both red and white wines, the whites being either dry or medium dry, well balanced, elegant wines with delicate bouquet and a fruity flavor.

SAUTERNES: This is the name of a district that includes the township of BARSAC, which produces the greatest naturally sweet wines in the world. Sauternes have a lovely deep golden color; they are mellow, very fruity, and with a long-lasting, rich flavor.

The greatest of the wines of Bordeaux come from Medoc, St. Emilion, Pomerol, Graves, Sauternes and Barsac, but there are also excellent wines produced in other districts within the region of Bordeaux. Among them are:

CERONS, SAINTE-CROIX-DUMONT, LOUPIAC, COTES-DE BORDEAUX-SAINTE-MACAIRE, PREMIERES COTES de BORDEAUX, SAINTE-FOIX, ENTRE-DEUX-MERS, GRAVES de VAYRES, CANON FRONSAC and COTES de CANON-FRONSAC.

Most of the wines may be drunk when young, but they age well, especially the red wines from Médoc, Graves, Pomerol, and St. Emilion. They may be kept for several years. Some of the greatest red Bordeaux may reach their peak between ten and twenty years; some have been known to last for half a century.

The white wines mature more quickly than reds, and the dry white Bordeaux are drunk when young, although they keep well for several years. The rich wines of Sauternes are slower in reaching their peak, and age very well.

CHATEAU, REGIONAL AND PARISH WINES

There are two principal types of bottled Bordeaux: regional bottlings and chateau bottlings. Chateau (meaning castle) is the Bordeaux term for vineyard estate, some of which do have real castles on them. A chateau bottled wine is one which has been bottled at the vineyard where the grapes were grown and, therefore, the wine will have come from that specific place.

Regional and parish bottlings also come from a specified place, except that meanings have changed. Instead of an individual vineyard, the place is the district or "Appellation d'Origine Controlée." There is a fine distinction drawn which is of interest. Whereas the Chateau wines stand or fall with the reputation of the owner of the vineyard, regional bottlings are guaranteed by the reputation of the shipper.

This is the way it works out in practice. The wines are brought from the different vineyards of a district called after the region whence they came: "St. Julien," "Barsac," "St. Emilion," etc. They are matured in the cellar of the shipper in Bordeaux, and it is the shipper's name one sees on the label. If a wine happens to be the special choice of the shipper or "monopole," it will be so identified.

Reading of labels can yield a great deal of information about a wine. The name of the shipper indicates that the wine is one of quality because reliable shippers will only sell, under their own label, wines which will be sure to maintain their good reputation. Another guide to quality is the ADEB seal affixed to the neck of a bottle of Bordeaux wine. This is a gold and black seal of quality of the "Association pour le Développement de l'Exportation du Vin de Bordeaux" (ADEB). It is awarded only to those wines which have been submitted for—and which pass the stringent tasting tests—approval by a committee of Bordeaux wine experts.

In France there is no more serious subject than that of wine. Politics take second place, which may well be why the country has gone through so many different governments. One can, therefore, be sure that French custom with regard to wines is strictly enforced. The standards set by the ADEB for granting their seal are high, and even more strict than those actually required by French law. The seal guarantees that all Bordeaux wines bearing it are of a high order of quality; each in its own class and price range, of course.

BURGUNDY

This region has been famous as long as Bordeaux. Sometimes people will have long discussions as to which yields the greatest wines, and go on drinking both in order to arrive at a conclusion, which they never do. Perhaps the outstanding characteristic of Burgundy wines is their "warmth" and a strong bouquet. They are full-bodied and mellow, and the whites are very dry.

Here are the divisions of the great region of Burgundy:

CHABLIS. The small town of Chablis is north of the town of Burgundy and produces a dry, white wine so famous that many countries have tried—unsuccessfully—to imitate it. The wine of Chablis is very dry, light and heady. Its characteristic flavor is difficult to describe; its color a light yellow with a slightly greenish overtone.

THE COTE D'OR. This great wine-producing section is divided into two parts.

A. The Cote de Nuits to the north

B. The Cote de Beaune to the south

Cote d'Or wines possess Burgundy qualities to the highest degree. They mature more quickly than the corresponding Bordeaux, but age well.

A. COTE DE NUITS: Very full-bodied and have a remarkable bouquet. The best known of these come from the following townships: FIXIN, GEVREY-CHAMBERTIN, MOREY-SAINT-DENIS, CHAMBOLLE-SUSIGNY, VOUGEOT, FLAGEY-ECHEZEAUX, VOSNE-ROMANEE and NUITS SAINT-GEORGES.

B. COTE DE BAUNE—These wines are a little lighter than those of Cote de Nuits. They have a very strong bouquet, are delicate and smooth. The whites are dry, fruity, and rank among the very best.

The principal townships are: ALOXE-CORTON, PERNAND-VERGELESSES, BEAUNE, POMMARD, VOLNAY, MEURSAULT, CHASSAGNE and PULIGNY-MONTRACHET.

SOUTHERN BURGUNDY

The wines from this region are lighter than the Cote d'Or, fruity, and with a delicate bouquet, excellent when young.

SOUTHERN BURGUNDY means the regions of: CHALON, MACON and BEAUJOLAIS.

Chalon produces the well known wines of:
MERCUREY, RULLY, GIVRY and MONTAGNY.
Macon produces both red and white wines, very fine, the most well-known perhaps being POUILLY-FUISSE, which is a dry, fruity, heady, white wine.
Beaujolais produces fresh, light wines with an earthy flavor and bouquet, best when young.

The principal wines of Beaujolais are:
SAINT-AMOUR, JULIENAS, FLEURIE, CHIROUBLES, MORGON, COTE DE BROUILLY and MOULIN-A-VENT.

The best known French Sparkling Wine of its type is called Chauvenet Red Cap. It is matured in the century-old cellars of F. Chauvenet in Nuits, the heart of Burgundy. It is fruity, elegant, a sparkling wine of deep red ruby color, made as champagne is made, carefully developed in the bottle. Its companion piece is Pink Cap, a rose sparkling wine of the same high quality and acceptance. F. Chauvenet also ship a variety of very good Burgundy still wines, their Pouilly Fuisse, a fresh crisp white wine, and their Beaujolais, a fine, light, fruity, red wine, or their Pommard, a hearty full red wine from the Cote d'Or area. Munson G. Shaw Company of New York, their United States representatives, tell us that F. Chauvenet own some choice vineyards in the Nuits-St. Georges area. It is a name worth remembering.

ALSACE

Along the French bank of the Rhine lies the region of Alsace which produces dry, fresh, fruity, white wines.

These wines are not named from the geographical locations of the vineyards, but after the names of the vines.

The principal wines are:

RIESLING—a very dry, elegant and classic wine.
GEWURZTRAMINER—a fruity, supple wine which holds the distinction
of having probably the greatest bouquet of any wine in the world.
TRAMINER—of the same family as the Gewurztraminer but lighter in
bouquet and flavor.
SYLVANER—a fresh, light, fruity wine.

They are served chilled, make delightful aperitifs, and may be served throughout the meal.

COTES DU RHONE

These wines are warm and full-bodied, vigorous, with a rich bouquet and luscious taste.

The principal wines come from:

COTE-ROTIE, CONDRIEU, HERMITAGE, CORNAS, SAINT-PERAY, LIRAC,
TAVEL and CHATEAUNEUF-DU-PAPE.

The pink wine of Tavel is famous as one of the best rosés produced anywhere.

THE LOIRE

This region lies along the bank of the Loire River and produces wines of red, rosé or white which are light, delicate and fresh.

The best known are the dry, still, white wines of POUILLY-FUME and SANCERRE; the still and crackling white wines of VOUVRAY which range from dry to sweet; the red wines of CHINON and BOURGUEIL: the white wines (dry or sweet) of SAUMUR; the wines of ANJOU, white or rosé (mostly sweet) and a few reds; the dry, white wines of MUSCA-DET.

These are young wines from the Loire, consumed when young and never allowed to age. The whites and rosés are chilled. The reds lose none of their charm by being cooled. The sweet whites are very well, however, and keep for a long time.

COTES DE PROVENCE

The Cotes de Provence (Cote d'Azur) produces some lovely wines of which the reds are full-bodied and full-flavored; the rosés are light, fresh and fruity. The whites are dry and full-bodied, sometimes slightly sparkling. They go very well with fish and shellfish. These wines should be drunk when they are young.

OTHERS

Some wines are not known outside of France. Because there are many fine wines in that country, some feel that those which are not great are worthless. This is not true as some of the lesser wines of France would be the pride of another country less fortunately situated for wine production.

In the southwest and south of Bordeaux are good wines but not too famous: BERGERAC, MONT-RAVEL, MONBAZILLAC; the Pyrénées (JURANCON); the Tarn (GAILLAC) and LIMOUX.

In the southern part of France, from the Rhone River to the Pyrénées, spreads the region of the LANGUEDOC Province called the MIDI (the south). Large quantities of wine are produced here, most of it served day in and day out on the French family table. Those of superior quality are labelled according to the V.D.Q.S. regulations.

Up in the north—between Burgundy and Alsace—the JURA produces some very good wines (COTES DU JURA, ARBOIS, CHATEAU-CHALON, L'ETOILE).

And then across the Mediterranean, ALGERIA also contributes wines: MEDEA, MILIANA, DAHRA, MASCARA. There, too, the superior wines have the V.D.Q.S. label.

TERMS USED WITH REGARD TO THE WINES OF FRANCE
(Bordeaux Wine Information Bureau,
17 East 45th Street, New York, N. Y.)

There is a language of wines which the gourmet or connoisseur uses:

AGING: this refers to the maturing period of the wine. At first the aging is very active in casks, and continues much slower when bottled. When over two years old, a wine is considered an excellent vintage, provided it has been bottled a year after the wine was made. When it is put in bottles from the casks two years after it is made, the wine has really reached perfection. Most wines are at their best from one to five years, depending on the region of origin and the conditions of the vintage.

AROMA: the scent of the wine. Red wine is swirled in the glass before tasting as contact with the air improves its aroma, which is the fragrance of the grapes producing the wine.

BODY: the density or consistency of a wine. Its body weight. When more than one wine is served at the same meal, the light-bodied ones are served first.

BOUQUET: Fragrance from the fermentation and aging of the wine.

BRUT: Maximum of dryness.

CHILL: To cool the wine prior to serving by standing it in an ice bucket.

CLARET: True Claret is red Bordeaux wine.

DRY: Opposite of sweet. The dry wines are served before the sweet ones.

FRUITY: Quality of a wine in which the aroma and flavor of the grape are recognizable.

LABEL: The label carries the credentials of a wine. By French law the label gives:

1. the name of the wine which is, most of the time, the place of origin, or sometimes a proprietary name.
2. the exact place, or at least the country of origin.
3. the mention of "Appellation d'Origine" or "Appellation Controlée" or "V.D.Q.S." if the wine is entitled to any one of them.
4. mention that the bottling was done by the owner of the vineyard, if such is the case.
5. name of the shipper.
6. name of the importer.
7. alcoholic content of the wine.
8. volume content of the bottle.
9. vintage, if any.

Bottles of Bordeaux may also have a seal bearing "Qualité Approuvée par ADEB" meaning that the wine has passed the special test of quality set up by the Association pour le Développement de l'Exportation du Vin de Bordeaux (ADEB).

MISE EN BOUTEILLE: Bottling. When these words appear on a label they are followed by an indication of who did the bottling. Any one of the following expressions means that the wine has been produced, aged and bottled in the same estate: "Mis en bouteille au Chateau": "Mise de la Propriété": "Mis en bouteille par le propriétaire": "Mis du Domaine": "Mis en bouteille au Domaine."

MEDIUM DRY: slightly sweet.

NON-VINTAGE WINES: Wines blended from several vintages to obtain high standard quality. Only non-vintage wines can be the same in quality from year to year.

ROSE: pink wine. Always chilled.

SEDIMENT: Deposit which results from aging in the bottle. It does not harm the wine in any way and very often indicates that the wine is a greater and older vintage. A bottle showing sediment should

188

be allowed to rest upright until the sediment has sunk to the bottom of the bottle. It should then either be decanted or poured carefully in order to allow only clear wine to pass into the glass. Most wines do not contain sediment.

SWEET: pleasant taste characteristic of sugar. French table wines, even when very sweet, are never sugary or syrupy because their sweetness comes from the fermentation of the sweet grape juice and not from the addition of sugar.

VINTAGE: the year of the harvest from which a specific wine was made. French law permits only true vintage dates to be mentioned on bottles of wine.

VINTAGE CHART: List of vintages with grading of quality for each one. Vintage charts may be reliable as a general indication of quality for most of the wines made during a certain year. It should be remembered, however, that they are useless as a guide to the quality of any specific wine.

CHAMPAGNE

This is perhaps the most famous of all the wine regions of France. No other wine has had the worshipful respect and joyous welcome of Champagne, which never varies in popularity except to grow even more welcome as time goes on. While everyone loves Champagne, not everyone is familiar with its origin and cultivation. Knowing a few important facts vastly increases the appreciation of the "romantic" of the wine families.

By French law, only wines made from grapes grown in the Champagne region may be called Champagne. The process of Champagne making, termed "Champagnisation," is widely used in other parts of France, as well as in other countries for the making of better sparkling wines. Yet even the best of the sparklers are not Champagne, because only in that region is the combination of soil and climate found which makes for the unique quality of the wine.

Champagne is not a large area. It is the most concentrated vine district of France, representing only one-hundredth of the land dedicated to vine cultivation. It is a narrow band, really, which runs midway along the slopes, a hundred miles or so in length, and from four to fifteen hundred yards wide. The quantity is limited, but the quality is superb. The grapes are small, with thin skins and few seeds. The vines are kept short by pruning, so there is no waste of either heat or sap.

The delicate vine demands constant and exacting care, as many dangers constantly threaten its life and health. The work of the vine-grower is intense and never-ending as he battles insects, disease, frosts and storms, any of which may bring disaster to the crop. When the harvest comes, the bunches are minutely examined and selected. The spoiled are eliminated. About four tons of grapes are placed on the wine-press and yield 444 gallons of must . . . so begins the life of the wine. The wines of each of the vine districts have their own special characteristics, and the successful blending of these wines make what we know as Champagne.

In the middle of the seventeenth century, Dom Pérignon, cellar keeper to the Abbey of Hautvillers in the Bénédictine Abbey of the Champagne country, quite accidentally discovered how to control fermentation, i.e. the secret of a second fermentation, the chemical action which puts the bubbles into Champagne. He was able to obtain wines which kept both their limpidity and their sparkle. At the moment of his find, the excited monk rushed from his cellars crying exultantly: "Come quickly, I am drinking the stars!" André Simon, world authority on wines, says that the story is apocryphal, but concedes that while Dom Pérignon did not create sparkling champagne (there is such a thing as *still* champagne) he undoubtedly did much for its fame. He produced the "cuvées" by blending wines of different growths, and this gave the wine a richer bouquet. His artistry was greater than that ever used before.

Champagne is the most festive and extraordinary of wines. Upon its entrance into the roster of world wines, it went directly to royalty. Each European court drank champagne at its celebrations, following the example of Louis XIV, then the Regent of France, Louis XV, and also the King of Prussia, and the English Court. The coronation of the kings of France took place at the ancient Cathedral of Rheims, and champagne was the drink of exultation in toasting: "Vive le roi . . . vive la France!"

The Wines of France

The district of Champagne lies about 90 miles East of Paris, a wide plain of cultivated land from which the world-famous city of Rheims rises. To the south, the "Montagne de Rheims" stretches in a series of long wooded hills on the slopes of which lie some of the finest vine districts of Champagne. On the southern side of the "Montagne de Rheims" runs the Marne River, with other French vine districts spreading on either side. Chief among these is Ay, which is classed as one of the very best. Epernay is the principal and renowned town of this section. Still further south, and across the Marne River, "Cote des Blancs" with Cramant and Avize conclude this general geographical survey of Champagne.

Nowhere in the world can be found such a favored combination of soil, climatic, geological and geographical conditions to make up the exact factors needed for producing the original Champagne. The average daily temperature for the year is 50°. This is precisely right for bringing the grapes to maturity. The vines are well sheltered from the North wind, and the slight altitude above plain level is sufficient in most cases to preserve them from Spring frosts.

In the prehistoric days of the Second Epoch, scientists say that an inland sea covered the vast basin which is now Champagne country. In the course of thousands of years, the sea withdrew and left behind large deposits of chalk, which make up the soil. If you are puzzled by chalk as a favorable factor, the vintners will tell you that the chalk soil reflects the sun's rays and provides the maximum heat and light needed by the vines. The forests nearby hold and regulate the variations of moisture; the lime and calcium of the soil help to make the wine what it is. You will find here in the country of Champagne deep cellars one hundred feet below the ground, dug out of the waterproof chalk foundations. The cellars stretch for more than a hundred and twenty miles, and are the resting places of millions of bottles which remain there waiting in a cool and even temperature, before they go out to the world to grace the festive board.

To know the history of the Champagne country is to touch the heart-beat of France. There is hardly a region more closely associated with the great events in its national history. In 57 B.C., Julius Caesar —with the avowed purpose of conquering Gaul—was confronted by a

Belgic tribe from Rheims. They were people who had an affinity for Latin civilization and offered Caesar their alliance, rather than pitting their strength against his legions, who would destroy what they had built. So it was that victorious Caesar made the town of the Belgians a fine Gallo-Roman city called Durocortorum. It became the capital of the province of Belgae the Second, the crossroads of eight main highways, and was famed for its magnificent monuments. Imagine when you are next in Paris, which has celebrated its 2,000 birthday, that at the time Durocortorum was a bustling city with statues and fine roads, Paris was still an obscure village known as Lutetia Parisorum.

The Roman Empire collapsed, early in the fifth century, when it was overrun by barbarian invaders. Rheims, too, was destroyed by fire, with Epernay and Chalons sharing a similar fate. But these tragedies brought some good. In the confusion of destruction, the archbishops of Rheims asserted their authority and prestige. In 496 Saint Rémi baptised—in the presence of Clovis—the Frankish monarchy, and thereby inaugurated the long tradition of coronations which made Rheims the holy city of France, and its metropolitan church the nation's cathedral.

As it turned out, the successors of Saint Rémi were later to intervene frequently in the affairs of the kingdom. They were given the title of Counts, then raised to that of Ducs de Rheims, becoming the first peers of France. Under the feudal system, they were temporal lords, quite independent of the Counts of Champagne, and governed as sovereign rulers. This applied as well to the Count and Bishop of Chalons, while Epernay, several times claimed by the Counts of Champagne, came under their domination.

In the course of time, out of so many seigneurial estates (comprising vast areas of land and skillfully cultivated vineyards) regions were founded with an intellectual life, which were known as: SAINT-REMI DE RHEIMS, SAINT-THIERRY, HAUTVILLERS, VERZY, ORBAIS, etc.

We shall not linger longer on history, except to bring it to the twelfth century, because this period marked the first crusade to the Holy Land of Jerusalem, in which the Champenois enthusiastically took part. Saint Bernard preached Christianity in 1147 in the shady glades at Chalons. It was an era of economic prosperity. Champagne Fairs were put on which attracted world travelers. There were movements of population, increasing circulation of merchandise and money; the building of magnificent Romanesque churches. The churches were the true fruits of an artistic genius which developed so remarkably in the twelfth century in the erection of the awe-inspiring Champenois cathedrals: Rheims, Troyes, Chalons and Soissons. They manifested in the highest degree the marvels of Rémois sculpture. And all of the beauty arose out of the gratitude of the human spirit to a beneficient God who gave them the gifts—the bountiful gifts—of the vines.

Well situated for grape cultivation, the northern part of Champagne occupied a dangerous position geographically for which it would pay in succeeding centuries. During the Hundred Years' War, it was the line of march of North-Eastern France, trampled upon, then ravaged, by the rival factions of the Armagnacs and the Anglo-Burdunians. Ramparts were built at Rheims which made it possible, in 1359, to repel the assault made upon the city by King Edward III of England. Edward, who loved the wines of Champagne, which made him feel both romantic and powerful, was determined to be crowned king at Rheims, but so well protected was the city that he was unable to enter. The less powerfully protected town of Epernay was lost and retaken, burned, ransacked and ruined, no less than twenty-two times. It was a vale of tears between the year 533 and the Fronde wars. But days of consolation were to come. The 17th of July, 1429, marked the coronation of Charles VII as King of France. He had been escorted to Rheims, with superhuman tenacity, by Joan of Arc.

Despite the Holy Wars of the sixteenth century, the period was fruitful. Troyes became the home of an admirable school of sculpture. Magnificent private residences were built at Rheims. After the reign of Louis XIV—on which Colbert, a native of Rheims, left the imprint of his genius—the seventeenth century was marked by fine architectural achievements in the towns of the Champagne region (Hotel des Intendants, now the Préfecture of Chalons; Place Royale at Rheims, etc.). The French Revolution brought destruction to many large abbeys in the vine-growing area, and the long period of wars which ensued began in Champagne with the battle of Valmy (1792) and ended with the dearly bought victories of Napoleon I during the French Campaign of 1814.

The nineteenth century, for the vine-growing region, was an era of extensive economic progress. The population of Rheims rose from 20,000 in 1801 to 120,000 in 1914; that of Epernay from 4,000 to 21,000. The war of 1870 subjected the area to foreign occupation, and the war of 1914 raged for four years over this part of France. It destroyed four-fifths of the City of Rheims. Further devastation was wrought by the Second World War. Yet because of its favorable situation, it was chosen by General Dwight Eisenhower as his head-quarters. It was here that the terms of surrender were met and the peace signed, on May 7, 1945, which brought hostilities to an end as far as Europe was concerned. The dearest hope of its inhabitants is that they will be allowed to tend their vineyards and pursue the destiny of the Champagne country amid the blessing of peace.

And this is how—they tell us—champagne is made. The gathered grapes are brought in baskets from the vineyards to the press house late in September, which is vintage time. People are happy and sing at their work. The grapes are weighed and emptied into large wine-presses which hold 4,000 lg. Great pressures extract the juice from the grapes, which runs into vats, and is eventually pumped into casks of 205 litres.

First fermentation takes place within a brief time, transforming the juice into wine by the decomposition of grape sugar into alcohol. After several months, when fermentation has been completed and the wine has reached the required degree of clearness, the blend is made up. Experienced tasters blend their wines of various growths to make up a "cuvée."

The art of blending is the secret of champagne. If it is a very good year, only the wines of the last grape harvest form part of the blend, and a vintage wine is obtained with a definite personality. In other instances, wines of preceding years may be added to improve the strength and the flavor of the blend. Once the blend is attained, the wine is bottled. It is then stored in cellars, where a second fermentation takes place in the bottle. The ferments work on the sugar, which has remained in solution in the wine, and transform it into alcohol and carbonic gas. The gas stays imprisoned in the bottle, accounting for the wine being sparkling or bubbly.

After some months, when the fermentation has taken place, the bottles are placed neck downwards in tilted racks. Each day for several months, cellar-men alter their positions by slightly shaking and turning the bottles. This is done to bring the sediment formed by the second fermentation down to the inside surface of the cork. After three months of this daily operation, the bottles are then placed upside down and the wine is perfectly clear. They may be left in this position for a year or several years, so that they age gradually in a cool and even temperature. This is how the wine obtains the desired delicacy of flavor.

Before shipping the wine, the bottles are uncorked to get rid of the deposit accumulated under the cork. At this moment, some liqueur is added (sugar in solution in a mixture of old Champagne). According to the amount of liqueur added, the Champagne is half-dry, dry, extra-dry, or "brut." Now the Champagne is perfected.

Each great Champagne firm has its own standard in blending, and the reputation of the Champagne producer is the best guarantee of quality. Non-vintage wines from a reputable firm often equal, or even surpass, a vintage wine from an obscure house.

Champagnes are labelled according to the degree of dryness:

> BRUT—the driest
> EXTRA-DRY—fairly dry
> SEC (dry)—sweet
> DEMI-SEC (medium dry)—very sweet

Champagne is the only region in which the word "sec" (dry) has such meaning.

The wines of Champagne are fruity, light and sparkling. Generally they are of a pale yellow color, although some pink Champagne is also produced.

We would like to include something of the interesting history of the birthplace of Champagne in Hautvillers, the picturesque village overlooking acres of vineyards which run down almost to the very banks of the River Marne. A Bénédictine monastery was founded there in 650 A.D. At that time the vineyards were already well known, producing a light sparkling wine. The House of Moet and Chandon (which is indissolubly linked with the fame of Dom Pérignon) has owned the abbey and its vineyards for more than two centuries. In the second half of the eighteenth century the monk discovered how to obtain the fine effervescence, which is one of the exquisite delights of Champagne. As has been said, he also evolved the art of blending grapes from the various vineyards, enhancing the quality of the wine in the formation of the *"Cuvée."*

Moet Champagne begins when the grapes are gathered in the second half of September. The finest growths come from the Montagne de Rheims, the Marne Valley, and the Cote des Blancs. Without delay, the grapes are taken to large presses at Epernay. The *must* runs from the presses into vats and casks, where the first fermentation takes place, converting the grape-sugar into alcohol.

In January the second operation occurs. The wine is blended from various growths, and the taste perfected by adding a proportion of old vintage wine held in reserve for that purpose. These delicate blends constitute the *cuvée*. In the Spring the *cuvée* is bottled before the second fermentation, or *prise de mousse,* takes place. The ferments in the wine again begin to work to create the sparkle. From the fermentation comes a deposit, and the bottles which have been lying *sur lattes* are put neck downwards on inclined racks. They are then turned every day for several months to work the sediment down to the cork. This is called the *remuage.* Then the bottles are binned upside down *en masse,* in which position they remain to mature for several years.

During the *remuage* period, sediment collects on the cork and must be removed by a process known as the *dégorgement.* The cork is quickly removed and the sediment escapes. Now a small amount of liquor made from cane sugar and older wines is added to each bottle and a perfectly clear and bright wine is recorked for the last time, the cork crowned with a metal cap and held in place by a wire muzzle.

The Wines of France

For the sake of accuracy, here are all of the Champagnes of the Champagne country, as listed by the *Comité National de Propagande en Faveur du Vin* from their headquarters at 40, rue Marbeuf, Paris, France.

The *Montagne de Reims* gives its finest vintages as:

VERZENAY, VERZY, MAILL, SILLERY, LOUVOIS, BEAUMONT.

Within this region is that of the *Petite Montagne,* which has interesting secondary vintages.

Between the *Montagne de Reims* and the valley of the Marne:

BOUZY AND AMBONNAY

AY in the VALLEY OF THE MARNE is considered to the chief vine-growing district. Here are found the well-known vintages:

MAREUIL AND DIZY
CUMIERE AND HAUTVILLERS

South of the Marne.

COTE DES BLANCS, CRAMANT AND AVIZE
OGER AND LE MESNIL
VERTUS

The slopes of Vertus produce black grapes.

Cote des Blancs

CHARDONNAY (A white wine).

After robing the bottle with labels and gold foil, the fabulous champagne goes out into the world to crown the festive board. It is probably more closely connected with laughter than any other wine, for champagne bubbles and laughs at itself in pure joy of being, which it quickly conveys to its guests. The warning pop of the cork brings its first surprised laughter as the Champagne gushes forth to be confined to the long-stemmed glass. Sir Richard Steele (1672-1729) put it aptly when he remarked: "Conversation never sits easier than when we now and then discharge ourselves in a symphony of laughter; which may not improperly be called the chorus of conversation." And it is champagne which sparks the laughter.

197

It is with great pride that the House of Moet and Chandon traces its family lineage at Hautvillers, the birthplace of Champagne. It was toward 1794 that Jean-Rémy Moet, by his decision to buy the vineyards and monastery buildings at Hautvillers, started a family on its way to world fame. It came about in this fashion: The buildings of the monstery were left uninhabited after the French Revolution. This seemed a waste, and the wise Frenchman who lived at the Chateau of Romont envisioned repairing and furnishing them. Thus revitalized, he gave the estate at Hautvillers to his daughter Adelaide Moet, who happily settled there with her husband, Pierre-Gabriel Chandon, and since that time the family has been attached to the village. Several became mayors of Hautvillers in the nineteenth century. Actually this firm was in existence since 1743 under Claude Moet (born in 1683) who owned and operated vineyards in the district. The House of Moet and Chandon preceded other great firms in the Champagne country.

Claude was succeeded in the vintner business by his son Nicolas-Claude (1719-1792) and his grandson Jean-Rémy Moet (1758-1840). Jean-Rémy proved to be a business man of acumen and inspiration. By this time the family was affluent. He had a good education and travelled to the great capitals of Europe. He was familiar with the cuisines of Paris, of course—of Vienna—of Rome—of London. Many times the villagers made him Mayor of Epernay. Members of the imperial family, and Napoleon himself, visited his estate. The Emperor decorated him personally in 1814. By 1832, the elegant Jean-Rémy Moet released the active control of the business to his son, Victor Moet, and to his son-in-law, Pierre-Gabriel Chandon. From there on, the company became known as Moet and Chandon, and has ever since remained in the hands of descendants of the two families. Paul Chandon Moet has proved himself to be a fine photographer, and we are indebted to him for many graphic photographs taken in and about Hautvillers, and covering the processing of Champagne.

The story of the wine families of France, told in the same detail, would prove beyond anything else how devotion, loyalty and continuity are the priceless ingredients which produce great wines. Enthusiasm for the land and its gifts is high in all regions of the vines. Frenchmen perhaps imbibe their own product more than any other nation. The whole world loves champagne, but Frenchmen naturally love it best. The growers and producers organization in the Champagne region of eastern France reported that two-thirds of the record production for 1957 never even left the country. Sales in 1957 totalled 48,400,000 bottles, which was up from 44,300,000 bottles in 1956. The French market alone took 35,705,008 bottles of the 1957 total. Sales to the United States have been increasing steadily since 1953.

1956 will always be remembered as a very great year, for France then produced more champagne than ever before in all history. Pierre Schneiter, Mayor of Rheims, proudly reported this new record to the press of New York City, where he officially represented the Ministerial Committee of the Council of Europe, and unofficially spoke in his capacity as first citizen of Rheims, the "Champagne Capital of the World." He said that the output for 1956 comprised champagne from Rheims, Epernay and Ay, the three principal cities of the Champagne District. He described the 17% increase over 1955 as "the greatest amount ever produced in the three centuries since modern champagne came into existence." In America, statistics are rendered in gallons rather than bottles. In 1955 Americans took just under 3,000,000 bottles or 589,000 gallons. In 1956, this was increased to 3,100,000 bottles or 623,000 gallons. As one should realize, a year's purchases come from stocks shipped also in the latter part of the previous year.

How does America figure as a Champagne consuming country? According to the Mayor of Rheims, the United States was 80,000 bottles behind Great Britain as France's number one champagne customer, yet he predicted that we would soon become Number One. It is interesting to note that, in the view of the French experts, economics, politics, and the development of taste by travel are all factors in the champagne market. Prior to World War I, two-thirds of all French champagne produced was shipped abroad, and a third was consumed in France. In the intervening years, the trend was reversed. Of the total for 1956, 32% was exported, while 68% was consumed in France itself. Enthusiasts claimed that the French wine harvest for 1956 was the best since 1900, considered the top year in vintage history.

All of this happy revelry from wine consumption did not quite please the French Government, which began an anti-alcoholism campaign. In April of 1959, the world press received reports that the wine merchants were exceedingly worried by their government's paternal interest. The embattled purveyors of the fermented juice of the grape complained it was bad for business. In an official interview with Premier Michel Debré, the dealers asked that the government show more pride in the glories of France and, instead of campaigning against wine, that it be declared the "national drink," and measures be taken to increase, rather than decrease, consumption. It is not the drinking but the excessive drinking by any individual which worries the government. It affirms, perhaps justly, that Frenchmen should know better. Meanwhile, the unhappy wine merchants blame the "hostile propaganda" of their government for the drop in consumption in the past few years. They insist that wine is healthy, and quote a French "Scientific" report which claims that wine is as good a germ killer as penicillin. That remains to be seen. Meanwhile, there is no question but that wine has inspired poets, politicians and philosophers. And most Frenchmen agree with Omar Khayyam:

> "I wonder often what the Vintners buy
> One half so precious as the stuff they sell."

The Englishman is well grounded in cuisine and wine drinking, to say nothing of the stronger spirits. It is interesting to recall that at one time parts of France were under English rule. Historically, part of south-western France, which comprises the Bordeaux country, was in the twelfth century ruled by England, and so remained for the next three hundred years. This is the land of Claret and Claret drinking became commonplace, and the upper classes have favored it to the present day. At that time, New York was under British rule and, during the seven-year siege by the red-coats during the American Revolution, Madeira and Claret were favorite wines.

In the fourteenth century, the French of the Bordeaux country were reluctant to part with their wines, and it was necessary to send over British ships to get the barrels of wine. Some marine authorities hold that this practice contributed to English sea power, which was maintained for many centuries. An honest thirst, apparently, may lead to anything, and very often does. "Yeoman of the Butlery," wine-drawers, gaugers, official brokers, and other government appointees, raised the cost of imported wine, as did the compliance with many royal and local licensing provisions. Nevertheless, for about five hundred years the wine trade thrived, and wine could be purchased at times for as little as a half-penny a gallon.

By the sixteenth century, consumption of "Gascon" wine had generally fallen off. Expressing fear and consequent hatred of the French in the early part of the eighteenth century, the British Government actually tried to wreck the French wine industry by discriminating in favor of other wines, particularly those from Portugal.

At this time, port became a favored beverage. In 1860, Queen Victoria's government sensibly adjusted the duty to the alcoholic strength of the beverages imported. However, the traditional and early taste for claret continued in the upper classes, despite the increase in cost entailed by the heavy tariff. An interesting exhibition was held some years ago in London, called "The Englishman and his Wine," which was reviewed on the spot by Monsieur André Simon, the noted wine authority. On display were wine glasses, decanters and corkscrews, created by English craftsmen in the seventeenth and eighteenth centuries.

The "bottle scrue" or corkscrew, as we call it, was invented at the time flush corking came into use, allowing for the proper aging and storing of wine. The earliest illustration of this device is in a print dated 1773. An item described in the catalogue of the exhibition was the "Cellarman's Leather Bottling Boot, With Strap Attached. For use during corking." We know from allusions in history and fiction that English country squires were notoriously heavy drinkers of claret. Many a four-bottle man who had slipped under the table was saved from choking to death by having his collar undone by a boy servant provided by the host for this purpose. It was a mark of masculinity to imbibe as much as possible before falling under the table. If a man could rise again, and drink still more, he was not yet considered drunk. Only when he could not arise and had to be borne out by the attendants, feet first, denoting the complete victory of Bacchus, was he deemed inebriated.

18

Cognac, Liqueurs, Bourbon, Brandy

"Claret is the liquor for boys; Port for men; but he who aspires to be a hero must drink Brandy."
—SAMUEL JOHNSON

IT WOULD BE IMPOSSIBLE TO COMMENT ON all the various wines, spirits and liqueurs in the world which contribute to conviviality. Some are better known than others. Many have interesting histories which bear retelling. It can safely be said that, even in the most remote parts of the world, at least two French words are familiar—Paris and Cognac. Cognac is the region which is the home of Cognac brandy. It is a work of art—a masterpiece of nature—which France offers to the world with just pride. Nothing is more pleasant than extended hospitality. When a restaurateur or a private host serves genuine Cognac, he honors both himself as well as his guests. After a good dinner, Cognac creates an optimistic relaxing atmosphere. It has a unique way of warming the spirit and lightening the burden of care. That is why it is averred the people in the Cognac district live for a long time, and are remarkably alert and spry in their old age.

There are approximately 150,000 acres planted with vines surrounding the ancient town of Cognac. From these vines come grapes which yield a natural brandy of unrivaled quality. Cognac brandy can only be produced from the wine of this district. By a stroke of good fortune—the peculiarity of the soil, of the climate, and the proximity of the sea—Nature has contrived by happy coincidence to combine these ideal elements which give a Cognac distinct taste and character.

Cognac is divided into seven sub-districts:

GRANDE CHAMPAGNE, PETITE CHAMPAGNE, LES BORDERIES, LES FINS BOIS, LES BONS BOIS, LES BOIS ORDINAIRES AND LES BOIS COMMUNS.

The Cognac shipping firms mix brandies of various vintages and different sub-districts so as to balance each other in the best possible "blend." For the last four centuries, most of the land in these various districts has belonged to the same families of vintners; and long and successful tradition has ensured them a place of their own within the economy of France. Cognac has gained its fame purely on its merits. In the seventeenth century, Cognac brandy was acclaimed by traders from foreign countries. In the busy port of La Rochelle, vessels departed bearing in their holds shipments of this precious liquid to all parts of the globe.

Cognac is made as it was in centuries gone by. The local distilleries continue to use the old-fashioned potstill, and no modern inventions have ever supplanted it. The farmer calls it "burning his wine." In the Forest of Limousin there grows a particular type of hard oak, suitable for making the casks in which the brandy is aged. If aged in any other type of wood, it takes on a different flavor. The oaken casks lie for long years in the heavily charged atmosphere of darkened warehouses. The action of the wood and of the air impart to the brandy its golden color and incomparable bouquet and flavor. The evaporation is substantial during that period.

There are other brandies in other countries which are sometimes called Cognac, but anyone who has tasted genuine Cognac can never be deceived. The French Excise and the National Bureau of Cognac control production, aging and distribution, which guarantee the brandy. The territory was delimited by decree on May 1, 1909.

Cognac, the fiery spirit of wines, is best taken in the balloon or tulip-shaped glass, and some cognac glasses are enormous. When the palm of the hand warms it, the subtle and marvelous aroma satisfies the most discriminating of gourmets. To take it this way after a meal is called *neat*. In a cocktail, it imparts a delicate and striking flavor. Some cooking recipes are made better by the addition of Cognac, such as Soufflés, some sauces, fowl or game, whose flavor is enhanced. A dessert wine is Pineau des Charentes, derived from selected musts, strengthened by cognac.

A very special liqueur is that called Chartreuse, which is produced by the Chartreuse Fathers of the Carthusian Order. This order was founded almost a thousand years ago (in 1084) by Bruno, a famed instructor at the University of Reims. Withdrawing into the desert of Chartreuse with six companions, he founded a monastery dedicated to prayer and solitude. The monks kept herbs, sold wood, and made the liqueurs which have become so respected. The secret of the formula has been kept since 1605. Only three monks participate in the production in their isolated mountain retreat.

The mysterious elixir was concocted of aromatic herbs, and the formula was so complicated that the old manuscript giving it was ignored until 1735, when Brother Jerome Maubec succeeded in perfecting the formula. He developed the green liqueur; the yellow liqueur was discovered in 1840 by Brother Bruno Jacquet. It has been called Queen of Liqueurs for its mellow softness. Both the green and yellow liqueurs were produced in the pharmacy of the monastery, and Brother Charles went on the back of a mule to sell them in Grenoble and Chambéry. They were widely imitated. Excellent base brandies are used from selected wines. The secret formula is known to use 130 herbs. The oaken vats in which the liqueurs are developed are truly enormous, with a capacity of 10,000 liters. The herbs and brandy are distilled together in the still, and the herbs give up their properties and aroma to the brandy.

The cellars of the Compagnie Française de la Grande Chartreuse are the largest liqueur cellars in the world, containing a double row of gigantic vats. When you are next in France, perhaps you will have the opportunity to visit Voiron, which is located in the midst of breath-takingly beautiful scenery. Only recently have visitors been allowed there by the Chartreux Fathers. (Every day except Sunday from 8 to 12 and 2 until 6.) Voiron lies directly on the main route between Paris and the French Riviera. Along the way are roadside inns where the food is simple but excellent; and the Monks of Chartreuse welcome the traveler.

The Fathers make the Elixir Végétal of La Grande Chartreuse (136 proof) but this is not available in the United States. The Green Liqueur (110 proof) is very pleasing to the taste, containing a large number of herbs, and is excellent after meals. The Yellow Liqueur (86 proof) is milder than the green and of a different taste. The sole Distributors in the United States are Schieffelin & Co. of 30 Cooper Square, which firm by coincidence happens to be the oldest pharmaceutical house in this country. They have been importing since 1794.

Another old French house which produces a distinguished liqueur of Fine Champagne Cognac is that of the Etablissements Marnier Lapostolle founded in 1827, deep in the chateau country, by J. B. Lapostolle. Eugène Lapostolle succeeded his father as director of the distillery in 1859. The distinctive cognacs which formed the basis of Grand Marnier were carefully stored in the family's large wine cellars. It was the son-in-law of Eugène, Marnier Lapostolle, who formulated what is today known as Grand Marnier. It was created from the Fine Champagne Cognac found only in the Charentes region surrounding their establishment. The strict formula has been followed ever since, and it is guaranteed by the French State Excise Department, which carefully guards the wine industry. Perhaps their most famous is the Grand Marnier, distilled from the peel of oranges and blended with Fine Champagne Cognac. It is the perfect accompaniment to Crepes Suzette. In France you will also find popular the Cherry Marnier, which has such a rich fresh cherry flavor.

The legendary liqueur of Old Ireland, is Irish Mist. The story of its origin goes back nearly 1,000 years . . . to the days when Ireland was ruled by warring clans. The drink of these ancient Irish warriors was "Heather Wine"—a cordial based on whiskey and wild heather extract.

The secret of making Heather Wine was carefully guarded. Then came the Danish and Norman invaders—and, in the 16th century, the armies of Queen Elizabeth I. Gaelic Ireland was lost—and so was the secret of making Heather Wine. Ireland's nobles, clerics and fighting men left their native land in a centuries-long exodus—known as "the flight of the Wild Geese" to enter France, Germany, Austria and Spain. And the secret recipe for Heather Wine went somewhere, somehow with them.

"Twas a sad loss for Ireland," said Daniel E. Williams, a fine nineteenth century Irish distiller. From his Tullamore Whiskey Distillery he began a search for the precious recipe among all the countries of Europe. At the same time he experimented with whiskey, heather honey and herbs at home, hoping to duplicate the Heather Wine formula.

His sons carried on the fruitless search, and his grandsons after them. And then, one day in 1948, into his great-grandson's office at Tullamore came an Austrian refugee. He brought a recipe for a liqueur based on heather honey and whiskey that had been in the family for generations and that he knew was of Irish origin.

The 100-year-long search was ended! For this was the recipe the Williams family had been looking for—and it excelled in quality, appearance, bouquet and taste anything their trial-and-error experiments had previously produced.

Heather Wine is now being produced at Tullamore Distillery under the name of IRISH MIST, the legendary and only Irish liqueur. And today, in the reign of the second Elizabeth, it is no longer jealously guarded by the Irish elite. Ireland cordially invites the whole world to enjoy IRISH MIST. The United States, Canada, New Zealand, Australia, Norway, Sweden and the West Indies are already discovering its pleasures.

Hennessy is a very famous Cognac brandy that had its inception in 1763, when Richard Hennessy settled in Cognac. He was an Irishman in the Irish Brigade who came to fight for the King of France, or perhaps for adventure itself. He was so delighted with the local brandy that he sent a few casks home to his friends. They overwhelmed him with praise and requests so that he began to export

Cognac brandy on a business basis. Richard's son James founded the firm of Jas. Hennessy & Co. and began to ship to all parts of the world. The House of Hennessy is now in its seventh generation of direct descendants of Richard.

Hennessy cognac was shipped in casks until 1860 and thereafter in bottles. The woeful looking Saint Bernard dog with the little oaken cask about his neck means he bears true cognac of France. An elegante of the old school places a bouillon or dessert spoon over a demi-tasse of hot black coffee in which there is a cube of sugar, adds an ounce of the cognac, sets it to blazing and, when the flame begins to fade, pours the contents into the coffee. Café Royale is considered the perfect ending to a fine dinner.

Bourbon is the proud production of America. Its origin, in fact, coincides with the birth of the United States Government in 1789 when George Washington took the oath as first President of the United States. Bourbon is the only whiskey truly native which, like the whalemen's scrimshaw carvings, can be considered indigenous to America. Bourbon, which at one time replaced currency, and was praised by Daniel Boone, Andrew Jackson and William Henry Harrison, was first distilled in 1789 by a Baptist minister, the Rev. Elijah Craig who used corn and rye with Bourbon County limestone water. The result was genuine old-fashioned bourbon.

After the Revolutionary War, hundreds of soldiers flocked to the Kentucky hills and began bourbon-making in Bourbon County, Kentucky. There the native corn, rye, wheat and malt were mixed with the iron-free water which had run over limestone rocks. Kentucky abounds in springs of water which rush upward through layers of limestone which filters out impurities and provides water generally conceded to be the best in the United States for the manufacture of bourbon. Kentucky is the home of most bourbon manufacturers but some important whiskey-distilling areas are located in the limestone water regions of western Pennsylvania and southern Indiana as well. After the American victory over the British at Yorktown, there were some 1,500 stills in operation. The most important factor distinguishing bourbon from all other whiskies is its distinctive flavor derived from American corn.

After several decades, the distillers began to float their whiskey barrels down river to New Orleans for export. It was the drastic effect on the young and important bourbon industry which helped to formulate national support for the purchase of Louisiana. Before the Civil War, bourbon was sold only by the barrel and there were no brand names when it was bottled. With the War, however, came professional distillers and bonded warehouses. This ended the back-yard-farmer production begun by the early Scottish and Irish settlers in the United States. These immigrants brought with them their native skills and magical yeast for their household craft of whiskey making. The conversion of surplus grain into profitable whiskey was a welcome economic expedient. In 1872, Isaac W. Bernheim established a distillery in Louisville and made a fine Bourbon which he sold through his salesman, I. W. Harper. Mr. Harper cleverly promoted the sale of his whiskey by putting it in fancy decanters, and the company by this name still dispenses some fine bourbon.

A prime example of Kentucky Bourbon at its best is "21" Brands' JOHNNY REB, which dates back to the halcyon days of the antebellum South where a man's ability to judge good whiskey was a matter of personal pride. To meet this discriminating demand the small, country distillers evolved a whiskey-making technique that has never been excelled. JOHNNY REB follows this proven formula exactly. It is made from a genuine sour mash, charcoal filtered, naturally aged and bottled at 90 proof.

While some writers say the Rev. Craig stored his whiskey in charred barrels, this is really a very controversial subject. Nobody knows who first used a charred keg for aging whiskey. The first historical reference to them dates about 1840, and it is doubtful—all legends to the contrary—that Elijah Craig ever saw a charred keg. The Bourbon Institute has researched three versions: A distiller to save money planned to use kegs in which fish had been stored and to get rid of the odor he scorched the inside of the barrels with a blazing pine knot. Subsequently he discovered that the whiskey had a more pleasant flavor and ruddy hue. Still another is that an early-day cooper carelessly burned some barrel staves which he was heating preparatory to curving them and decided to use them any way. Months later a customer told him that the whiskey from the charred barrel was very good. Still another version is that the discovery was made in Jamaica when a rum warehouse burned and it was found the rum from the charred barrels was better than from others.

Bourbon is aged in charred kegs made from *new* wood, preferably white oak either from the Ozarks or the hills of Tennessee. The cost of these kegs runs about $22 to $25 each and *cannot be used again.* Once used, they are sold to Scotch and Canadian whiskey people who buy them up at $1.00 or $2.00 each. This adds a great deal to the price of the product. Another serious factor in its cost is taxes. The first excise tax was levied in 1791 for a badly depleted federal Treasury and enforced by the Secretary of the Treasury, Alexander Hamilton. The farmers in Pennsylvania took exception to the levy of 11¢ a gallon which resulted in the Whiskey Rebellion of the history books.

In ensuing years taxes and regulations, both federal and state, have proven a heavy burden to the industry. In 1897 came the Bottling-in-Bond Act; in 1913 the Webb-Kenyon Act; in 1919 the Eighteenth Amendment; the Repeal Amendment of 1933 and in 1935 the Federal Alcohol Administration Act. During the War of 1812 the tax was 9 cents a gallon. During the Civil War it went from 60¢ to $2.00. Moonshining forced the tax down to 50 cents. During World War I, it rose from $2.40 to $6.40 just before Prohibition. In 1934 it was back to $2.00. Today the federal tax is $10.50 a gallon. In its general usage this excise tax is levied by the United States Government on distilled spirits, malt beverages and wines.

Bourbon has many expressions and many moods. The bourbon devotee is faithful to his own. Connoisseurs have for a long time been cooking with sherry and other wines after the manner of the great French chefs. What is less known is that some chefs have been flavoring foods with American whiskey for many years. Cooking with liquor provides new and unusual ways in which the golden touch of hospitality can be added to entertaining. A pride of Kentucky is the presentation of Bourbon Paté, which is not difficult to prepare and is very festive with latitude in the choice of interesting molds.

BOURBON PATÉ

1 lb. fresh chicken livers
1 small onion, minced
1 lb. butter
2 tbs. Marsala
½ tsp. paprika
⅛ tsp. allspice

½ tsp. salt
⅛ tsp. white pepper or Tabasco
1 clove garlic, minced
⅓ cup Straight Bourbon
1 cup roasted California Walnuts,
    chopped

1 envelope unflavored gelatine
1 can or 1½ cups clear chicken broth

Sauté onion in ½ lb. butter until tender. Add chicken livers cut in small pieces and cook for ten minutes, stirring occasionally. Add ½ of the chicken broth. Marsala, paprika, allspice, salt, pepper and garlic. Cook for five minutes more.

Place mixture in electric blender. Gradually add remaining butter, melted and bourbon. Blend until smooth. Stir in walnuts.

In saucepan, sprinkle gelatine over the rest of the broth. Heat and stir until gelatine is dissolved. Pour part of gelatine-broth into mold and arrange any garnishes desired. Chill mold for ten minutes. Fill mold with chicken liver mixture and top with remaining broth. Keep in refrigerator for at least six hours before unmolding and serving.

For a century and a half a certain refreshing drink has been the symbol of hospitality, the grace and elegance of the art of entertainment in the nation's Southland. A Lexington, Kentucky attorney and wit once set down a classic recipe for the very dream of drinks—the Kentucky Mint Julep. Judge Soule Smith's description and instructions have done more than anything else to keep alive the drink which he termed "the zenith of man's pleasure."

"Take from the cold spring some water, pure as angels are; mix with sugar until it seems like oil. Then take a glass and crush your mint within with a spoon—crush it around the borders of the glass and leave no place untouched. Then throw the mint away—it is a sacrifice. Fill with cracked ice the glass; pour in the quantity of bourbon which you want. It trickles slowly through the ice. Let it have time to cool, then pour your sugared water over it. No spoon is needed, no stirring is allowed—just let it stand a moment. Then around the brim place sprigs of mint, so that the one who drinks may find a taste and odor at one draught . . . No other land can give so sweet a solace for your cares; no other liquor soothes you so in melancholy days. Sip it and say there is no solace for the soul, no tonic for the body like Old Bourbon Whiskey."

Now let us catalogue whiskeys to untangle the mystery of their meanings. The Irish had a word for it. Long ago in Gaelic they called whiskey "Usigabeatha" for the Latin "aqua vitae"—water of life. The Anglicized form is whiskey.

STRAIGHT WHISKEY: By federal regulation, this is a whiskey such as bourbon, rye, corn or wheat, an alcoholic distillate from a fermented mash of grain distilled at not exceeding 160 proof and withdrawn from the cistern room of the distillery at not more than 110 and not less than 80 proof, and aged for not less than 24 calendar months in new charred oak barrels. Aging brings out the character as in the aging of tobacco or cheese and is nature's way of awarding an excellence for patience. And character has been defined as "that combination of a whiskey's sensory qualities which distinguishes it from another whiskey." Why, indeed, are there so many brands? Because each distiller has his own favorite formula, a time for mashing, temperature, and the particular proof at which to distill off his whiskey. A master distiller gives his skill and in the end process talented tasters render their judgment.

BOURBON: First distilled in Bourbon County, Kentucky, 51% of the grain used is mash corn. This makes America's most popular straight whiskey (spelled with an "e"). It is wonderful for blending and a truly American product. Distilled from mash of corn, rye and barley malt with corn as the determining factor, to qualify as bourbon, at least 51% and less than 80% of the grain must be corn, distilled out below 160 proof and aged for two years. The white oak for the new barrels comes from the Arkansas Ozarks and the Cumberlands of Kentucky and Tennessee.

BLENDED WHISKEY: In many states, this drink is first man on the totem pole. Blending is the combination by judicious means of carefully selected straight whiskies with grain neutral spirits. From the straights, the new whiskey derives its aroma, flavor, character and body. The grain neutral spirits give the result a lightness and velvetiness which does not eliminate character. It is possible to secure by the science of blending a uniform product which always turns out identical to the desideratum.

CANADIAN WHISKY: Canadian law permits greater freedom than American law. In Canada, a distiller may use any grains he feels suit his needs. He uses barley malt, corn and rye, and is not limited to proof nor to methods of blending. The government bows to the knowledge of the distiller, and his skill is recognized in world markets. New casks are not needed and used cooperage is acceptable. Proofs of imports vary from 80 to 90.4; a whisky which is light-bodied and pleasant, it contains no distilled spirits less than two years old. Canadian distillers may blend their whiskies either before aging or during the aging period and most Canadian whiskies exported to the United States are blends. United States regulations do not permit the labelling of Canadian whiskies as "straights."

IRISH WHISKEY: Spelled with an "e," this is a full-bodied straight Irish whiskey or a blended Irish whiskey which is much lighter. Straight and malt whiskies are distilled off the pot stills at about 140 proof from fermented mash of barley malt and some small grain. The smoky taste of the barley malt is eliminated by drying out in coal-fired kilns. Usually sherry casks are used for aging Irish whiskies. When imported, they are at least four years of age.

SCOTCH WHISKY: Barley was used exclusively in the traditional products of years ago, with the Highlands providing the most abundant of grains. In producing the malt whiskies, barley lends a distinctive character not to be imitated elsewhere. Its popularity in world markets began a hundred years ago. To suit palates other than those of the cold, northern hills of Scotland, a blend was achieved with other grains. In 1934 (first year following Repeal) America imported 2,132,235 proof gallons. In 1959 this figure had risen to 18,332,786 proof gallons. More than 50% of the production since the last war comes to these shores. Yet shortages prevail because a four-year waiting period is required.

Whisky in a blend is not used until fully developed, which sometimes takes eight years. The malt whiskies come from the Highlands, Lowlands, Campbeltown and Islay. They have a smoky aroma due to the drying of the sprouted barley malt over open peat fires. The oldest distiller in Scotland is the House of Haig which was established in 1627. Distilled by the pot still method, the whisky ages for at least three years in uncharred oak barrels or used sherry casks.

SCOTCH TYPE WHISKEY (A Blend): A mixture made outside Great Britain composed of not less than 20 per cent by volume of 100 proof malt whiskey or whiskies distilled in pot stills at not more than 160 proof, from mash of malted barley dried over a peat fire and aged for not less than three years in new, plain or re-used oak barrels, *and* not more than 80 per cent by volume of whiskey distilled at more than 180 proof and less than 190 proof, aged for not less than three years in new, plain oak barrels or re-used charred oak barrels.

SOUR MASH WHISKEY: A type of whiskey which is produced as a result of using part of the previous day's mash instead of water to start and to assist in the fermentation of a new batch of mash.

CORN WHISKEY: Whiskey distilled from a fermented mash of grain containing at least 80 per cent corn. It need not be stored in *charred* wooden containers.

WHISKY: To clarify confusing spellings, whisky is the name identifying the distilled spirits of Scotland and Canada. Some American distillers use this spelling to label their products and the U.S. Treasury Department uses it in regulations.

TAX GALLON: The unit of distilled spirits subject to the federal excise tax. It is a U.S. gallon (231 cubic inches at 60 degrees Fahrenheit) of 100 proof alcoholic strength on which the federal tax is $10.50. On the other hand a wine gallon is a physical measure of actual liquid volume; the standard U.S. gallon containing 231 cubic inches as compared to the British Wine (Imperial Gallon) which contains approximately 20 per cent more by volume than the U.S. wine gallon. The British Imperial Gallon contains 277.4 cubic inches with the Canadian Wine (Imperial) Gallon the same as the British wine gallon.

BOTTLED-IN-BOND: The U.S. Bureau of Internal Revenue affixes a strip stamp tax-paid over the closure of every bottle of distilled spirits. Green stamps are used for bottled-in-bond spirits and reddish-pink stamps for all other distilled spirits.

1. Straight Whiskey distilled in one plant in one season.
2. Must be aged in new charred oak barrels for at least four years.
3. It must be bottled at 100 proof.
4. The Internal Revenue Department affixes a green stamp over the cork and neck of the bottle.
5. The Federal Government does not guarantee quality, but does guarantee that the regulations have been complied with.

U.S. Government Bonded Warehouse: A warehouse established under the laws and regulations of the Internal Revenue Service in which distilled spirits are stored in bond, before payment of tax. Although the proprietor of a bonded warehouse is a private individual or firm, the operations as well as the warehouse itself are kept under the direct supervision of officers of the Internal Revenue Service who carry the keys to the warehouse, keep a governmental record of all entries and withdrawals of spirits, etc. The warehouse owner may enter the premises only in the presence of a governmental officer and no spirits may be withdrawn except with the Government's permission.

RYE WHISKEY: Early Americans, including George Washington, distilled a good rye whiskey which was popular in the eastern part of the country. Taste patterns were disturbed by Prohibition so that the taste for a full-bodied malty rye whiskey has since declined, although some "old faithfuls" still remain. Rye is defined by Licensed Beverage Industries, Inc. of New York City as "Whiskey distilled at not more than 160 proof from a fermented mash of grain containing at least 51 per cent rye grain." When a man asks for rye, he gets either a blended whiskey or Canadian whisky, which is what he anticipates. It has a darker color and a heavier body than bourbon.

GIN: The main flavoring agent is the juniper berry. It is made in a pot still, and has been since discovered by a scientist at the University of Leyden in Holland. The Spanish called it *ginebra;* the Dutch *genever;* the French *genièvre* (juniper). Gins are not aged and are colorless. Some acquire a golden hue from being stored in wood, as has been done in recent years. Sometimes gins are flavored with orange or mint. The re-distilling takes place in the presence of juniper berries and other botanicals, anise seeds, caraway seeds, almonds, cassia bark, fennel, orris root, licorice, bitter orange peel, lemon peel. Old Tom is a dry gin slightly sweetened by a small amount of simple syrup. It is ready for bottling immediately after distillation and has no aging requirements.

VODKA: Varying spirits have their graph line of popularity. After World War II, there developed a fad for vodka. The name appealed as something exotic and daring. Getting a start in California, the idea spread throughout the nation and permanently changed the drinking pattern of many Americans. Vodka is a neutral spirit, distilled usually from grains, and filtered through activated carbon to remove any taste of the spirits. Vodka, to deserve its classification must be devoid of flavor or aroma. It is colorless and not aged. Therefore, it lends itself well to combining with any other liquid. It becomes a "Screwdriver" with orange juice, a "Bloody Mary" with tomato juice, with dry vermouth it is a "Vodka Martini," and it can be taken with cider, coffee or tea, if desired.

In this country, the good vodkas are distilled from a grain mash, including portions of malt, rye, wheat, etc. Vodka is called neutral spirits because it is distilled out at 190 proof or higher. Then it is treated with charcoal (carbon) so that the end result is tasteless. Contrary to general belief, most of the vodka consumed is produced in the States. In 1958, 15,100,625 gallons were used. Of this amount 99.9% was produced in the United States. People like to say *Vodka.* The name associates itself with the Volga boatman and the romance of the old Russian regimes. Therefore, its brand names are usually Russian, and it is true that most of the firms in the United States have foreign roots. No special bottle shape is used for vodka. In Russia, this is the general name for distilled spirit and *wódka* is the Polish spelling. In some areas of Poland and Russia, vodka has been distilled from a potato mash, but this is unusual, and the standard method is from the grains. The myth about vodka's virility has as little validity as that applying to oysters. Vodka is no stronger than any other 80 proof beverage, and 100 proof vodka is no sturdier than Bottled-in-Bond.

RUM: This spirit belongs to our own hemisphere rather than to Europe. It was probably the first beverage distilled in the United States, with its roots in the tropics. The black-strap molasses the New Englanders used came from the Americas. Sugar cane is a tropical plant, and it is from the residue of sugar manufacturing that rum was born. The left-over portions were distilled and alcohol created, then aged in the wood. Usually the dry, light-bodied rums, distilled out in column stills at fairly high proof, come from Puerto Rico and Cuba; the full-bodied ones from the British West Indies come from old-fashioned pot stills at a much lower proof. The more pungent rums of this sort marketed here come from Jamaica, Trinidad, Barbados, British Guiana, Martinique, Madagascar and Reunion Island, and from New England, too. It is known as Rum, Rhum, Ran, Cana and Batavia Arak. The latter is from the Island of Java in the Indonesian Republic. It is a very pungent rum, yet light-bodied.

BEER AND ALE: To round up our classifications, we should add the ancient beverage which has served the thirst of man, rather than his esthetic needs, from ancient times. References are found in the records of the Aryans, Chinese, Egyptians, Greeks, Romans and Babylonians to the brew from farmers' grain. Involved are barley malt, some rice and corn, brewer's yeast, hops. American beers, fashioned after the English and German, are produced from bottom fermentation with temperatures no higher than 48° F. Stout and Porter come from Ireland and England. Ale, a top fermentation brewed at temperatures from 50° to 70°, has more body and is less dry. With the Dutch who settled New Amsterdam, before the English changed it to New York, the breakfast beverage was beer. Traveled and cultivated Englishmen introduced table wines for dining. The beers, however, were the common denominators, a substitute for water, which was not always obtainable or potable. Governor Bradford wrote in his journal that it was necessary for the Mayflower to seek harbor because "we could not now take time for further search or consideration, our victuals being much spent, especially our beer . . ." The landing, therefore, according to some narrators, took place at Plymouth Rock as of December 19, 1620, storms, weather and illnesses being other factors accounting for the delay. Descendants and others who comprise America's population have not neglected this beverage. Figures for 1959 show a production and consumption in the United States of beer and ale of 2,697,000,000 gallons.

A number of years ago, a famous Italian firm began distributing to the States its brandy, vermouths, cordials and liqueurs. This is the Distillerie Stock Company, which was founded in Trieste in 1884 by Lionello Stock, when he was seventeen years old. At that time there were no major brandy distilleries in Europe, only local production for local consumption. Stock set up a widely operating organization which concentrated on quality. The Stock family, now in its fourth generation, currently employs more than 10,000 persons throughout the world.

Up to Stock's time, producers sold brandy in casks. He pioneered in selling his products bottled and labelled with his name on each one. He refused to sell brandy in casks for fear the liquor might be diluted along the line. Realizing the importance of experiment and scientific application, Stock was the first to work with universities. Now, too, universities at Trieste, Vienna, Zurich, Rome and Bologna collaborate with Distillerie Stock to produce an even finer product. Their Italian brandies are truly superb.

The story of this brilliant innovator is fascinating. He wanted to control his own shipments and so acquired his own ships, trucks and railroad cars. While this would be natural procedure for a steel tycoon in America, it was a bit unusual for an entrepreneur of the wineries. His after-dinner liqueurs are justly famous, including blackberry, cherry, peach, apricot, anisette, crème de menthe, crème de cacao, crème de mocca, crème de Marsala and Maraschino liqueur. Often liqueurs are a blend of extract, natural or artificial, with spirits. However, Stock's liqueurs are made of ten-year-old brandy with pure distilled fruits. They are truly delightful in flavor.

By 1918, this company (founded by a very young man with the determination to attain his dream), had factories and distilleries in Austria, Poland, Switzerland, Yugoslavia, Hungary, Egypt, Israel, Brazil and France. When Stock died in 1948, it was after an entire lifetime devoted to the growth and prosperity of his company, with high honors bestowed on him. Perhaps he prized the most the fact that he was designated as purveyor to the Vatican.

There is usually some difference of opinion with regard to alcoholic beverages for the reason that each distiller, vintner and rectifier does things in an individual way, and often by secret formula. This accounts for the distinction between brands. However, a minimum of essential knowledge will serve as a reliable guide in this field. We will cover the Brandies and Cognacs first, then Cordials and Liqueurs.

BRANDIES AND COGNAC: While cognac is the oldest commercially produced spirit, today the largest volume of sales is accounted for by brandies produced in the United States. Brandy has been defined as "a potable spirit distilled from wine or a fermented mash of fruit and usually aged in the wood." In practically all countries which grow fruit, brandy is produced locally.

BRANDY (CALIFORNIA). This State accounts for 66% of the brandy consumption in the United States. Everything is done by one organization: growing grapes, making wine, distilling, aging, bottling marketing. In contrast to this American method, European farmer-distillers sell their brandies to the blender-shippers. Since Repeal, many fruit brandies come from abroad.

218

Cognac, Liqueurs, Bourbon, Brandy

COGNAC: Considered by experts as the most famous brandy of them all. It is usually aged in casks made of limousin oak from the forest of Limoges. On cognac labels we found the various symbols of the individual shippers: V—very; S—superior; O—old; P—pale; X—Extra; E—Especial; F—Fine.

ARMAGNAC: After cognac, this is the best known brandy. It is produced in Southern France and often shipped as a vintage brandy, i.e. the distillation of a particular year. Often it has a fuller body and is drier than cognac.

APPLE BRANDY: This has been covered in the chapter on California. Wherever apples grow and cider is fermented, Apple Brandy or Apple Jack can be produced. The latter is the best known in the United States. Apple Jack Brandy is aged in charred oak barrels for 4 to 7 years and bottled at both 84 and 100 proofs. In the United States, it was one of the first distilled spirits in pot stills. Its history in this country goes back to the 1600's.

GRAPPE: This is a very popular brandy in Italy, a distillation from the grape pomace of the wine press. It is clear, without color. Some is distilled in California.

SLIVOVITZ: This brandy is distilled from a fermented mash of prunes. The stones are allowed to remain during fermentation. In France, brandy distilled from this fruit is called Quetsch and Mirabelle, and is brown in color. Slivovitz is the national drink of the Balkans.

KIRSCH OR KIRSCHWASSER: A brandy distilled from a fermented mash of cherries. The stones are left in during fermentation. The most famous of the Kirsches is the Schwartzwalder Kirschwasser the Cherry Brandy of the Black Forest. The French have their Alsatian Kirsch, the Swiss their Kirschwasser. This brandy is colorless.

BARAT PALINKA: Brown in color, this brandy is distilled from a fermented mash of apricots and is made only in Hungary.

CORDIALS: Much has been produced in the United States and 90% of the sales since World War II have been of native production. The imported cordials are made of secret formulas which cannot

219

be reproduced elsewhere. According to U.S. Federal Regulations, cordials and liqueurs are produced by mixing or redistilling neutral spirits, brandy, gin etc. with or over fruits, flowers, plants for flavoring, to which has been added sugar or dextrose, not less than 2½% of the weight of the finished product.

Man has known the comfort of cordials and liqueurs since earliest history. In the tombs of the Egyptian Pharaohs have been found formulas and replicas of stills. The Athenians wrote of the delight of cordials. Actual production for commercial channels, however, dates from the Middle Ages. They were the creation of physicians, alchemists and monks searching for an elixir of life. The methods of making them still are proprietary secrets.

NAMES	FLAVORINGS
Anisette	Anis seed
Arrack Punsch } Caloric Punsch }	Batavia Arak
Blackberry	Blackberry
Cherry	Wild Black Cherry
Crème d'Ananas	Pineapple
Crème de Bananes	Banana
Crème de Cacao	Cacao and Vanilla
Crème de Fraises	Strawberry
Crème de Framboises	Raspberry
Crème de Menthe	Peppermint
Crème de Noyaux	Fruit Stone (Bitter Almond)
Crème de Roses	Rose and Vanilla
Crème de Vanille	Vanilla
Curaçao	Orange
Danziger Goldwasser	Orange, Spices and Gold Leaf Flakes
Kümmel	Caraway Seed
Mandarine	Tangerine
Maraschino	Marasca Cherries
Ouzo	Anis Seed
Peach	Peach
Prunello	Plum
Sloe Gin	Sloeberry
Swedish Punch	Caloric Punch (above)
Triple Sec	White Curacao

Cognac, Liqueurs, Bourbon, Brandy

MOST PROMINENT CORDIALS

Amer Picon	France	Bitter Cordial
Bénédictine D.O.M.	France	A drier Bénédictine Liqueur
Chartreuse	France	Aromatic Plant Liqueurs Yellow . 86 proof Green . 110 proof
Cherry Heering	Denmark	Wild Black Cherry
Cointreau	France and United States	Triple Sec
Cordial Medoc	France	Blend Cognac, Curacao
Crème Yvette	United States	Violets and Vanilla
Drambuie Scotch Whiskey	Scotland	Heather Honey, Spices
Forbidden Fruit	United States	Grapefruit
Grand Marnier	France	Curacao
Gilka Kümmel	Germany	Kümmel
Pernod	United States	Star Anis
Southern Comfort Whiskey	United States	Peach and Bourbon
Strega	Italy	Plant Liqueur
Van der Hum	South Africa	Spicy Plant Liqueur
Vieille Curé	France	Plant Liqueur

The Brand Names Foundation, which is now in its eighteenth year, has done a notable job of strengthening public confidence of consumers by joining stores with manufacturers and advertising media in stressing the importance of the brand competitive system of America. Many a brand name which was familiar to Europeans during our Colonial days still enjoys a faithful following. Crosse and Blackwell dates from 1706; Royal Worcester porcelains from 1751; Wedgwood china from 1759 and the Britannica Encyclopaedias, fount of so much knowledge, from 1768. There are over 300,000 trade marks and 20,000 brand names in use which stimulate sales and it is interesting to note that the oldest brand name on record with the Foundation is Cherry Rocher, a French cordial. The oldest American native brand is alcoholic, too. It is Old Medford Brand rum which dates from the Revolution—1776. James E. Pepper distilled spirits and Caldwell's rum came along in 1790.

19

Italy, Mother of Wines

*"Nothing more excellent or valuable than wine was
ever granted by the gods to man."*

—PLATO

SINCE THE ANCIENT DAYS BEFORE ROMULUS
and Remus founded Rome, the cultivation of vineyards has been one
of the important agricultural pursuits of the people of Italy. Wine
has been a nutrient, a medicine, a spiritual ritual, a way of life for
her people. Natural water not being very palatable, mineral waters
and wines are the customary beverages. Italy is the second largest producer of wines in the world, second only to France. The country from
the Swiss and Austrian borders in the north down to the Straits of
Messina and over to Sicily is one sprawling vineyard.

The marching troops of Caesar brought vine cuttings to France and
Germany. The vineyards in these countries have required far more
cultivating and selection of varieties because the soil and climates are
less hospitable than that of Italy. In certain blessed areas, other countries have been able to produce extraordinary wines, while there are
also areas which produce ordinary wines. It is said that Italy has
always had the climate and soil devised by the gods for their purpose.
Taking more or less for granted this gift, Italy issues very few truly
great wines, though on the other hand, none of the wines can be
said to be poor or bad. All of the table wines are pleasant.

Wine, they say, is a necessity of life, and Italians are born with a taste for it. Eating or dining without wine is inconceivable. It is the natural beverage, inexpensive, dietary, advantageous, safe. It is the sunshine of the grapes converted into liquid warmth, which soothes the soul.

While the Italian Riviera is eye-filling, the ruins and culture in the old cities are impressive, the lakes nestled in mountain tops are breath-taking. Italy as a whole has not been fortunate in the possession of natural resources. She imports gasoline and petroleum. American-owned or franchised Shell Oil stations dot the land. Even coal for the railroads must be imported, for there is no local coal. After centuries of using wood for stoves, the forests have been depleted. When they vanished, they took the rivers with them. The great rivers of antiquity, such as the Po and the Tiber (which the ancients called Father Tiber), are in mid-summer narrow struggling streams with scraggy banks of rocks and weeds. But there are waterfalls, and water power is Italy's "white coal."

Italy pays for her imports with olive oil, native products, wool cloth, textiles and wines. Music and art—of which there is abundance—has little commercial value within the country. Two wars have drained Italy of man-power and money. In the north—as late as 1956—though railroad stations bombed to the ground had been replaced, the ruins were left behind them. Bombed houses still stood with new buildings erected next to them. It costs money for dynamiting and rubble removal. The Lend Lease program of America has injected new life into Italian industry and brought the country in general to a better standard of living.

Barolo, a village in Piedmont, sitting on an extinct volcano, grows on its slopes the Nebbiolo grape, which gives Italy a fine red table wine with a ruby red color that grows darker as it ages. The surrounding hills produce wines not as great as Barolo and known as Barbaresco. Grignolino is a red wine light in color with a good body from the grignolio grapes, the choice of table wine for the well-to-do of Northern Italy. A half brother to Barolo is the Barbera grape, a dry wine. On the type of Burgundy, it comes to as much as 14 proof.

Another wine you will meet in Italy is Freisa, which has a strawberry bouquet. These three may be sweet or dry in taste. There are too many varieties in Piedmont to catalogue them all. Asti, a little village in the center of the Muscat grape-growing region, produces sparkling wines—Asti Spumante—Moscato Spumante and Lacrima Christi.

From Lake Garda East up to, around and beyond Verona are the vineyards that produce the ruby red Valpolicella. Though having a slightly bitter tang, this wine has softness and a delicate bouquet. Wines come from the grape varieties—Corvina, Molinara, Roassar and Negrar—grown along the eastern slopes of Lake Garda. The Red Bordolino is from land further east and around Verona. Beyond ancient Verona, the Garganega and Trebbiano produce the very aptly called Bolla Soave—a light, dry golden white wine, velvety in texture and with a haunting bouquet, distributed by Fontana-Hollywood Corporation of New York City.

In Italy, Veronese sparkling wine is very popular. It is garnet-red Recioto Nobile de la Valpolicello. Racioto means "ears" in Italian. The upper part of the grape cluster, as it hangs heavily on the vine, has the appearance of ears, and these ripen earlier than the rest of the bunch. By the time the whole cluster has ripened, the ears are overripe and a nobile mold develops. The recioto grapes are gathered and pressed apart to produce by Champagne methods a richly perfumed, delightful wine.

It is tempting to dwell a little on Tuscany, that rugged country whose hills are dotted with mournful cypresses, its fields lush with asphodel, the ancient Tuscan flower. The Road Aurelia of the Romans leads from the capital city to the northern stronghold. Some forty years ago, D. H. Lawrence captured the mood of Tuscany in *Etruscan Places* (Viking Press). "There is a queer stillness and a curious repose about the Etruscan places I have been to," wrote Lawrence, "quite different from the weirdness of Celtic places, the slightly repellent feeling of Rome, and the rather horrible feeling of the great pyramid places in Mexico . . . or the amiably idolatrous Buddha places in Ceylon. There is a stillness and a softness in these great grassy mounds with their ancient stone girdles, and down the central walk there lingers still a kind of homeliness and happiness. True, it was a still and sunny afternoon in April, and larks rose from the soft grass of the tombs. But there was a stillness and a soothingness in all the air in that sunken place and a feeling that it was good for one's soul to be there."

The Etruscans flourished in the sixth century before Christ, and the paintings on their tombs which they left behind show them to have been a vivid, gay, life-accepting people, in whose veins ran the rich red juice of love and life. They wined, dined and danced to the music of seven-stringed lyres and flutes, amid the grey olive trees, which one sees gnarled, twisted and old, like feeble men, on the rocky hillsides. Etruria and Tuscany was their land, and music and merriment the center of their life. Etruscan archeology reveals more than ever the vitality of this warm-blooded people. It is a potent premise for the importance of food and drink in the promotion of happiness and well-being. We are indebted to the fine article by Raymond Bloch in *Horizon* for May, 1960 for current findings on the Etruscans: *In Search of the Etruscans.*

Mr. Bloch uses as one of his arresting illustrations a banquet scene painted about 475 B.C. Remarkably preserved in the Tomb of the Leopards at Tarquinia, it shows a wine bearer leading a flutist and a lyre-player wearing colorful scarves. These paintings, which were created as a solace for the dead, tell a joyous story of Etruscan life and times. The Greeks and Romans, who were themselves highly advanced in the art of living, were scandalized by the privileged role women enjoyed in Etruscan society. There is evidence that they reclined beside their husbands on the banquet couch. The terra-cotta lid of a sarcophagus shows a handsome young couple of wealth and splendor commemorated as they dined together. This sculpture is now in the Museum of the Villa Giulia in Rome.

Poets and writers of many countries found their inspiration in this region. One thinks of the English poet, Robert Browning, and his poet wife, Elizabeth Barrett Browning, who lived fifteen years in this memory-laden place, where Elizabeth died and was buried. I believe everybody knows that Tuscany is the home of Chianti wine, and one cannot mistake Chianti because of its special packaging in straw-covered fiascos to identify its source of origin. It may not have been the wine of the ancient Etruscans, but we do know that its recorded history goes back a thousand years. It was praised by Dante, Boccaccio, the Borgias; even St. Francis of Assissi loved the wine of Tuscany—all long before the straw fiasci came into general use.

Chianti Classico is limited to a special area and its characteristics are established by the *Consorzio per la Difesa del Vino Tipico Del Chianti*. Such wine is entitled to the use of an emblem picturing a black cockerel on a golden background. Each of the seals is numbered, and its issue is controlled. The Chianti Classico region lies between Florence (Firenze) and Siena and includes the parishes of Radda in Chianti, Castellina in Chianti, Greve, San Casciano and part of Castelnuovo—Berardenga.

This wine is a blend of 70% Sangiovese grapes, with the balance of Canaiolo Nero, Trebiano, Malvasia and, in several great vineyards, some Caberenet and Malbec grapes. Chianti marked for aging is bottled in regular claret bottles because the straw tends to deteriorate. Chiantis in fiasci are intended to be drunk within five or six years from its bottling, at the most. From the rolling hills of Umbria come the white wines of Orvieto which, like Chianti, goes to the market place in straw-covered fiasci. Orvieto comes secco (dry) and abbocato (sweet), straw-colored, with a fruity freshness. Frascati is the name of the Tusculum of which Horace, the poet of the ancients, spoke. This white wine cannot travel gracefully, but when consumed locally, it has charm, freshness and fruitiness.

There are many fine houses which market Chianti, among them the House Ruffino established in 1877, which purveys to the Holy See of the Vatican and, in his time, to the King of Italy. Large cellars and bottling plants are maintained at Pontassieve in Chianti. Ruffino Red Capsule is the traditional Chianti, lively, ruby red, with a warm and brisk taste, naturally matured. The Blue Capsule, long matured, has balanced roundness and rich refinement. The White Capsule is a white vintage wine, which has a limpid and brilliant color, delicate bouquet and graceful taste, delicious when served chilled. The Rosatello Ruffino is their Rosé wine from the must of choice selected grapes made by a special system of vinification. Its distinctive bottle in the shape of a pyramid is patented, and still has the wickered basket flask to protect it. Ruffino Orvieto is a white vintage wine from the

Aging cellars at The Christian Brothers Winery in Napa Valley, which has the largest total gallons of oak cooperage for the aging of wines in the U.S.A.

Sun-drenched vineyards surround the chapel and school of The Christian Brothers of California, Mont La Salle, Napa County, California.

Kentucky Hunt breakfast arrangement by interior designer Valerian Rybar of Mint Juleps and Bourbon decanters, an established American tradition, as exhibited in the Fourth Annual Exhibition of Table Settings at Tiffany's by leading New York decorators.

"The Vintage in California" from a drawing by P. Frenzeny in Harper's Weekly for August 5, 1878, depicting California wine-making in the middle and late eighties.

Drawings by P. Frenzeny

Sketch of early days in Beaulieu Vineyard (B.V.) and estate in Rutherford, Napa Valley, California.

←————

Left to right, Fred C. Taylor, president, Greyton H. Taylor, vice president, and Clarence Taylor, vice president of the family-owned Taylor Wine Company, Inc., of Hammondsport, New York, examine the distinctive French hybrid grapes which their viticulturists have been developing for fifteen years in their Finger Lakes vineyards. These grapes have made possible the delectable Pink Champagne, a sparkling addition to the Taylor list.

Entrance to the Monastery of Le Grand Chartreuse near Grenoble, France. Nearby the Carthusian Monks cultivate the numerous herbs for the secret formula known only to four monks. The formula for their Green and Yellow Chartreuse Liqueurs, calling for a blend of 130 different herbs, dates back to 1605.

Huge barrels in which the Chartreuse Liqueur is aged by the Carthusian Monks in the mountainous area in Voiron, France. The liqueur gave the color, chartreuse, its name.

Gifted with an exceptionally fine taster's palate, author Robotti is shown at his fabulous international wine cellar beneath the Richelieu, sometimes used for private parties.

Photo by Bakalar-Cosmo

There is nothing static about the restaurant industry. The intelligent owner makes tours abroad to the principal cities of the Continent as often as possible. The co-authors on board the S.S. Independence.

Photo by James Kozik

The Peter Robotti School replaces an old landmark, the castle of a noble built in 1776. For its construction and furnishing, President Giovanni Gronchi of the Republic of Italy awarded the author the Gold Star of Solidarity (first class) with the title of Commendatore and Cavalier. This is the highest award given to a native son who has become the citizen of and resides in another country.

Photo by Alfredo, Alessandria

"It is always my aim to visit Italy at the harvesting of the grapes as this is the most enjoyable time of the entire year. Gathering grapes in my family's ancestral vineyards during a summer vacation."

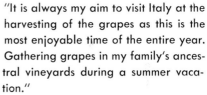

"My native village, Fubine, the little medieval suburb of the railroad town of Alessandria, tucked away among the hills, slopes and green valleys of Piedmont. The Cathedral on the highest hill dates from 1496; its spire is the first sign of welcome of the returning native." This was completely restored by the Robottis.

The Waldorf at Fifth Avenue and Thirty-third Street built by William Waldorf Astor opened March 13, 1893. In 1896 the hotel built by John Jacob Astor IV was merged with the Waldorf, the combined buildings having a thousand rooms. The new Waldorf-Astoria, with 2000 rooms was opened September 30, 1931.

Mr. Robotti's famed Richelieu occupies the ground floor and lower level of his own modern seven story building with the Columbia Broadcasting System tenanting the upper six floors. Paul Resnick and Harry F. Green were the architects and Murray J. Friedman, builder.

Orvietan vineyards, and matured in the closely situated cellars at Pontassieve. The shape of its flask is known as "pulcianella" and it is velvety smooth and spring-time fresh.

In the winter, northern Italy is cold, her streams and rivers fed by melting snows and glaciers. Most of Italy was, at one time, in the direct path of glaciers. When they rolled on, they left a rocky terrain. Dry and rocky mountains cover much of the country; the rest is of volcanic origin. In between there is land which is tilled to the very last inch. In the north one finds the most beauty. There are gentle hills, long ago deforested and cultivated into vineyards which stretch lazily toward the Alps. The earth is a rich, reddish loam. There are thousands of acres of vineyards uninterrupted by dwellings. The people own parcels of what were once the vast estates of the nobility, the Dukes and Counts who governed before Italy was unified. The present vineyard caretakers and workers live in nearby villages and go to and fro to their land parcels. Small proprietors still work with oxen and horses, leaving at dawn and returning at sundown.

Piedmont is perhaps the best known and most important wine region in the country. The cold streams with their glacier origin constantly contribute to the fertility of the soil. Monferrato is the great wine producer. Much of what is made is consumed locally and enjoyed by diners in Genoa, Milan and Torino. Italy lacks the organization, so imposingly evident in France, which makes wine producing a great industry. It would be difficult to describe the Italian regions completely as they do not fall into the neat category of the French. However, there are varieties which have achieved recognition and some fame.

It was my great privilege to have a share in conservation of the traditions of my own birthplace, Fubine, a village like the others where in the olden days the caretakers of the vineyards lived in contentment. From my childhood I saw the tall spire rising against the sky, of Fubine's pride, the cathedral which dates back before the time of Christopher Columbus. There are birth records there from the year 1496 still cherished in its archives. My earliest memories of Fubine are of the fragrant family vineyards and of the orchard sprawling behind the house. My blessed mother's efforts helped to erect an altar to St. Anthony in one of its side chapels and until I was twelve I served Mass there wearing a lace surplice my mother made. Putting on that surplice and assisting in the Mass was the greatest thrill of my boyhood. My mother hoped I would be a priest. I spent hours in the vast old building, peering up at its lofty nave, studying the remnants of the moat and the old walls, admiring the marble statuary and gold-framed paintings: treasures bestowed on it by the Vatican during its earlier years.

As I mentioned elsewhere, I might have stayed in Fubine if it had not been for an insect invasion. The plague did tremendous damage to the family vineyards and many vintners emigrated to the United States. They later returned, bringing with them American vines and techniques that restored the family business. But talk of America, the instinct of youth for adventure brought me to New York and a career as a restaurateur, where the background of the fine cuisine of Piedmont, and the land of vineyards of my people for generations, were to be my greatest assets in a highly competitive field. Kay Sullivan in her story of my life for *Catholic Digest* (December 1958) told how I was able to help the place of my birth when it was hurt by war. Request for assistance came in a letter received at the end of the second World War, written by Dr. Peter Garlasco, a friend from boyhood, and doctor of the town of Fubine. Dr. Garlasco told how badly off the townspeople were with refugees streaming in, and many persons, especially the older ones, in need of food and medicines.

The good doctor was deputized to care for anyone needing provisions and medical attention, with the bill sent to me. In this way he had a standing list of 200 families receiving aid. When I returned in 1948, even the lovely vineyards did not look the same after the war years. The place of my boyhood was a happy town. Everybody sang, the harvesting of the grapes in September was the highpoint of the year. Everybody was friendly and crowded into the cathedral for Mass on Sunday mornings, and then stood around in the square afterwards to chat and laugh. Now the people were too frightened to stand in the square or even to go to church. The Communists were very powerful. There had been violence and death in Fubine.

One afternoon as I sat with my old pastor, Eg. Emilio Don Buzio,

228

who once had been a Professor at the University of Padua, and rector of the church in Fubine for thirty-five years, we hit upon a unique plan. This was the purchase and installation of an enormous loudspeaker. Thereafter when Mass was celebrated and the organ played, everybody in the village heard it. Before long people began to return to services. The familiar liturgy pouring out over the loudspeaker did more to touch their hearts with courage to face the jeers of the Communists than any amount of exhorting would have done. This was only the beginning. In 1956, the town fathers proposed that we save the church from ruin. The roof leaked and the moisture was ruining the priceless paintings. The pews were falling apart. The floor needed attention. The restoration of the cathedral involved an extensive roof repair, new pews, renovation of the entire interior, windows replaced, to bring the ancient history-laden edifice to its former glory.

This led to the realization of how the war years had hurt the core of the town in the matter of education. The few schools were widely scattered, overcrowded, badly in need of repairs and without heating facilities. It was then that we saw the old castle on the crown of the hill overlooking miles of vineyard country. My wife found the legend of its building. The date was 1776, the year of American Independence. We walked through it from room to room, from floor to floor and thought with a little fixing up here and there we could make a school out of it. We were so wrong. The architects' report said "Impossible. How can you get plumbing fixtures and heat into a building nearly two hundred years old?" So the old castle was torn down. New foundations put in and an impressive building replaced it, with a fine courtyard, lovely little chapel, modern gymnasium, and classrooms. Dr. Garlasco was chairman of the committee for the school project. And that is how the Peter Robotti School of Fubine came into being. It was the culmination of many vintages and thousands upon thousands of dinners faithfully served on this side of the Atlantic.

To return to Italy's adaptability to grape cultivation—glaciers and volcanos, too, have contributed to the fertility of the vine. In a sense it is a process similar to the earth's transformation of carbon into diamonds and the conversion of matter into other precious stones. Volcanic dust has fertilized the land for centuries on end in the shadow of Vesuvius in the Neapolitan region. Two wines of some note are found here: Lacryma Christi and Gragnano. Grown near Vesuvius, the Lacryma Christi is for the most part a golden wine, not too dry and with an aromatic bouquet which comes from the volcanic soil. It is said that the driest sparkling wine in Italy, with an intense richness all its own, originates here. When we walked through Pompeii's cobbled streets (which archeologists long ago laid bare to the surface after its burial under volcanic lava and dust), we could sense that here—like the Etruscans—lived a people of high order, enjoying life to its fullest with sumptuous cuisine and elegant wines. Evidence of it was on every side. We noted the ruins of the great dining rooms, the baths and swimming pools, the small shops for the artisan, all of which Bulwer-Lytton resurrected so movingly in his *Last Days of Pompeii.*

Around Gragnano the grapes for the red wine which bears this name are grown. It is dark red, rich and fruity. It is said to come closer to greatness than the present-day Falerno does to the legendary Falernum, beloved of the ancients. From the region of volcanic ashes and dust come wines touched by fire from this very productive soil. Mt. Etna is Sicily's most famous lava-belching volcano, and it is interesting to note that the rich Marsala is obtained from the Insolia and Calaretto grape varieties grown here. The methods of production are similar to those used on the island of Madeira to produce an old-time favorite. The wines are baked in heated warehouses and fortified with brandy distilled from wines of the district. They are always blended wines. Muscat and malvasia grapes come from the islands of the Inland Sea, famous for the luscious, rich headily perfumed sweet dessert wines of these grapes. The most famous of these are: Moscato di Pantalleria, Malvasia di Lipari and Moscato di Sirausa. Those produced in Sardinia are consumed in Italy and not available to our markets. The only exception is Vernaccia di Sardegna, a dry, very heady, strongly flavored wine.

California, America's Wine Basket

"Before dinner men meet with great inequality of understanding and those who are conscious of their inferiority have the modesty not to talk: when they have drunk wine, every man feels himself happy, and loses that modesty, grows impudent and even vociferous."

—SAMUEL JOHNSON (1709-84)

MOST OF THE NATIVE WINES OF CALIFORNIA are outstanding, as many fine wines come from the Golden State. A respected name in the California wine industry is that of Wente, who produce some of the finest white table wines of the country, especially the sauterne and white burgundy varieties. The Germans have long been expert at wine growing and production and it is, therefore, not strange that this firm was founded by a native of Hanover, Germany, who came here in 1880. Carl H. Wente received his training under Charles Krug, the pioneer viticulturist of the Napa Valley. Soon feeling confident enough to branch out for himself, in late fall of 1883, Carl Wente bought some vineyards in the Livermore Valley, south of the town of Livermore. It is on this land that the original Wente winery still is located.

Carl Wente developed a market for his good quality table wines at above the average prices of the time. He found that the Semillon and Sauvignon blanc grapes of the Sauternes region in France could adapt themselves to the soil and climate of Livermore. Later on, the noted vines of the Pinot Chardonnay of white burgundy and champagne were imported, and thrived in this area. Carl's sons Ernest and Herman, the present owners, extended the acreage and buildings, and acquired the El Mocho vineyards. This occurred when Louis Mel, pioneer of the Livermore Valley, retired and released his treasured property to the Wentes. Today many say that Herman Wente is the greatest of the wine makers of California.

It is interesting how some famous varieties of vines came to be imported to California. It appears that Charles Wetmore was sent by the California Vinicultural Society to obtain choice cuttings in France. Wetmore, the founder of Cresta Blanca, went to France armed with a letter of introduction from Mrs. Mel-de-Bire to the Marquis de Lur-Saluces, who owned the world-renowned Château d'Yquem in Sauternes near Bordeaux. Wetmore obtained choice cuttings of the Semillon, Sauvignon blanc, and Muscadelle du Bordelais vines from the vineyards of Château d'Yquem. Some of these he gave to Louis Mel, who propagated them in his El Mocho vineyards. When the present proprietor of the Château d'Yquem (who bears the family title of Marquis de Lur-Saluces) visits California, he calls on the Wentes and inquires how his California Yqem children are faring, and to sample what the California climate can produce in the way of sauternes.

Visitors often wonder how the gravelly dry-looking soil of the vineyards can produce good crops. Strange as it may seem, much of the soil of the Wente vineyards is alluvial deposit, washed down from the hills to the east, which contains considerable heavy gravel apparently well suited to the finer grape varieties which mature in the hard way that nature has devised for them.

The grapes are picked by variety at the peak of ripeness for wine making. The juice is pressed in small batches, the wines placed on racks in a small cooperage, then aged in oaken puncheons, and finally aged again in the bottle to full maturity. The wines marketed under the label of Wente Bros. are the white table wines, which carry their vintage date on the labels. All the wines—white, red and rosé—are labeled with the Valle de Oro brand. The Valley of Gold is the romantic name given to Livermore Valley by the Spaniards who first colonized there. This is what an Easterner notices so particularly in California: the abundance of Spanish names for towns and sections and cities. When you ask for Wente wines, you have a choice of:

WHITE WINES

Dry Demillon (this is similar to a French Graves, though it is less sweet; vintaged)

Sweet Semillon (produced from late-picked grapes to ensure maximum richness and sweetness—non-vintaged)

Sauvignon Blanc (from the grape, vintaged)

Grey Riesling (popular, vintaged)

Pinot Blanc ⎫
Pinot Chardonnay ⎰ both vintaged

VALLE DE ORO WHITE WINES

Chateau Wente—Blend of Semillon and Sauvignon blanc grapes, with the addition of a little Muscadelle du Bordelais, produces a fine sweet sauterne.

Chablis

VALLE DE ORO RED WINE AND ROSÉ

Burgundy

Rosé

Claret (obtainable only locally from the winery in large containers; ideal wine for home bottler—pleasing and inexpensive)

The Beaulieu vineyard at Rutherford in Northern California has a great name for its wines. The trade designation is B V for its selection of red, white, sparkling, aperitif and dessert wines.

RED

Georges de Latour Private Reserve. (This is a vintage Cabernet Sauvignon from that grape, produced only in better years, and considered the premier claret of California.)

Beaumont (A vintage wine principally from the grape, but with small proportions of Merlot and Petit Verdot added, as in the better Red Bordeaux of France)

Burgundy (from Pinot Noir, Napa Valley Gamay and Mondeuse de Savoie).

WHITE

Chateau Beaulieu (vintage sweet Sauterne from late-picked Sauvignon blanc and Semillon grapes, with a bit of Muscadelle du Bordelais added.

Pinot Chardonnay (vintage wine from that grape; limited production)

Beauclair (vintage Johannisberger or White Riesling)

Dry Sauternes and Sweet Sauternes (both from Semillon and Sauvignon blanc grapes)

Chablis (from Pinot Chardonnay, Chenin blanc and Melon de Bourgogne)

Riesling (from Johannisberger or White Riesling and Sylvanter)

Rosé (Beaurosé—from Cabernet Squvignon mainly)

SPARKLING WINES (bottle-fermented)

The Beaulieu Champagnes (dry and medium dry in character, were first available in 1955, followed by a Sparkling Burgundy)

APERITIF AND DESSERT WINES:

Pale Dry Sherry

Sherry XXX (medium sweet)

Cream Sherry (sweet)

Port XXX

Muscatel XXX

Muscat de Frontignan (from the vines of that name whose cuttings were imported by George de Latour in the early part of the century)

Georges de Latour came from the Bordeaux and Burgundy regions of France, where the name of the family of de Latour was well known. He had read of California being a country suitable to grape culture. When he arrived there at the turn of the century, he traveled through the State searching for the ideal location for his purpose. In 1900, he finally settled in the Rutherford area of the Napa Valley. Today the Beaulieu estate, with its Versailles-like gardens, well-kept orchards, spreading mansion, is a showplace of the Valley.

Georges de Latour found the soil and climate favorable. He possessed inherited skill and, furthermore, had been gifted with a sensitive palate for tasting, which is of primary importance to those engaged in the wine industry, especially in the producing end. In forty years of application, he established a good reputation for the Beaulieu wines throughout the United States. There is a French atmosphere about the estate and the winery itself which is a part of their success. Prohibition shut down the winery's activities except for the production of sacramental wines. Becoming proficient in this specialty, Beaulieu did not surrender that part of the business when Prohibition ended, and it still provides Altar Wines to the clergy.

TABLE WINES
> Cabernet Sauvignon and Burgundy in the reds and Château Beaulieu, Sweet Sauternes, Dry Sauternes, Riesling, Rhine and Chablis in the whites.

SWEET WINES
> Muscat de Frontignan and Muscatel XXX, Tokay XXX and Angelica XXX.

Georges de Latour died in 1940 and Madame de Latour presided in her husband's place until her death in 1951. She is remembered in wine circles as the *grande dame* of California viticulture, with grace and charm in the French manner, making of her home a true Château. Now their daughter Hélène and her husband, the Marquis de Pins, continue the work of upholding the de Latour tradition. The Marquis de Pins is a landed proprietor in France, with an expert knowledge of vintages throughout the world, and is a connoisseur and able judge of wines. He and his wife pay periodic visits to the wine regions of France, and maintain a home in San Francisco for their social activities. Daughter Dagmar is a wine expert, too, married to Walter H. Sullivan, Jr., a San Francisco realtor. Thus California has been able to produce a wine dynasty of its own with the French touch.

Aldo Fabrini of Beaulieu, and his charming wife, drove us one fine morning from San Francisco, where they live, to the winery at Rutherford. At the winery we were given the grand tour and were the guests of the winery at lunch with André Tchelistcheff as our host. It was he who introduced us to the Marquis. André Tchelistcheff with deep-set blue eyes, a tanned heavily lined pleasant face, small and wiry, vastly intelligent, is a French-trained Russian brimming over with wine lore. He seemed to us something of a magician and reminiscent of the infamous Rasputin of the late Czar's imperial court, and Rasputin my wife and I called him thereafter in our private conversations, charming, affable and hospitable as he was. We learned that André joined Beaulieu in 1938 and presides as production manager in charge of the winery and the vineyards. He is the Beaulieu key man who skillfully adapts American chemical techniques of producing quality to his storehouse of Old World wine-making experience. He pointed out that there are actually four Beaulieu vineyards, two at Rutherford, which we saw, and two more at Oakville, each planted with varieties suited to the soil and location sun-wise. Beaulieu Vineyard is the brand name, but everyone is familiar with the more simple designation B V.

News was made in the American wine industry with a new era beginning June 6, 1959, when Paul Masson opened the Champagne Cellars at Saratoga, California, where four million bottles of champagne and still wines were placed for rest and aging. The beautiful winery, costing many millions, and designed by John S. Bolles, has the distinction of being the first ever built in the United States for the primary purpose of producing and aging bottle-fermented champagne. It is the first, too, designed to welcome guests from all over the world. American wineries have become increasingly cordial in their public relations, extending invitations of guided tours so that people may learn first-hand and be initiated into the fairy realm of the wines.

Paul Masson, the master vintner of France, a gay and handsome Frenchman, came as early as 1870 from his home in Burgundy to work in Santa Clara Valley with Charles Le Franc, who later became his partner and son-in-law. In the Santa Cruz Mountains, Masson discovered a soil and climate similar to his native Burgundy. He imported choice vine cuttings to begin the vineyards. Today the gleaming new winery and cellars cover seventeen landscaped acres off the San Jose-Saratoga Highway. The great wine-tasting hall and reception room measures 11,000 square feet. A glass wall faces a 9,000 square-foot pool where a sixty-seven-foot fountain symbolizes the effervescence of champagne. It is a befitting monument to the joyful wine of laughter. The opposite wall is covered with sixteen transparencies showing the various bottles of Paul Masson wines, champagne, vermouth and brandy, each associated with the variety of grape from which it is made. While visitors stop at the tasting counter, they can appreciate these instructive transparencies.

One enters the winery by ramp, deviously devised to show on its inner face a mosaic depicting the history of wine making. It was created by Jose Moya Del Pino, the Spanish artist who has adopted California as his home. There are 21,600 square feet in the main building devoted to the making and aging of wines, especially champagne, and to blend and bottle brandies. The sightseeing is done from the mezzanine level of the five main areas; champagne cellars, bottling and packaging departments, finished goods, storage cellar, and the brandy blending and bottling room. Kurt Opper presides as head wine master, John Hyba is champagne maker, and Leo Berti is production manager.

With typically American enterprise, the vast plant has incorporated all mechanical and scientific progress known to this time. Knowledge gleaned from the wineries of Germany, France and Italy by Otto Meyer, President of the Paul Masson vineyards, has been put to good use. Here one sees glass-lined steel tanks, used by modern Germans, the new way of aging wines before final aging in the bottle. In effect, the tanks are enormous bottles of 5,000 gallon capacity.

Near the chalet, high in the hills, one finds the original Paul Masson Winery, the historic land-mark, whose owner could never have imagined the growth and changes which time has brought. Going up the curving mountain road for three miles, one reaches the chalet. Here in private tastings, wines were selected by the State Department for showing at the Moscow Trade Fair of July 1959. The particular wines chosen for display were: three champagnes, Brut, extra dry and Pink; two table wines, Pinot Noir and Pinot Chardonnay, all recipients of awards of merit.

In the oak-beamed reception room of the chalet, with its log fireplace, Paul Masson long ago entertained the great people of his day, attracted by the quality of his wines and the culinary excellence which his household provided. Good wine, good food, and handsome men and women to enjoy them were the dreams out of which Paul Masson built his life. Today the wall facing the Santa Clara Valley has been removed and, in true Californian architectural style, has been replaced with window pane, so that one sits seemingly suspended in space above the valley overlooking San Jose, Sunny Vale, and Mt. Hamilton, beyond.

It would be of benefit to visit each winery which extends an invitation to the public. Some, in particular, are unforgettable. Not many realize The Christian Brothers, which produce a superlative line of California wines, is a bona fide religious order. For over eighty years, The Christian Brothers of the Roman Catholic Church, have produced wines which rank with the finest the Old or New World can offer. The primary responsibility and interest of these Brothers lie in education—"To give a Christian education to youth, especially to the poor" were the words of its founder, St. Jean Baptiste de La Salle, who set forth this aim at Rheims in France nearly three hundred years ago. The first American school was opened in 1848. Today the Order operates nearly 1,500 schools or colleges in some 72 countries throughout the world, providing teachers in 119 institutions of learning in the United States alone.

In California, the Brothers are occupied in an avocation, with the approval of the Church, as viticulturists and makers of fine wines, brandy and champagnes. Activity centers at Mont La Salle, Napa County, some sixty miles north of San Francisco in the beautiful foothills of Napa Valley. The headquarters of the Novitiate for the Western Province of the Order is located here along with The Christian Brothers' vineyard estate. The famous aging cellars are located at St. Helena. While the Brothers at first produced wines exclusively for sacramental purposes, when the Mont La Salle Novitiate was built, extensive vineyards were acquired for production of table wines as well. The vineyards were originally laid out in the 1880's in volcanic soil of which there are today a thousand acres.

The vines are exclusively of European stock, costly to raise with an average yield of only $1\frac{1}{2}$ to $3\frac{1}{2}$ tons of grapes to the acre in the Mont La Salle's mountain vineyards, which are non-irrigated. Brother Timothy is in charge of the quality of the grapes; Brother John is president and general manager assisted by Brother Gregory, business administrator of the various wineries. Distribution of the wines, champagnes, vermouths and brandy is handled by Fromm and Sichel, Inc. of New York, Chicago and San Francisco. There is no other connection between this firm and the Order except for the long and friendly cooperation between independent producer and independent distributor. Many have wondered about the income earned from the business. All proceeds from the operations of its wineries is vested in the Order and used by the Christian Brothers for maintenance of Mont La Salle and for educational work. There is no personal compensation for the Brothers who have taken the vow of poverty. Proceeds help to support young men in training to become Christian Brothers and toward the maintenance of schools. One may have the opportunity to see the Brothers at work, for the Winery and Novitiate situated high in the beautiful wooded foothills, welcome about 80,000 visitors yearly, to go through the cellars at St. Helena, Napa County.

A new wine of which the Christian Brothers are rightfully proud is their Chateau La Salle, a pale gold wine of delicate bouquet. From 1955-1959, the wine, still unnamed, was awarded nine gold medals at the California Wine judgings at the California State Fair held in Los Angeles. The Brothers decided to name their wine after a beautiful old Château in Rheims, France, the home of the founder of their order, St. Jean Baptiste de La Salle who was born there in 1651. Some years ago, the Christian Brothers in France, part of a teaching order, which encircles the globe, became the owners of the old Château. The wine produced in an old stone winery high on the western hills surrounding the Napa Valley, California, commemorates the possession of the French Château.

California, in general, produces a wide variety of red table wines called California Clarets, Red Burgundies, and some Red Wines of the Italian type; also the White Table Wines known as California Sauternes and White Burgundies; Rhine Wines; Rosé Table Wines and Sparkling Wines. The latter are the California Champagnes (among these the Korbel Brut and Sec, Paul Masson Brut and Extra Dry and the Cresta Blanca Brut.) There are also the California Pink

(Rosé) Champagnes comprising Almadén Pink, etc., and the California Red Champagnes and Sparkling Burgundies which include Korbel Rouge, Almadén Sparkling Burgundy and the Paul Masson Red Champagne.

The remaining classification includes the Aperitif and Dessert Wines of the California Sherries, dry and sweet. Not to be over-looked are the California Ports, among which are found the Louis Martini Tawny Port and the Buena Vista Vintage Port. We visited the Louis Martini plant and winery and found a very fine establishment and received a cordial welcome. The Muscat Wines are chiefly from the Napa Valley (Beaulieu Muscat de Frontignan) and from the Livermore and Santa Clara Valleys. Black Muscat is also produced in Santa Clara and goes by the intriguing name of Novitiate of Los Gatos Black Muscat, with the Southern Alameda County contributing Weibel Black Muscatel or Cream of Black Muscat.

One often hears of the California Wine Association, which has its headquarters in San Francisco and, over the years, has played an important part in the progress of the wine industry of California. The history of this organization dates back to 1884. In that year, a number of well-known wineries decided to join forces and call themselves the California Wine Association. It was re-organized in 1929 as Fruit Industries, Ltd., but, in 1951, reverted to its original name.

The grand old man of California viticulture, A. R. Morrow, was long the dominant figure of the association, and his memory has been perpetuated in one of its well-known brands. The Association is presently headed by Sydney C. Wortley, Fred Snyde, Chairman of the Board, and Mario Perelli-Minetti, general manager. Actually the Association comprises eleven cooperative and other wineries, to which some 1200 wine growers contribute their grapes in a well-organized system. These wineries are located in the four major wine districts: one in Sonoma, which features dry table wines; six in the Lodi-Sacramento district, mostly for sherry, tokay and brandy; two in the Fresno-San Joaquin district, especially for muscatel and grignolino; and one in the Cucamonga district, which produces port and other sweet wines. The Association controls the production of the various types of wines with regard to regional suitability and quality. There is an enormous winery for blending, finishing, aging and bottling in San Francisco.

It must not be thought that the Association covers the entire state, but it is one of the three largest wine producers, and the wines enjoy national distribution. Its table and dessert wines are marketed under the brand—*Ambassador District*. 75% of its volume comes from grapes grown in the district designated on the label, which assures the purchaser that the wine has been produced from vines famed for each particular type. There is a prominent brand known as *Eleven Cellars,* named for the eleven wineries of the Association. These happen to be Red Wines, Zinfandel, Burgundy and Claret, and also White; Sauterne and Chablis, as well as Rosé and Vin Rosé.

TABLE WINES:

> (In addition to Eleven Cellars)
> Ambassador District Red: Cabernet, Grignolino, Zinfandel and Burgundy; White: Dry Sauterne, Sauterne, Haut Sauterne, Riesling, Rhine and Chablis; Rosé: Grignolino Rosé.
> Dolly Madison: Red and white, produced from 100% vinifera grapes and marketed mostly in the East.
> Sparkling Wines (bottle-fermented)
> Ambassador Champagne and Sparkling Burgundy
> Sparkling Wines (Bulk Process)

APERITIF AND DESSERT WINES:

> Ambassador District: Pale Dry Sherry, Sherry and Creme Sherry (sweet), Port, Muscatel and Tokay.

ELEVEN CELLARS:

> Pale Dry Cocktail Sherry, Sherry and Cream Sherry, Port and Ruby Port, Muscatel, Tokay and White Port.
> Ambassador: F. I. Dry and Sweet Vermouth.

A great deal of the activity of wine culture flourishes in northern California, but the Southern Districts contribute their share. The Southern California Region centers in Los Angeles County and City, and in San Bernardino County (Cucamonga District). Roughly the entire state is divided into the Northern Coastal Region, comprising the Sonoma-Mendocino District, Napa-Solano District, Livermore-

Contra Costa District, the San Francisco District (mentioned above) and the Santa Clara-Santa Cruz-Central Coastal District, with its Santa Clara County and Valley, Santa Cruz, San Benito, Monterey and San Luis Obispo Counties.

The Great Inland Valley Region comprises the Lodi-Sacramento District, the Escalon-Modesto District (Southern San Joaquin and Sanislaus County) and the Fresno-San Joaquin Valley District with its Madera, Fresno, Tulare and Kern Counties. There are many other wineries deserving of mention, but we are noting here only those varieties which are particularly familiar to those interested in the native wines of California. One may sometimes run across the brandies of California, a spirit distilled from the wine. California law requires that distillation from fruits other than grapes be labeled with the particular fruit used. A federal regulation defines brandy as a distillate obtained solely from the fermented juice or wine of the fruit, distilled at less than 190 proof and bottled at not less than 80 proof. There are also some high-proof brandies produced which are used in the making of aperitif and dessert wines.

The alcoholic strength of spirits or liquors is measured and known by the ancient term—*proof*. This varies in different countries. In the United States, 100 proof spirit means that which contains 50% alcohol by volume, absolute alcohol being 200 proof spirit. Wines are always labeled with the percentage of alcohol they contain by volume, but brandies, on the other hand, like other spirits, indicate their proof. Most California brandies are about 84 proof (42% alcohol by volume). The bottled-in-bond brandies are 100 proof (50% by volume) like all bonded liquors. California Brandy is distilled from grapes, and Apple Brandy (Apple Jack) from native apples.

The State has not been too successful in its attempts to produce the fruit brandies so well-loved in Europe. Perhaps the most familiar native brandy of this country is Christian Brothers, which is a blended type, 84 proof, from Napa County. Beringer Brandy is also 84 proof, varying in age from 11 to 14 years, and featured by Beringer Bros. Inc. of St. Helena, Napa County. The East-Side Winery of Lodi, San Joaquin County, markets the Royal Host brand. One is a six-year-old straight brandy, and the other a blend, both 84 proof. The Italian

Swiss Colony at Asti in Sonoma County (now owned by the Petri people) purchased the Hartley and Lejon brands from National Distillers in 1954. Most of the brandies marketed under these following brands come from the Shewan-Jones plant at Clovis, Fresno County.

Hartley—a straight brandy of fine quality, 84 proof, and from 5 to 6 years old. There is also a bonded 100 proof under that label.

Lejon—a blanded type 84 proof, named after a famous figure in the wine industry—Lee Jones—who founded the Shewan-Jones enterprise shortly after the repeal of Prohibition.

Masson—a light-bodied blend of straight brandies, 84 proof, marketed by Paul Masson Vineyards at Saratoga in Santa Clara County.

There are other establishments producing good brandies, among them that of Schenley Industries, Inc. which owns the Roma Wine Company in Fresno, where the Roma Wine Company plant is located. Most of their brandies are produced there, although they may be bottled in other states. They are merchandised by Brandy Distillers, a Division of Associated Brands, a Schenley subsidiary. The best known, perhaps, of the Schenley brandies is *Coronet* V.S.Q. (Very Special Quality) 84 proof blended. Other similar brandies are *J. Bavet, Old Monastery* Brand, and *Louis* brandies, all blended and 84 proof.

There is a company which devotes its entire efforts to the production of brandy which it markets by bulk sales, with some bottling done by a special contractor for the *Zanbro* brand. George Zaninovich, Inc. Orange Cove, Fresno County, is headed by George Zaninovich, a rugged individualist who has been owner, president and general manager ever since setting up his distillery in 1937, where he had been growing grapes since 1915. A great story could be written of the California wine makers.

The Almadén Vineyards at Los Gatos are credited with the introduction of Rosé or Vin Rosé or Pink Wine. This wine did not exist in this country prior to 1942. News of a pink wine was brought by travelers who had tasted it in Southern France—generally Tavel. A little was imported, even though it was predicted that it could not travel. The first time that Rosé was judged in a California fair was at Sacramento in 1947, where it received a gold medal. Here was a fresh, gay and pretty wine to be served chilled. When it appeared in

New York, it became a conversation piece. The Vin Rosés of France and Italy were not available during the war years, so when the Almadén Grenache Rosé was introduced it found much favor. It went with all foods, was simple, delightful, and easy to serve.

Rosé was born at Almadén on a July afternoon in 1941. The climate provided warm days and cool nights, very like that of Provence in Southern France, and from the Grenache, the principal grape of Tavel, came a Vin Rosé. Frank Schoonmaker, as consultant, had suggested that it be made—and it was produced by Oliver Goulet, cellar-master at Almadén. Louis A. Benoist, president, was final arbiter. The color comes, during fermentation, from the skins of the grapes. It is easy to have too little or too much. During fermentation, it has to be watched day and night, and drawn off the skins the moment the desired color has been reached. The color remains unchanged for its lifetime, which is short. Its lightness, freshness and fruitiness are the attributes of a young wine. No Rosé has ever improved after its second birthday. A Rosé is *not* a mixture of red and white wine. *This is forbidden by French law.* A Rosé is a pink wine made from black grapes. The pigment of the grape skin is soluble in alcohol and becomes a part of the wine during fermentation. If the grape skins are not removed until fermentation is complete, the wine becomes red.

1959 will go down in vintage history as a fabulous year for wine, both here and abroad. The growing weather was ideal, except for early frosts in upper New York State which reduced the crop by about twenty percent in that region. By and large, there was just the right amount of sunshine balanced by the right precipitation, plus the added advantage of a warm and lengthy autumn. New Yorkers were treated to a long Indian summer that extended up to the Christmas holidays. These conditions, ideal for the vineyards of New York, pertained favorably to the vineyards of California, as well. The result was that the sugar content in the grapes of 1959 was very high. The Autumn of 1960, it may also be noted, was a similarly mild one of an extended summer and time will tell how the vintage of 1960 fares.

It is customary for Europeans to complain that Americans do not drink, like, or know wines. Statistics prove that this is not quite true. A great deal of wine is consumed in this country. $754 millions in wine is used annually, which includes 145 million gallons produced in the United States, and 9 million gallons imported, chiefly from Europe. Production of wine is a growing American industry. In 1958 it produced 1,042,000 cases of sparkling wines compared to 170,000 cases in 1936. Before World War II, 75% of the champagne drunk in the United States came from France and 25% was American. Now these figures are reversed. Today Americans drink almost four times as much champagne as they did twenty years ago, much of it subsidized by the credit card systems. An odd fact worth noting is that although 75% of the nation's vineyards are in California, 55% of the quality Champagne is produced in New York in its Finger Lakes region, while California leads in the production of quality still wines. (The Finger Lakes region, the home of the Taylor Wine Company of Hammondsport, New York, is about forty miles beyond Corning.)

Even in a year such as 1959, no more than 5% or 6% of the wine produced, either here or abroad, is a fine wine. The balance is *vin ordinaire*. The production of 1959, a great vintage year, will not reach the shops, restaurants and hotels until 1962 or 1963. As everyone along Madison Avenue knows, statistics do not climb up the graph chart of their own volition. The Miracle of American Business is the motivating force. The power house behind the Pacific Coast wine industry (in addition to the promotion efforts of the wineries themselves) is the Wine Advisory Board in San Francisco. In *The Server,* the house organ for all wines and spirits, the Board announced, as of August 12, 1957, that nearly $1,000,000 had been allocated by them for the advertising and sales promotion of California wines, on an industry basis, during 1957-1958 season. The fund was expended nationwide through various media to stimulate retail wine sales by augmenting the brand advertising of individual wineries and bottlers. The campaign covered advertising placement in national consumer magazines, newspapers, trade publications, medical journals, television and radio.

A portion of the $490,000 earmarked for the half-year period was devoted to new and colorful store banners, counter cards, leaflets and other reading material, to push wine sales at the point of purchase. Roy S. Durstine, Inc., advertising counsel for the Wine Advisory

Board, was responsible for ad placements in *Life, McCall's, Cosmopolitan, Redbook, Gourmet,* the *New Yorker* and *Sunset.* The Board provides for a National Wine Week in the fall of the year, during which it is stressed that California wines are all-purpose, all-year beverages, inexpensive, and always appropriate for meal-time, as a refresher, for cooking, and for entertaining guests.

There is one point the Board insists on: American wines must be presented as *native* wines, or United States wines. Nothing is more injurious to their acceptance than being designated in print or speech as *domestic.* The buyer is fearful of being less than elegant if he accepts a non-imported label, flatly said to be *domestic.* The words *native, United States,* or *American,* however, provide an entirely different connotation and atmosphere. There are some food writers and columnists who still commit the error of using the word *domestic,* just as there are writers commenting on the fine restaurants who say *eating* instead of *dining.* The Board also educates the dining room staffs of all restaurants in the proper presentation of American wines.

In his daily column *Tips on Tables* for the *New York World-Telegram and Sun,* Robert W. Dana wrote that "The cause of wine, delightful table companion of good food, is being done a disservice in many of the city's fine restaurants more through carelessness and ignorance than intent. American Wines are particular victims of this oversight, which often places them in an inferior position under the heading of domestic. Such an appellation, I know, is anathema to the many wine growers in California, New York and other states whose product is winning an increasingly appreciative audience.

"The worst offenders are not the French, Italian, Spanish and other restaurants whose wine lists naturally feature imported vintages. They respect a wine's origin and give their American selections their proper names, be it brand or name of grape. It is the American restaurants, fine well-run establishments with excellent food, that either reflect an inferiority engendered by the debacle of Prohibition or refuse to face the fact that American wines are fully as palatable as comparable European wines—and less expensive."

"The other day," continued Dana, "I tried to buy a half bottle of wine listed as domestic burgundy. The place sold it only by the glass.

I asked who made it. When I was told it was Louis Martini Burgundy from Napa Valey, I bought it with confidence. In Westchester, a delightful country restaurant had two cellars, one for European wines, one for American vintages. A New Jersey restaurant featuring Americana had no American red wine that wasn't chilled. After some search in the cellar, they finally offered a Beaulieu Cabernet Sauvignon at the proper room temperature.

"Let me say right here that I'm fond of all good wine from anywhere. The best in the world, the great wines that are costly treasures and the everyday wine that is sound and companionable, belong on the same wine list according to the financial capabilities of the restaurant. Like a brand name of any product, they deserve the mark of their own quality. For this quality to be properly appreciated, the wine should be served, but often is not, in a large enough glass (preferably tulip-shaped) so that when the glass is half full the wine's bouquet or aroma can be appreciated. A pea-size glass may be all right for a shot of liquor. For wine it is a libel."

Outside of California, the most important wine-producing areas in the United States center in the Finger Lakes district of New York and the Sandusky-Lake Erie Island region in the northern part of Ohio. Other places produce some wines such as the Puget Sound District and the Yakima Valley in Washington State, the Willamette Valley in Oregon; the Council Bluffs area in Iowa; areas along the Missouri River in Missouri; the whole of southwest Michigan; the Cincinnati district of Ohio and the Hudson River Valley of New York.

In the north central part of New Jersey, grapes for wine production are cultivated in the Egg Harbor District. There is an area around Charlottesville in Virginia, where the grapes are grown from cuttings brought by Thomas Jefferson, third president of the United States, from France and which he planted around his hillside home at Monticello in the Blue Ridge Mountains. Vineyards are cultivated as well in the eastern coastal-plains of North Carolina. In the Midwest there are vineyards in the Ozark Mountains in Arkansas, where we least expected to find them. Aside from grape cultivation, many of the southeastern and northwestern portions of the country produce a wide variety of fruits for wines and brandies.

The State of California is well organized in the production and promulgation of its wine industry. The Wine Institute is a voluntary, non-profit association which includes 225 of the state's wineries, with membership of 95% of the productive capacity. Its work is directed by a Board of 47 directors chosen annually on the basis of district, the number depending both on the production volume and the number of members within the district. Income derives from dues. Individual wineries pay in ratio to their production volume. By contract with the Wine Advisory Board, the Institute conducts a valuable Wine Study Course, compiles industry statistics, is interested in the orderly marketing of wine, in promoting the industry, issues weekly bulletins and maintains offices in San Francisco, Washington, D.C., New York City and Chicago.

The California wine industry promotes the sale of its wines with the assistance of the Wine Advisory Board. This is a state sponsored, cooperative effort with funds collected through assessments on every gallon of California wine sent into trade channels. Funds are expended in ways it judges best. With assessments of two cents per gallon on dessert wine and one cent on table wine, revenue is produced in the neighborhood of $2 million a year, depending on volume of business. Most of this purse goes to bring the story of wine to consumers. The resulting increasing interest in wine benefits other states and wine producing countries as well.

As its name implies, the Board acts in advising or making recommendations to the California Director of Agriculture under whose jurisdiction it operates and can proceed only after the Director approves its recommendations. Nineteen industry members, and a like number of alternates, serve and meet several times a year. Its growth has been noteworthy. When the Board first met in 1938, consumption of California wine was just under 55 million gallons. By 1955 this had increased to 117 million gallons.

In his excellent article for *Esquire Magazine,* November 1960, Forrest Wallace of Chicago, who is engaged in writing a book on French wines, appraised the California wines, gauging them by the same standards he applies to the wines of France. "On the basis of what I tasted in California on a recent trip," wrote Mr. Wallace, "I would certainly say that the time has come to try the market for great California wines. A few wholesalers, most notably Bercut-Vandervoort in San Francisco itself, are willing to age and care for high-quality California wines." (Bercut-Vandervoort has even revived the practice of wholesaler-bottling. I tasted a Bercut Frères 1945 California Pinot Noir which this firm has nursed with the great imports in its magnificent cellars—a lovely, full-bodied, mellow red wine.)

"And there are unquestionably a number of retailers whose own love for wine would convince them to give the best care to a great wine from anywhere. Production is not necessarily so limited as is sometimes claimed—BV bottled two thousand five hundred cases of its splendid 1946 Pinot Noir, which is as much as almost any of the great French châteaux can produce even in a bumper year. The problem in many vineyards is that the best wines are used to "stretch" the less good, producing a standard which is fine only as far as it goes, which is not very far."

CHAPTER

Some Wines of New York State

> "From crystal goblet quaffs the King
> Of wine whereof his minstrels sing;
> From earthen bowl, if it have wine
> His vassal like a king doth dine."
> —A ROUNDELAY

THE FIRST COLONISTS TO SETTLE IN AMERICA found here a profusion of wild grapes. It is said that when Leif Ericson and his blonde Vikings visited the Atlantic Coast in the year 1000, they called the land they found "Vineland the Good" because of the grape vines they found growing everywhere. The name "Vineland" appears in many of the old records of New England. On Martha's Vineyard one summer we noted the lush growth of wild grapes which gave the little island off the Atlantic Coast its name.

When Lord Delaware was Governor of Virginia in 1616, he proposed to the London Company, who financed the settlement, that wine-making in the colonies be developed on a business basis. The suggestion was followed by those familiar with viticulture, and cuttings of European vines were shipped to America. Many wine-growing and wine-making experiments continued until the eighteenth century, all of which were doomed to failure. Late in the 1700's, however, John Dufour was able to domesticate the wild native vines of Kentucky, which intiated the development of American grapevines. After that, many native grapes were cross-bred and domesticated.

250

Some Wines of New York State

An officer in the American Revolution, Major John Adlum was one of the earliest of the mercenaries to extoll the native American grape. In 1823, he attempted to obtain from the United States government a lease of a portion of public ground in Washington, D.C. for establishing a vineyard and conducting experiments. Though his efforts were unsuccessful, he continued to spread cuttings and information to people with whom he corresponded in various parts of the country. Thomas Jefferson, James Madison, Benjamin Franklin—who all enjoyed the hospitality of the French courts and the marvelous French way with food and wines—were eager to see America begin its career as a wine-making country.

Few think of New York State as a wine-producing area, yet it creates many good and even brilliant wines which are much enjoyed and appreciated. In the aptly named city of Naples, New York, are located the Widmer's Wine Cellars, whose sherries are particularly well known. Their Neapolitan Sherry is an aperitif which is not too dry. Smooth, flavorsome, it is golden brown, while Widmer's Cocktail Sherry is a brilliant, pale sherry, fragrant and nutty in flavor, yet very dry, and excellent as an aperitif.

While New York is not generally thought of as a wine state, wine lovers are becoming more and more conscious of the part it plays in bringing wines to American tables. There isn't space, unfortunately, to mention all of the wineries in New York, much as they deserve recognition. The history of Widmer's Wine Cellars, and the manner in which their wines are produced, may be of interest as indicative of New York's participation in this industry. Here, once more, we have an Horatio Alger pattern. The founder, John Jacob Widmer, came from Switzerland, in 1882, at the invitation of his brother, who had preceded him to the fertile valley in the famed Finger Lakes Region. There the soil, climate, and the west hill of the Valley, seemed well adapted to grape culture as practiced in Europe. In October of 1882, John Widmer bought his first plot of hillside woodland with borrowed money, cleared it, and planted his first vines the following spring. The old vineyard, located directly west of the homestead, still faithfully bears its excellent fruit. In 1888, Widmer began wine production in the basement of his home.

Swiss people in Rochester, New York, and Patterson, New Jersey, were among the first buyers of the wine, which was then sold in kegs and barrels. Bottling began in 1891 in a rented warehouse, purchased in 1905, which has a Lehigh Valley Railroad siding. This plot (across the street from the original homestead of the Widmers) is now completely covered by winery buildings and offices. On January 1, 1924, the business was taken over by John Jacob's three sons, Carl, Frank and William, while the father remained active until his death in 1930. During Prohibition, the plant was kept going by producing unfermented grape juice, fruit and wine jellies, syrups, and a limited amount of wine sold for sacramental and medicinal purposes. After Repeal, the plant was well equipped to proceed with the production of fine New York State wines.

So great was family harmony and trust that the enterprise was not incorporated until September, 1933, when William Widmer became President, a position he still holds. In 1936 and 1937, a large stone cellar, referred to as Building No. 5, was constructed which covered the entire plot of land purchased in 1915. The Widmer Cellars presently ship forty different varieties of wine, with a plant capacity of 2,500,000 gallons; 700 acres of land support 375 vine acres with 640 vines to the acre. William Widmer appreciates the value of combining American methods with the Old World skills of his father, and has learned much about this ancient industry in the Royal Wine School of Germany as well as from observing the methods used in other wine-producing countries of Europe.

Widmer's Sherries are quality wines: Neapolitan Brand Sherry, Special Selection, Cocktail Sherry, Golden Cream Sherry. They age their Sherry by a unique process, first aging the wine in oak barrels which rest in the sun *on the roofs* of the winery. Then it is clarified through modern, scientific equipment and blended to complete the cycle, reaching its maturity before bottling. The wines for Sherry rest on the large rooftop through summer suns and winter snows until they are mature. It is quite a sight to see hundreds of barrels blanketed under a soft covering of Nature's gift of white. Weathering for years by exposure of the barrels to sun, rain and cold has been found to mellow the wines to perfection. The Widmer process of aging Sherry is unique in this country.

The famous Finger Lakes area yields many varieties of grapes at different times in the harvest season. In the order of their ripening, they are:

Delaware	(light red)
Elvira	(white)
Fredonia	(medium black)
Niagara	(light green)
Concord	(black)
Ives	(jet black)
Clinton	(purplish black)
Isabella	(deep black)
Catawba	(light purplish red)

Each of these varieties is individual and easily distinguishable from the others. Experimenters in this country and in Europe continually work to produce new varieties from seedlings, hybridization and crossings. For almost two centuries, viticulturists worked to marry the European Vinifera species with the American Labrusca, out of which union the French-American Seibel grapes have been recently developed. French-American hybrids and labrusca varieties are usually more expensive than the vinifera grown elsewhere in the United States. It is interesting to note the price differential within the species grown in the Finger Lakes. The Delaware, a fine vine grape, costs about three times as much as the Concord, which is an all-purpose grape. Other grapes of the Finger Lakes Wine District are used for wines, such as Eumlan, Iona, Dutchess, Diana, Salem, Campbell's Early, the Diamond, Norton, Noah, Sheridan, Vergennes and others, but they appear in small editions.

When vintners or wine merchants speak of American Wines, they mean any wine produced in the United States. However, more specifically, the term is applied to those wines grown *east* of the Rocky Mountains, because they are made from grapes *native* to America. Furthermore, the wines grown *west* of the Rockies, i.e. California Wines, are not native since they are made from vines originally brought from Europe. Technically, however, "United States Wines" aptly describes all wines produced in the United States.

The Finger Lakes District in the upper part of New York State produce the best known of the American Wines. Made of native grapes, they have enjoyed a good reputation for the distinctive natural flavor Nature has given to these grapes.

TYPES OF AMERICAN WINES

Appetizer Wines	*White Table Wines*	*Red Table Wines*
Pale Dry Cocktail Sherry	Sauterne	Burgundy
Extra Dry Vermouth	Rhine	Claret
Sweet Vermouth		Rosé

Dessert Wines	*Sparkling Wines*	
Port	Dry Champagne	(Royal Quality)
Tawny Port	Brut Champagne	(Very dry)
Sherry	Sparkling Burgundy	(Champagne Rouge)
Cream Sherry		
White Tokay		
American Muscatel		

The first vines to be cultivated in New York were grown in 1830 in Hammondsport in the Finger Lakes District. This region enjoyed a rare combination of climate and soil well suited for the growing of wine grapes. The waters of the Finger Lakes, deep and clear, act as a thermostat on the vines. In the spring, the frigid temperatures of the lakes keep the buds dormant until the danger from the frosts has passed; and in the fall, their stored-up warmth protects the vines from the early frosts. It was in April of 1880 that Walter Taylor moved into this district, with his young bride, and bought a seven-acre vineyard near Hammondsport, on the western slopes close to Lake Keuka. He grew and shipped grapes for two years and then purchased a seventy- acre farm where he set out thirty-five acres in Delaware and Ives grapes, white and red varieties.

Soon Taylor brought his parents, George and Maria Taylor, to assist in the expanding endeavor, and the family began producing table wines, which they barreled and shipped to New York City, later adding dessert wines. From the original seven-acre vineyard in 1880, the Taylor Wine Company's vineyards grew until they now have 550 acres in grapes, and also use the harvest from 1500 adjoining acres under the guidance of their own agronomist. It is still a family enterprise, owned and operated under the management of Walter Taylor's three sons. Fred C. Taylor is President; Clarence W. Taylor is Vice President in charge of production and Greyton H. Taylor is Vice President of public relations and promotion.

The pride of the family is Bully Hill Farms, located in an area of scenic beauty, owned and operated by Greyton H. Taylor and his son, Walter S. Taylor. It includes the former family homestead and the first winery and vineyards of Walter Taylor, founder of The Taylor Wine Company. Large plantings are currently being made there of the special French Hybrid grapes that grow so well in New York's Finger Lakes wine district: White Varieties—Seibel 5279 (Aurora), Seibel 9110 and Red Varieties—Seibel 13053, Foch, Seibel 5898. The adoption of balanced-pruning and bud-counting in pruning the hybrids is of utmost importance, Mr. Taylor advised us. The internodes are much shorter than those of our native varieties and an excessive number of buds can be left on a relatively short cane if not closely counted. Spacing, length of rows, marking, soil management, line posts, end posts, trellis engineering are all subjects of importance on the Bully Hill Farms.

Harvest time extends normally from September 15th to October 20th, with each variety of grape picked separately at its peak of perfection, when its flavor and natural sugar are judged by the vineyard and winery experts to be at their maximum. I have found that no matter how European-oriented a restaurant is, there are many diners who like to taste and enjoy some native quality wines. It has become a necessary part of culinary education to be familiar with what our own country produces. Wines in the dining rooms of even excellent restaurants go unsold because of lack of proper promotion at the point of sale. We have in our cellar—aside from spirits—no less than 150 qualities of well-selected wines, and for each there is a diner desiring his own preference, or waiting for an introduction to a new and unique experience. New York columnist Robert Dana merits commendation for constantly reminding his readers about the excellence of United States wines which, he says, deserve better treatment in restaurants. Managers of banquets honoring foreign guests are likewise to be commended for featuring with each course an appropriate United States wine, thus stating the fact that this country can offer suitable wines.

I cannot overstress the matter of timing with regard to the service of wines. It is after the Captain has taken the food order, and the appetizer is served, that the precise moment arrives for the Sommelier to suggest wines—unless, of course, the host has already specified his wishes in that respect. It takes an average of some ten minutes to record a food order. The host is then anxious to give his attention to his guests. Unless the matter of wine has come up naturally, I believe it best to wait until the guests have had an opportunity to taste the first dish. After they have had a chance to comment on it, there is a natural opening to suggest wine with the main course.

Selling wine is a matter of feeling your way with delicacy. However, the Captain must be imbued with the conviction that table wine will add to the enjoyment of the food served. If he has any hesitation in believing that philosophy, he does not belong in the restaurant business at all. Perfection in a restaurant is principally that of satisfying the patron. I would go even a step further—it is a matter of anticipating his satisfaction. The service of a fine wine leads to that goal.

GLOSSARY OF WINE TERMS

(Supplied by the Taylor Wine Company
Hammondsport, New York)

Appetizer Wines

Served before meals to stimulate the appetite.

Aroma

Fragrance of wine originating from the grapes used in its production.

Some Wines of New York State

Body

Consistency or thickness of a wine.

Bouquet

Fragrance which originates from the fermentation and aging of a wine (see aroma).

Brut

Driest type of champagne.

Cuvee

An especially prepared blend of wines used in making champagne.

Dessert Wines

Still wines ranging between 15 and 20% alcohol by volume, and tending more to sweetness than other wines.

Dry

When the natural sugar of the grape has been consumed by fermentation, the wine is considered dry—the opposite of sweet.

Fruity

A frank taste of the grape found in good wine.

Generic

Wines which have similar characteristics are called by traditional or generic names such as Burgundy, Claret, Vermouth, etc. When generic names are used they are generally qualified by the wine's geographical origin.

Lees

Sediment left in vats and casks by the fermentation and storage of wine.

Must

The juice of the grape before and during fermentation.

Red Wines

Any wine that has red coloring, obtained from the pigment found in the skins of certain varieties.

Sparkling Wines

Wines which have undergone a second fermentation within closed containers. Upon opening, the natural carbon dioxide gas causes the cork to pop and the wine to effervesce.

Still Wines

Wines which go through only one fermenting process.

Table Wines

Still wines having not over 14% alcohol by volume, usually dry or less sweet than dessert wines; most often served with meals.

Varietal

A wine named for the principal grape variety used in producing it. By regulation, a varietal-named wine must consist of 51% of the grape variety whose name it bears.

Vermouth

A wine flavored with herbs and other aromatic essences. There are two kinds: dry (pale yellow in color) and sweet (dark amber in color).

Viticulture

The cultivation of the vine; grape-growing.

Wine

The naturally fermented juice of freshly-gathered ripe grapes.
    —also—

mellow

Well natured, soft, ripe.

must

Crushed grape pulp and juice for fermenting.

Premium wines

Above average in quality and price.

Ripe

A wine at maturity, at its best.

Smooth

Having no harshness of taste.

258

Some Wines of New York State

Solera
A continuous blending process, combining the finest of several years' Sherry or Port.

Sparkling wine
Made effervescent by natural fermentation within a closed bottle or container.

Special natural wines
Natural wines with natural (not synthetic) flavors added.

Tart
Having agreeable fruit acidity.

Varietal
Any wine named for its variety of grape.

Vintage
Each year's harvest of grapes and the wines therefrom.

CHAPTER

 22

Travel Molds Tastes

"To be a good traveler, argues a philosopher: A sweet landscape must sometimes atone for an indifferent supper, and an interesting ruin charm away the remembrance of a hard bed."

—HENRY THEODORE TUCKERMAN (1813-71)

"Some are found to travel with no other intent than that of understanding and collecting pictures, studying seals and describing statues; they travel from one cabinet of curiosities to that gallery of pictures; waste the prime of life in wonder; skilful in pictures; ignorant in men; yet impossible to be reclaimed, because their follies take shelter under the names of delicacy and taste."

—OLIVER GOLDSMITH (1728-74)

AN INSIGHT INTO SOME OF THE MYSTERIES OF the operation and management of restaurants may prove of interest to the dining public which, as time goes by, becomes more qualified to judge the best and to expect higher standards of restaurateurship. Perhaps at no other time have people been so aware of the culinary arts, and so receptive to further understanding which leads to greater participation and pleasure in the delights of the table. With science shrinking the earth and bringing people closer together, world cuisines previously foreign and exotic have won their adherents in America. Wide travel abroad has opened up vistas of taste to dishes and wines once known only to the fortunate few. The tendency is toward greater luxury and elegance than ever before, and the need for the knowledge of performance, operation, and familiarity with the culinary arts themselves.

Before World War I, and up to the Prohibition Era, Americans were great gourmets. After the dry period blighted the land, the heart of the great luxury hotels was crushed. Wealthy people who wanted to enjoy dining as it should be, accompanied by fine wines, had to resort to speakeasies. For a long time fine dining was retarded. An entire generation grew up with little or no knowledge of wines. Young people had to go to speakeasies, where liquor was obtainable, but the cuisine was poor and the service lacking in atmosphere because illegality cast a shadow over the legitimate pleasures of the palate. The folly of Prohibition thus set gourmetism back nearly a generation.

However, a full recovery is in the making, what with continuing prosperity and increasing travel. Although European standards have also suffered because of the war, there remain some fine establishments in England, Italy, France, Switzerland and Germany, where the culinary art is still revered. Americans are now far better informed on good wines, and eager to learn about their variety and qualities. Upon returning from Europe, they continue the wine customs to which they were so pleasantly introduced abroad.

World travel does broaden tastes in cuisine, art, clothes, and customs. At one time, certain dishes were known only to a few wealthy world travelers. Since World War II, the American public has become conversant with many gastronomic offerings of the Old World, such as the Provencal fish soup-stew called *Bouillabaisse,* with Spain's *paella,* and the cheese-and-onion pie known as *Quiche Lorraine.* Of course, in every vanguard, evils trail behind. The pizza of Italy's southland, for example, is libeled by most American imitations.

There are more cheeses now on the market, with well-known European brands available to restaurant diners. Many travelers cannot forget the delicious cheeses enjoyed abroad and hunt for little-known varieties here at home. Unfortunately, most of them are consumed locally and rarely imported to America. Yet tastes have advanced. Up until recently, most people knew only Cheddar, Swiss, and some of the processed cheeses. Only a more alert group of gourmets were familiar with Roquefort, Camembert and Bel Paese. Now these are commonplace at the Food Fairs, and more people ask for Gruyere, a sharper Swiss cheese, and for Brie and Port Salut. Taleggio, Pipo Crem' and Brie all go well with wines. Taleggio, an Italian cheese, is similar to Bel Paese but sharper. Pipo Crem' is French and half-way between Roquefort and Brie, a creamy cheese. Visitors returning from France remember Bleu de Bresse, which is not available here, though its substitute, Pipo Crem', is.

In New York there are many fine cheese stores to satisfy legitimate yearnings for a primary food which has become an Epicurean delight. Watching over the interests of the cheese industry is the Cheese Importers Association of America with headquarters at 51 Chambers Street. A unique and delightful store which calls itself Cheeses of All Nations, Inc. is located at 235 Fulton Street, this city, operated by Phil Alpert, who is inspired on his subject. This youngish man has established the Cheese of the Month Club, an idea in food distribution which has been followed by other gift-minded businesses.

This is the way it works. A donor may have sent to a fortunate recipient a different cheese each month. Mr. Alpert has also established a Gourmet Club, membership of which is open to those who answer correctly some fifteen questions on a Cheese Quiz. Random House published a book called the *Complete Book of Cheeses* authored by Bob Brown and Clifton Fadiman which was dedicated in appreciation to Mr. Alpert for his valiant efforts in behalf of disseminating knowledge of the beloved cheese.

The store maintains a fine Cheese Cellar at 295 Greenwich Street which is a library of known and rare specimens from every country. It can be visited by special arrangement and Mr. Alpert told us enthusiastically that his company is at the present time negotiating with the Department of Parks to secure some old caves which have been discovered near the Manhattan side of the Brooklyn Bridge, once used in colonial times for the storage of wines and rums as a natural cellar. Every cheese connoisseur should be aware of Cheeses of All Nations which publishes a comprehensive catalogue and is most worthy of a personal visit.

Airplanes have taken precedence over ships for transatlantic crossings in the past ten years. The easy-going traditions of the luxury liners, with their own travel rituals, were indoctrination grounds where passengers became acquainted with the cuisines of France, Italy, Germany, Scandinavia, etc. In August of 1960, at Idlewild Airport, an average of 30,000 persons from overseas arrived daily, and a similar number went abroad. Their journeys emphasize speed, efficiency and detachment. Viewing this attitude, one wonders if the trans-Atlantic liner may soon be thought of only as a way of life for the few who have treasured leisure. A quick drink at the airport bar substitutes for the bon voyage champagne party at which one can show off a beautiful suite on board a luxury liner; light luggage replaces the steamer trunk filled with its formal party clothes, baskets of fruit and bouquets of flowers are replaced by a corsage.

It is certainly tempting to substitute the quick processing of customs at Idlewild for the tiresome waiting on the piers where passengers huddle in alphabetical groups for the maddeningly slow inspection which takes the glow off the trip. In 1959, 212 customs officials handled the baggage of almost a hundred thousand air passengers. The chief incentive is speed. People are interested in getting to their destination quickly, and with a minimum of discomfort. The jet age is here. However, some elegants will never accept it. Sanche de Gramont, writing for the *Herald Tribune* (August 22, 1960) tells of an elderly gentleman from Montevideo, Uruguay, who said he flew only out of sheer necessity. "I hate planes," he said. "I would rather spend six months on a ship than eighteen hours on a plane." He said a plane was nothing more than a "luxury bus that flies." He described his trip from Montevideo aboard a Transcontinental flight very graphically: "I was herded into a waiting room. I was put on the plane like a sardine in a can. I was fed all day long like a baby. I couldn't sleep. And I couldn't smell the sea. I like the smell of the sea. I like the roll of the sea. In a plane, you don't realize you're moving, and all you can see are clouds."

It is impossible to prognosticate how this swift locomotion among the stars will affect the culinary arts. The fact remains, however, that increasing knowledge of other lands is being made available to vast numbers, and many of them will not be immune to the grace and

263

charm of foreign inns, cafés, restaurants, pensions and hotels. They will come back with epicurean tastes for excellent cuisines. And gradually, I believe, American purveyors will provide them with the best in food and drink for their gustatory delight. The air lines are not backward in supplying passengers the best in food and drink available when airborne.

Aboard Air France jetliners, authentic French cuisine reaches a high in elegance along the milky way. Perfection begins on the ground at the airline's own kitchens where scores of recipes are tested and re-tested. Final selections such as *le paté de faisan en croute* (Paté of pheasant) and other courses are then grouped according to seven distinct regions of France for preparation at Air France's kitchens throughout the world. For example, on the *Epicurean of the Atlantic,* the seven hour flight from New York to Paris, course by course service with Limoges porcelain, Baccarat crystal, and Cristofle silver becomes a 1600-mile Lucullan repast, with regional wines of excellent quality correctly served. Every year, the world's largest airline prepares nearly a million meals with French chefs' meticulous attention to detail, attaining perfection for in-flight service in the grand manner, which is truly luxurious.

CHAPTER

23

Wine in a Changing World

By Frank Schoonmaker

"*My manner of living is plain: a glass of wine and a bit of mutton are always ready, and such as are content to partake of that are always welcome.*"
—George Washington (1732-1799)

The title of this chapter indicates an *awareness on the part of wine authorities that wine drinking is affected by economic and social changes. With the permission of its author, Frank Schoonmaker, editor of* News from the Vineyards, *as well as that of Mr. Louis A. Benoist, President of Almadén Vineyards, Los Gatos, California, which issues the interesting little quarterly, we are including Mr. Schoonmaker's informative and entertaining comments:*

"Twenty-odd short years ago, which hardly amounts to a ripple in the long history of wine, worldly travelers on crack trains—the Twentieth Century Limited, the Super-Chief, the Simplon Orient Express —could sip their Riesling or their Claret while rolling dizzily along at fifty or even sixty miles an hour. And there were a few resorts in the Swiss Alps and possibly in the Andes and the Rockies, where a man could drink a bottle of Champagne at seven or eight thousand feet above sea level.

"This year, in 1960, travelers will be served over a quarter of a mil-

265

lion bottles of Almadén wine at altitudes higher than Mount Everest and at speeds in excess of nine miles a minute. You can drink Burgundy with your lunch in Paris, and dine, the same day, with California wine in San Francisco.

"Wine and wine-drinking, one would have thought, were of all things, among the least subject to rapid change. The vineyards the Romans first planted, in Italy and Germany and France, are still producing wine after eighteen hundred years, and in the popular mind, at least, good wine has long been associated with venerable, dusty bottles and ancient cobwebbed cellars—'old wine, old friends.'

"But in the matter of wine-drinking, as in practically all other fields, the past twenty years have produced something almost in the nature of a revolution. This is not true in America alone, but the world over, and the most striking thing, perhaps, is the trend toward younger wine. In the great restaurants of France you will still find listed the Chateau Lafite of 1900, 1869 and even 1806; alongside these noble veterans, and gay and fresh and attractive, come the Chablis and the Rieslings, the Beaujolais and the *vins rosés* of 1959, brought cheerfully to table when less than a year old. Most of the superb German Rhine wines of 1959 were safely in bottle by the time they had reached the age of eight months, and by now many of them have already been consumed and enjoyed.

"Naturally, not all wines can be brought along so rapidly—the great red Bordeaux and California Cabernets, the sturdier French Burgundies and Pinot Noirs from the North Coast Counties, these require time. But even these are made quite differently today from the way they were at the turn of the Century, and they are ready to drink in a matter of a few years, not a few decades.

"Tastes, on the whole, have changed in wine just as they have in food: we no longer serve seven-course dinners with five different wines; our meals are lighter and we like our wines that way; we eat more fruit, the year round, and we prefer fruity wines; our desserts are less elaborate, and the drier table wines are increasingly the more popular. Naturally, wine makers in California, just as in Europe, have gone along with the trend.

"One of the first straws in the wind, twenty years ago, was a sudden interest in and enthusiasm for *vin rosé*. Almadén produced this country's first rosé, almost exactly two decades ago—which was a success from the start, and Americans are now drinking about a million bottles of Almadén Grenache Rosé a year—this is just about as much as the whole Tavel district produces (also from the Grenache grape) in France.

"Purists and traditionalists have a way of looking down at *vin rosé*, saying that 'rosé is never a great wine.' Of course, they are right and we agree, and what of it? But how many people, except on some very special occasion, want to be faced with a 'great wine' when they sit down to luncheon or dinner? Far less than 1% of the world's wine could conceivably be called 'great'; most Frenchmen have rarely if ever tasted a 'great wine'; and *no* connoisseur and *no* expert would want to drink such a wine every day. Meanwhile *rosé* is pleasant and easy, fun to drink and not too expensive. We never claimed more for it and we never will.

"When Almadén *rosé* first came on the market, many wine-drinking people accustomed to the idea that wines were either red or white, looked at it a little suspiciously, as if we had produced some sort of freak, or made a blend of white and red. By now almost everybody is aware that all good *vins rosé*, whatever their country of origin, belong in a special category and are made in a special way, from black grapes which (like almost all black grapes) have white juice and their pigment in their skin.

"Pressed as soon as picked, they would yield white wine; fully fermented with their skins, they give red, and all red wines are so made. In between the two there is a sort of limbo, and if you draw the wine off at precisely the right moment, leaving the skins behind, you get something pink in color, somewhere between the tint of what our grandfathers called 'partridge eye,' and that of a nectarine, a strawberry, or a rose. The wine remains this color throughout its short life, and, quite frankly, it is as good when six months old as it ever will be. A *vin rosé* at the age of three years (whether it comes from California or France or elsewhere) is already past its prime—it has 'withered,' lost its freshness and fragrance and charm, like the roses from which it takes its name; at Almadén we bottle and ship it as soon as it is ready, and it comes to you, engaging and sprightly and appetizing, in the flower of its youth.

"Some ten years ago, a sensationally good new sort of winepress, the Willmes, was invented in Germany and soon began to replace the old hydraulic presses in the best cellars abroad: Almadén had the first Willmes press in California.

"When Prohibition ended, twenty-five years ago, fermentation—by which grape juice becomes wine—was a hit-or-miss matter of Nature and good luck in those days; today we know, from laboratory experience, the precise temperature at which our yeast cultures do their most effective work, and our wines are fermented at that temperature. Our wine storage cellars are air-conditioned, that for red wines at 60° and that for white to 55°, the optimum in both cases. Our young wines are watched over as carefully as babies in a modern hospital: we know their qualities, their deficiencies, and their requirements almost from the day they are born, and through frequent analyses and comparative tastings, we follow their evolution, until the day they are shipped.

"The really significant point is that this is not just an example of American efficiency, but part of modern, worldwide progress. No little Burgundian producer, today, would bottle his wine before asking the advice of the government laboratory in Beaune: he works, in his small artisan's way, as nearly as he can as we do. All of us are making better wine than we did, with far fewer spoilages and failures, and this is the consumer's gain.

"On the other hand, those of us who have known wine and loved it for most of our life, cannot help feeling a certain regret and nostalgia at the disappearance of so many things that were picturesque, and apparently permanent, and old. Near San Francisco, in San Mateo County and to an increasing extent in Santa Clara and in Livermore as well, many of the famous old vineyards have disappeared, replaced by shopping centers and subdivisions; but in Bordeaux, too, Chateau Haut-Brion and La Mission-Haut-Brion, are both surrounded and besieged by suburban villas. Even at Schloss Johannisberg, shiny, glass-lined, metal tanks are replacing the polished old oak Fässer—the wine will doubtless be better, but the great vaulted cellar will never look the same.

Wine in a Changing World

"It is easy to forget that such changes, perhaps less rapid but equally farreaching, have often taken place before. In the years before the Civil War, Americans drank more Bordeaux wine than they do today, and our leading domestic vineyards were on the banks of the Ohio River, near Cincinnati; then came the Trans-Continental railway, cheaper and better wine from California, and the end of the era. In France the vineyard acreage in Burgundy declined by 50% (this in marginal vineyards, to be sure) almost as soon as there was a rail line from Marseilles to Paris, and the far cheaper Midi wines could be shipped for a reasonable price up to the populous north.

"Madeira was a great American favorite in colonial days and during the first decades of the Republic—this was because the clipper ships, taking the trade wind route on their way back from Europe, found Madeira a convenient stop for supplies and water and (once there) for wine. What really matters in all this is that the wine is better, that the vineyards eliminated are those which are less good (this alas! is not invariably the case) and that a real respect for traditions and high standards be preserved."

A wine bottled at six months, eight months or a year should preferably be consumed in the locality of its birth within the first year, or if it lasts, within the second year of its life. As for export, it is a matter of chance. If it survives traveling, it can maintain its fragrance and bouquet for a year or two. Mr. Schoonmaker's comments on the trend toward young wines, which he correctly terms "something almost in the nature of a revolution" recall the traditions of the Europeans in regard to the aging of wines. My father, who was a very meticulous vintner, followed the traditions of his forebears and as his son I, too, was reared with these traditions:

A wine was never bottled until it was two years old. In the beginning, it was moved from one vat to another every month for six months. Thereafter it was moved every two months until bottled. In this way it was so purified it could stand being exported by land or sea any distance and could maintain its vitality. If kept at the right temperature, a wine prepared in such a traditional manner could remain healthy for many years. Such a wine as I describe was shipped by my father to his family of children who lived in New York in the year 1910. They were all enjoyed years ago. However, my brother Gene Robotti still has a few bottles left of the 1910 shipment. Lacking a wine cellar, he keeps his precious store in the closet of his suburban apartment and brings it forth for great occasions, such as the marriage of his daughter or the arrival of his grandsons.

CHAPTER

 24

The Changing Face of New York

*"If great change is to be made in human affairs, the
minds of men will be fitted to it; the general opinions
and feelings will draw that way. Every fear and hope
will forward it; and they who persist in opposing this
mighty current will appear rather to resist the decrees
of Providence itself, than the mere designs of men."*
—EDMUND BURKE (1729-1797)

NEW YORK CITY HAS BEEN PERPETUALLY SUB-
jected to demolition and reconstruction since the Americans in 1783
retook the town from the British. For the past decade or so there has
been a positive mania in Manhattan for erecting new office buildings
and multiple apartment houses. In this shifting landscape, a noteworthy development has been the movement of long-established restaurants to other locations, and the appearance of new ones under the
direction of experienced hosts, well-known and well thought of because of their previous connections. There is space here to trace only
a few of the migrations of hosts from old to new places.

The smart Harwyn Club was, for one, manned by defectors from
the imperial Stork Club. Some even defected from the Harwyn to still
newer pastures. And there is, for instance, Maurice D'Eufemia. This
handsome host began his career as a doorman at the swank Fefe's
Monte Carlo, progressed in gradual stages to higher ranks at the Stork
Club and the Harwyn, and finally graduated to ownership and management of his own restaurant on Second Avenue in the Fifties. He

calls it after himself—Maurice. The migratory trend extends to kitchens. Chef Fernand Desbans of Maurice was previously long in charge of Maud Chez Elle.

Another important facet of the hotel and restaurant world is that of interior design. The decorator often mentioned in this connection in New York City is Russell Patterson. The white-maned Patterson decorated Maurice's place with the extraordinary, extravagantly untraditional flair he has used for dozens of smart New York dining places. At Maurice's, for instance, he used black velvet walls for the main dining room with white and red satin overdrapes. It was designed to startle people. For the ceiling, he applied black satin with red satin surrounding the candelabra. Only Patterson would dare to use such a free hand. In another room, he directed the painting of a Paris mural on white satin walls, and complemented it with a ceiling of pale candy-stripe blue and white.

Speaking of designers, Norman Bel Geddes, who died at a premature sixty-one, left many memorials to his talents. An industrial and theatrical designer, Mr. Bel Geddes was as well a writer, producer, inventor, and the father of the noted actress Barbara Bel Geddes. He is known chiefly for his design of the beautiful Roxy Theater, recently demolished, the Ukrainian State Opera House in Kharkov, Russia, and for the Futurama exhibit at the 1938 World's Fair in Flushing Meadows. Bel Geddes pioneered in the design of the streamlined automobile, ocean liners, and airplane interiors. It will be long before the name of Norman Bel Geddes fades from the New York scene, which he did so much to change. Certainly he was deserving of publication by Doubleday who produced his biography, "Miracle of the Evening."

Mr. Bel Geddes designed the restaurant known as *The Playbill* for the Hotel Manhattan at Eighth Avenue and Forty-fourth Street. This was apropos, as Bel Geddes had produced and directed many Broadway plays, for which he designed scenery, costumes and lighting, and the restaurant was suitably inspired by the theater magazine of the same name.

New buildings and new restaurants need the creative imagination of decorators. Expansion is a golden era for those upon whom rests the responsibility of creating lasting and pleasing effects, yet utilitarian enough to suit the standards of the hotel and restaurant industry. While there are many fine decorators, some are outstanding. Shaw and Draper, Inc. A.I.D., N.S.I.D. of New York (Otho Shaw, who is skillful, and Dede Draper, (Mrs. Richard Draper) who is inspired) add elegance to lobbies, apartments, and restaurants, too. In a traditional spirit, they successfully recreated, at Le Chateau Richelieu, the seventeenth century consultation room of the Cardinal de Richelieu of the Palais Royale of Paris, regally applying to the walls a red silk damask by Scalamandré of a two-hundred-year-old Italian design, relieved by golden sconces, a royal red carpet, and other suitable accoutrements. It is said to be one of their masterpieces.

New York City itself is becoming a glistening metropolis. Thomas Wolfe loved this town and called it "a magnificent jewel in its fit setting of sea, earth and stars." Many others did not agree with him. Once known as the most unkempt of cities, it has buckled down to better housekeeping, provides waste receptacles along the streets with the invitation devised by the public relations department of the City— "Cast your ballot for a clean city here"—and sanded public ash-trays on Madison Avenue and elsewhere. It has belatedly recognized the problem of air pollution and, since the Fusion days of the late Mayor Fiorello La Guardia, its odors have been less distressing. The Little Flower's administration erected four modern sewage disposal plants and drew plans on the basis of New York's estimated 1970 population for complete disposal through thirty-two plants at a cost of $170 million or more.

Under the aegis of Robert Moses, the Department of Parks, in conjunction with the Department of Commerce, has landscaped some of the streets. Ponderous cement pots planted with shrubbery and flowers give Fifth Avenue (and some side streets, too) a festive look, not only for the "New York is a Summer Festival" months, but all the year round. These and other improvements make the city more desirable as a place to live, to work, and to entertain the constant stream of visitors from out of town. The hotels and restaurants, for their part, renew and expand to keep pace with the demands made upon them.

While, in themselves, the avenues and streets remain permanent,

273

they are subject to changes in the neighborhood and the type of structures built upon them. The Sixth Avenue El—with all of its Victorian memories—has long since been removed. While the West Side has been, as a matter of course, considered outside the social perimeter, the appearance of some fine buildings promises a brighter future. The new Time and Life Building, opposite Radio City's Music Hall, with plaza and playful fountains, has brought a touch of elegance to the section. While some may consider as a silly conceit of the Fusionists the name "Avenue of the Americas," this has the sincere support of the Avenue of the Americas Association which has installed handsome plaques from the street-light poles from Fifty-ninth Street to Canal Street, bearing the shields of the United States, its twenty sister American republics and Canada at a cost of $100 each.

After the Ninth Avenue overhead line was demolished, there still remained 350 miles of elevated track to scatter dirt and obscure the view, until the Second and Third Avenue structures were taken down. This quickly brought a renaissance to the forgotten avenues of the East Side. Sidewalks were repaired, trees planted, and new restaurants cautiously opened along First, Second and Third Avenues to accommodate the tenants of new apartment houses. The dispossessed from Park Avenue now are taking over the numbered avenues all the way to the East River, and smart diners are seen in those local restaurants. Nevertheless, the "name" restaurants remain a social necessity. The dividing line for most is Fifth Avenue. With the exception of the "21" Club, and a few other landmarks, society remains on the East Side and seldom crosses the Avenue to dine. Restaurants nestle along the mid-town side streets from the Hudson River to the East River, but those East of Fifth Avenue are considered the most socially acceptable.

Once upon a time Madison Avenue was the pride of homeowners, and the location of many little specialty shops which still remain ensconced along Ad Alley, realm of the taste shapers, the Men in the Grey Flannel Suits. Well over a century ago this avenue was first opened to traffic. Extending from Twenty-third to One Hundred and Thirty-eighth Street, it was named for ex-President James Madison, who died in retirement that year. Like Lexington Avenue, Madison had not been provided for in the original City Plan of 1811 which checkerboarded Manhattan by removing hills, dales, trees, and filling in brooks and streams. When the Street Commissioners planned the original system of numbered streets and avenues, they expected that this scheme would greatly increase the East-West traffic. However, by 1833, it was apparent that the existing North and South thoroughfares were not sufficient, so in 1836 two new avenues—Madison and Lexington—were opened.

While the development of Madison Avenue was slow, there was an early tendency for the specialty shops to cluster in mid-town. In 1845, one could still pick blackberries at the present corner of Thirty-fifth Street. The section was enhanced in 1857 when Columbia College moved from its original downtown site at Park Place, where it began as King's College, to Madison Avenue between Forty-ninth and Fiftieth Streets, and touching Park Avenue, where it remained for the following forty years. A plaque on the New Weston Hotel tells about it. The Hotel's pleasant custom of serving afternoon tea, with light refreshments in the London manner, makes the New Weston perhaps the most English spot in the city, perpetuating the bond of the once English College originally known as King's College, with its present occupant of the site.

Park Avenue—to become in time the most glamorous street in the world—had the customary humble beginning. It seems its first settler was an adventurous man named Jacob Kipp, who left New Harlem in Holland in 1653. He settled in the present section of Thirty-fifth Street, where he built a fine house, and cultivated vegetable and flower gardens on his estate, which extended to the bank of the East River. Now Kip's Bay recalls this pioneering Dutchman, who brought with him much of the gaiety, love for good food, good company, the dancing and singing of his countryman to Manhattan. He was in occupancy half a century before a regular road connected the northern villages, where his house was, with the tip of Manhattan, which was then the center of the town.

Travel was slow. A monthly coach, which covered the distance from New York to Boston in two weeks, was introduced in 1732. The route taken was the Boston Post Road. It crossed the present Park Avenue at about Eightieth Street through pleasantly rural scenery. Along about Fiftieth Street, there was a bridge over a brook where it was customary for an escort to pause with slacked reins and salute his fair partner. For many years early New Yorkers used this Kissing Bridge.

It was the coming of the railroad which was the decisive factor in evolving Park Avenue into a route of importance. In 1832, when the Harlem Railroad laid tracks at Murray Hill, it was still three miles out of town. Until 1860, only a few factories and breweries stood along the first city railroad, which connected New York with Harlem. For decades the area was a sprawling maze of railroad tracks and shanties. Only one major building dominated the section. This was the piano factory of Steinway and Sons, erected alongside the tracks in 1858, one block south of the new National City Bank and facing the Plaza of Seagram House.

Another railroad was the true starting point of civic development. This was the work of Commodore Cornelius Vanderbilt I, who must be mentioned in any reminiscence of Park Avenue as he was its true architect. The founder of the richest of social families in the United States was born in 1794 on Staten Island to a Dutch farmer and ferryman who spelled his name Van Der Bilt, and his wife Phebe Hand, a daughter of a New Jersey farmer. The Van Der Bilts were miserably poor squatters who came here in the seventeenth century to wrest a living through four generations, from a stony and sandy soil. Cornelius' mother kept a dairy and garden and was a leader of her Staten Island circle, attending all weddings and funerals. She lived to a ripe old age without ever leaving her farm house. Cornelius was her favorite child, yet none of his persuasions to move to better quarters were effective. She followed his soaring career with interest, however, and in 1853 had the unusual honor of being saluted with rockets and guns as her devoted son passed Staten Island in his palatial yacht, the *North Star,* on a European cruise.

To this day, all of the Vanderbilts return to rest in the Valhalla of Staten Island where their ancestors are entombed. The Commodore still reigns over the railroad he founded, for as you approach Grand Central Station by car from the South, toward Forty-second Street, you see his bronze statue. He is bearded and wears a high-collared fur-lined overcoat. Every inch the mighty tycoon, he built a family fortune on the strength of two maxims: "Never tell nobody what yer goin' to do, till you do it," and "Don't you never buy anything you don't want nor sell anything you hain't got." Secretive, aggressive, hot-tempered, and the most fluent master of profanity of his generation, Vanderbilt (who was not too scrupulous in his business dealings) was loyal to those he liked. At the time of the Gold Conspiracy in 1869, a Wall Street broker said begrudgingly, "The old rat never forgets his friends.'

In 1871, the Commodore (a title he won by popular acclamation) incorporated the railroad of the Harlem Line into his rapidly expanding New York Central. The following year, a major face-lifting began. The tracks were sunk a little lower into the ground, and streets were bridged across the tracks. Then New Yorkers began to build homes on stilts, tall metal and wooden piles sunk down alongside the railroad bed.

At this time, among the rocks of the present Central Park, there lived about 5,000 squatters who busily searched the waste piles along the avenue and collected fuel from the ashdumps of the railroad. They lived mainly on the sale of goat milk, which they distributed on regular routes along Park Avenue. In 1888, the railroad bed was sunk lower but the residents were still nearly asphyxiated by the clouds of grimy smoke from the coal-fed locomotives. By this time, it had become a middle class neighborhood of brownstone homes.

The name Park Avenue was applied in 1888, although there was much progress to make before deserving it. Its true success began ironically in tragedy. One January day in 1902, an engineer who was blinded temporarily by the smog of the switchyard, crashed his engine into a parked commuter train. Seventeen people were killed. This was the baptism of sacrificial blood which launched the avenue. As a consequence, the State Legislature banned coal-burners from the city and, by 1907, electrification was complete. The roadbed no longer needed open air for its smoking locomotives, so the covering-over began.

The road is neither a street nor an avenue but an artificial bridge which still covers the railroad tracks of the New York Central Railroad, an area which is now planted in greenery and flowers for its entire length. After the roadbed was enclosed, the avenue was invaded by socialites such as the Beekmans, Whitneys and Livingstons, who made their homes there for half a century. To serve them were the elegant Voison, Sherry's and the Marguery, while uniformed doormen in the garb of Royal Hungarian Hussars held open the door for the elite coming for cocktails at Delmonico's.

The Park Avenue Association, of which Mr. Edward B. Lockwood is President, is the civic organization responsible, since 1922, for the planting of shrubs for a pleasing vista, and, in 1944, for the planting of the Christmas trees as a memorial to the war dead. Mr. Lockwood concedes that commerce has practically displaced residences between Forty-sixth and Fifty-ninth Streets, but feels the press places too much emphasis on this segment of Park Avenue. He points out logically that the glamorous avenue is far from abandoned, as the journalists would have one believe, that, indeed, between Fifty-eighth and Ninety-sixth Streets there are 115 apartment buildings of which 71 are cooperatively owned. Many prominent people call Park Avenue home, with the Angier Biddle Dukes at 740, Senator and Mrs. Herbert Lehman at 820, Princess Helena Gourielli (Helena Rubinstein) occupying a 26 room triplex at 625, and Mr. and Mrs. Thomas Stilwell Lamont at 765. A cooperative apartment in the Seventies brings $155,000 for a penthouse of 9 rooms, 4 baths and $105,000 for a 4 master bedroom apartment with library, 3 maids' rooms, handsome fireplace, and three planted terraces.

There is no doubt about it: Park Avenue was once to New York what the Place Vendome is to Paris and the Grand Canal to Venice. Chinchilla, mink, French poodles, Russian greyhounds, high hats and canes, Ivy Leaguers gave the avenue the tone suitable to Hearsts, Rockefellers, entrenched wealth, and members of the Princeton, Union, and Racquet and Tennis Clubs. Five thousand of the nation's richest once lived there in duplexes, triplexes, and penthouses, giving the Midas touch to that Golden Mile between Grand Central Terminal and Fifty-ninth Street. Some still live in the few remaining apartments, and others in the Ritz Towers. But most have moved to greener pastures in Westchester and on Long Island and some to Third, Second and First Avenues in the newly built apartment houses.

More than any other street, Park Avenue, until its present commercial character was assumed, was a symbol of metropolitanism. Its residents all had the common denominator of luxurious living. They were the ones who gave the New York scene its glossy patina: young businessmen with good incomes, pretty wives and healthy children, paying extravagant prices for living in the metropolis, and without gaining any prestige in the community. Twenty years ago, this sophistication could be managed on $15,000 to $20,000 a year, but not today. Now most families of this class have shifted to the suburbs. The executive either commutes or becomes a businessman in suburbia. Actually, an evening out for this man and his wife can better be afforded than those who insist on living right in town. Here, too, another phenomenon is to be noted. The trend to suburban living has brought the mountain to Mohammed, for the suburbs have developed their own restaurants and night clubs.

The problem resolves itself into just how strong is the compulsion to live in Manhattan, divided by Fifth Avenue and Central Park. Many West Siders are as well off as East Siders, whose incomes may be higher, for the West Siders are not as concerned with fashionable living. Central Park West is the symbol of city-born West Siders, some wealthy, a few social, but on the whole caring less for swank than for solid comfort. They are New York-wise and home-loving. In that area live the smart lady buyers, writers, painters, and stars of music and the theater. On the West, rather than on the East Side, is the good homemaker's castle. Occasionally some wander over to the Park Avenue area of fine restaurants, but they are too provincial to appreciate the aplomb and éclat, and too wallet conscious to enjoy spending lavishly for the purchase of true elegance.

In addition to out-of-towners and the suburbanites, New York's entertainment and dining industries depend upon the Metropolitanites rather than the average city dwellers. The latter might as well live in Detroit, Philadelphia or Chicago, and are in the vast majority. They reside in obscure places around Manhattan and are violently upset when forced to move out by the bulldozers. Though some are leisured and well-to-do, this class lives within the horizons of its neighborhood eateries and smaller restaurants. Upon rare occasion, they may take in a Broadway show and select a downtown restaurant.

On the other hand, the Metropolitanites, either native-born New Yorkers or adopted, are continually excited by the size and complexity of the fabulous city. They get around to all parts of Manhattan, and are pleased when mentioned by the columnists. They may be intellectual and frequent museums, shops, foreign movie houses, concerts, sometimes the fine restaurants. Their horizons are unlimited, and they are alive to the invisible and unexpected. They realize that the resources and possibilities of New York are far too great for any one individual to comprehend.

Park Avenue was once a state of mind rather than a swank address, for the side streets with their shade trees and shrubbery are smarter, and the apartments overlooking the East River more pleasant. For many years, this avenue with the electrified trains speeding through its bowels has been the spine of residential metropolitanism. It symbolized for many the whole smart East Side with its truly wealthy and nearly rich, its plush restaurants, shops displaying perfumes, furs and diamonds, fashionable physicians, the clubs, and the strolling debutantes. The only avenue in the world to have a magazine, the *Park Avenue Social Review* ably presents a colorful panorama of elegance, wealth and luxuriousness unequalled by any other city in the world.

A major revolution erupted in the middle 1950's as corporate giants invaded this urban residential paradise, usurping space between marble-faced apartment houses with their elegant canopies. One by one they disappeared, falling under the bulldozers and dynamiters. The tenants of the Marguery went to court time after time in a vain attempt to save their homes, but each and every one was relentlessly ousted. The Marguery Hotel (across and just south of the Waldorf-Astoria) was replaced by the 52-story stainless steel and glass skyscraper of the Union Carbide Corporation. Sherry's, too, is gone. The Pepsi-Cola building has raised a modern monolith to thirst. Lever Brothers hold court in their glass tower, as do Colgate-Palmolive, Aramco Oil, and Universal Pictures, all of whom have built national headquarters, each with an identifying tower defying the skies.

280

The Changing Face of New York

At 375 Park Avenue, between Fifty-second and Fifty-third Streets, rises the imposing House of Seagram building, a 38-story bronze-cased tower, the first to use this metal. While corporations are not reputed to have souls, the men who run them often strive to give them a prestige which goes beyond mere commercialism. This has given rise in our times to a category of architecture which may be called the showpiece office building, an enlargement of the idea of the showplace executive office. The Seagram building, a monument to the demise of Prohibition, cost over $35,000,000. Set back on a twin-fountained, granite and marble plaza which serves as its pedestal, it is said to be the definitive statement of what a skyscraper can be, by the architect whom most purists hail as the master of glass-and-steel design. German-born Ludwig Mies Van der Rohe of Chicago, now in his seventies, received this opportunity through a young woman, Mrs. Phyllis Bronfman Lambert, daughter of Seagram President Samuel Bronfman, who instituted the search for an architect. Mies van der Rohe used the maximum of economy with deceptive simplicity, meeting zoning laws with the plaza, and it became his strongest work. Corporations seeking social status on Park Avenue are presently restricted by the city's zoning laws to the area south of Fifty-ninth Street, thus preserving the old spirit of the avenue as a residential area in the stretches beyond.

Adjacent to the Seagram building on the North, from Fifty-third Street to Fifty-fourth Street, was to be erected a fabulous Astor Plaza to challenge Rockefeller Center with a labyrinth of stores, restaurants, fountains, sunken gardens. It was envisioned by Vincent Astor, the fifth lineal descendant of John Jacob Astor (who landed at the Battery in 1784 with five golden guineas and some musical instruments to become in time the "Landlord of New York") as the ultimate achievement of the landed tradition of the family. The 42-story office center alone would have cost some $50 million. However, the plans died in the borning with the death of the sponsor, and the site was taken over by the First National City Bank.

Many will regret the old days of the Magic Mile where a few landmarks like the Waldorf-Astoria and the Church of St. Bartholomew still remain unperturbed in their traditions. The famous Ritz, where the smart set supped and danced all night, is now the site of a bank topped by 25 floors of business offices. New York's changeability has always been part of her alluring excitement. The sound of the pneumatic drill is her theme song.

Fifth Avenue, which runs straight up through the middle of Manhattan, became the residence of some of America's richest and most powerful people during the period of the city's greatest expansion from the Civil War to the great Depression of the Thirties. With some exceptions, the prominent families of New York gravitated to this avenue, the city's most glamorous thoroughfare. The J. P. Morgan residence was on Murray Hill, bounded by Madison Avenue and Thirty-sixth and Thirty-seventh Streets. Others, however, were not enticed. The George F. Bakers did not live there, nor did the Rockefellers.

Every city or town has a street or a district in which it is accounted a special privilege to reside. In the idiom of our own times, it is the "status street," and Fifth Avenue was once such an address. In London, it has always been Belgrave Square. In Paris there is the Boulevard St. Germain. In Baltimore, it is Charles Street. In Spokane, Washington, there is Rockwood Boulevard, and in St. Louis it is Lindell Boulevard. At one time the aristocrats of Philadelphia gravitated to Rittenhouse Square and upper Walnut Street, while the wealthy on the Pacific Coast took over Nob Hill in San Francisco.

The evolution of Fifth Avenue paralleled that of New York's first families. In the 1860's, the lower Avenue from Washington Square to Twelfth Street was occupied by the Rhinelanders, Delanos, the de Rhams, the Schermerhorns. In the 1870's, came the parvenus, the new railroad barons, Vanderbilts, Goulds, then the steel tycoons, Frick and Carnegie. By the time of World War I, the limits northward for residences were about what they are now. The mansions, chateaus and palaces stretched from Fifty-ninth to Ninety-fourth Street along the east side of Central Park. During the Twenties came the final invasion of the unpedigreed as bull-market operators, such as Charles E. Mitchell, shouldered their way in among the financial giants.

It is said that never in the history of the world, which has known many a Croesus, has so much private wealth been concentrated in a single street. Not one king, but dozens ruled there in splendor, vying for social position and power, the accumulation of art treasures, and the consumption of tremendous meals from kitchens large enough to service a hotel. Like new brash wine, their lives and houses symbolized the social growth of a particular vintage, the unregenerated money-makers of the late nineteenth and early twentieth centuries. To be "On the Avenue" was the symbol of success in a land of unlimited opportunity. Flemish tapestries covered great walls up to the high ceilings. Ballrooms for private parties could accommodate five hundred dancers. Marble bathrooms were fit for a Roman emperor. Homes were staffed by a score of servants attired in extravagant livery. Butlers and footmen received guests in immense foyers, and wide marble stairways led to music rooms dominated by large crystal chandeliers and massive plush chairs.

By 1939, of the seventy-two private houses left standing on Fifth Avenue, thirty-three were closed. Today almost all have been either razed, closed, or converted to public use. Influential families have moved to lavish apartments. Among the last to maintain homes on the Avenue were Bernard Baruch, Gordon Rentschler, Edward S. Harkness, Joseph Feder, James W. Gerard, and Mrs. Harry Payne Whitney. The turning point in the collapse of Fifth Avenue as a residential section was increasing taxes. Twenty years ago, the Vanderbilt mansion on Fifty-first Street on Fifth Avenue was assessed at $2,450,-000, and the tax bill for Mrs. Cornelius Vanderbilt was $197 a day. It remained vacant for a long time before it was demolished. Finally federal and state income taxes made the real estate tax insupportable.

A small Fifth Avenue mansion, in 1940, had to have a staff of ten servants—butler, chef, valet, lady's maid, footman, parlormaid, chambermaid, two kitchenmaids and a laundress. Today the payroll would total some $30,000 a year, while $14,000 sufficed then. A householder could feed such a staff on $80 a week, but to outfit the butler and footman cost $600 a year. Maintenance and repairs ran up to a minimum of $30,000 annually. So that is how it came about that the wealthy abdicated their thrones and their kingdoms and have bought smaller brownstones on the side streets where they can still live luxuriously. Meanwhile, they have relinquished the Avenue to the apartment dwellers and the merchandisers.

In 1907 the Fifth Avenue Association was founded by a group of merchants dedicated to making this thoroughfare the mecca of shoppers. This they achieved beyond the founders' dreams. In September of 1957 the golden anniversary of the association was marked with Grover Whalen as spokesman. In the words of the brilliant columnist for the *New York Journal-American,* Phyllis Batelle, Mr. Whalen was bristling with animation from his white-tipped moustache up as he declared: "She's a great old street." Then seventy-one, Grover Whalen, called "Mr. New York" and identifiable at all public rallies and parades by a lapel carnation, and the fact that he's squarely in the middle of the crowd running things, was chairman of the celebration.

"It will begin with a torchlight parade up Fifth Avenue on Thursday night, October 19th," he announced "that should be the most colorful spectacle since Charles Lindbergh came home. Then for a week, we'll have unusual events. The Sanitation Department will show us how they cleaned the streets fifty years ago and the Transit Commission will show its progress since the first Fifth Avenue bus." It all transpired as he predicted, with prizes awarded for the best store window exhibits, the New York Public Library having a reminiscences display, and a great ball and pageant at the Waldorf-Astoria. Rockefeller Center's famed channel gardens grew golden chrysanthemums for this golden anniversary. For fifty years, Grover Whalen was associated with the parades and problems of the Avenue. In 1907 it was a relatively short, fine residential street, with the merchants beginning to move in. Very little now bears resemblance to the Fifth Avenue of Mr. New York's own youth.

The architect who perhaps did more than any other to save some of the old mansions from oblivion was the late James E. Casale. He transformed into apartment houses the French chateaux, Italian palaces, baronial manor houses, and various villas which once were the requisite of social standing. Some became museums and educational institutions while others were tenanted by the consulates of foreign governments. Mr. Casale converted the somber Florentine palace on Madison Avenue, between Fiftieth and Fifty-first Streets, with its twenty-foot ceilings and candelabra, into habitable quarters. It had been built in the 1880's by the railroad magnate, Henry Villard, and occupied in splendor by Ogden Reid, ambassador to the Court of St. James, and his family, who later became prominent in their ownership of the *New York Herald Tribune,* now headed by John Hay Whitney.

The amiable and popular Bennett Cerf, President of Random House, is surely a king in his own right and deserving of such fine quarters as Villard's Italian palace. When he lunches or dines, he walks to a favored restaurant, such as "21" or the Richelieu, where he is ensconced at his regularly reserved table. He holds court just as his literary predecessors did in the days of London's Mermaid Tavern where Shakespeare, Boswell, Jonson and Goldsmith supped and drank. The rest of the great Villard mansion was converted to quarters occupied by the Roman Catholic Archdiocese of New York, and are conveniently adjacent to the Cathedral of St. Patrick.

One of the first mansions to be converted into apartments was that of Joseph Pulitzer, at 11 East Seventy-third Street. This was a sixty-room dwelling, an Italian palace of truly noble proportions designed by McKim, Mead and White in 1904. Mr. Casale made seventeen apartments out of the space, leaving intact most of the luxurious interior with its marble fireplaces and marble baths. The town house of Kermit Roosevelt, son of Theodore, at 29 East Sixty-ninth Street, was bought by William A. Garrigues, Jr., who put in five apartments, while reserving a handsome duplex for himself. Since he began his practice in 1907, Mr. Casale, a true gentleman of the old school, suave and handsome, has been responsible for remodeling, in addition to the Villard and Roosevelt mansions, the imposing total of some three thousand houses, mostly on the fashionable East Side. One of them was converted into the late André Pagani's Brussels Restaurant, at 115 East Fifty-fourth Street, whose progress of conversion and design I watched with keen interest.

All of this activity is symptomatic of the social changes resulting from economic upheavals. The era of the single dwelling of sixty rooms has passed, just as have the scattered offices of great corporations. As a consequence, now more than ever the restaurant is in demand for the fulfillment of social needs, and as the stage upon which the social game is played. The restaurateur and maitre d' hotel are paid hosts, and their large staffs act, for the time engaged, as the servants of yesterday. The dining rooms and cocktail lounges, maintained at great cost to management, are substitutes for the private chateaux and baronial mansions of an earlier day. Viewed in this light, entertainment away from home is a miracle of economy, no matter how steep the tab seems. And in such a place, there is a freedom of movement, and lack of proprietary responsibility, which make the party givers of our own times true princes of the blood.

New York in its role of world's most populous city, and host to all of America and every other country, will continue to expand its services for the entertainment of visitors. There is always a time gap between the building of a hotel, which is a city in itself, whereas restaurants quickly appear and disappear with regularity. The first hotel to open since the Waldorf in 1931, was the reconditioned Hotel Manhattan in 1957. Then was planned the great Zeckendorf Hotel for occupancy at Fifty-first to Fifty-second Streets and Sixth Avenue, which never got past the blueprint stage. In its stead two great hotels have been planned by Loew's Theatres, Inc. Americana East and Americana West.

The Americana West will be located on Seventh Avenue, between Fifty-second and Fifty-third Streets, on the site of the seventy-five-year-old Manhattan Storage and Warehouse, that ugly brooding fortress with its melange of furnishings long unwanted and forgotten. The plot was bought from Webb & Knapp, Inc., as announced by Eugene Picker, president of the theatre chain. Its 2,000 rooms will not make it Manhattan's biggest hostelry—the Hotel New Yorker has a larger capacity—but Americana West will have the distinction of being the world's tallest hotel, with fifty floors, each one dedicated to a state of the Union. It will, of course, have its own parking garage with space for 350 cars. A special feature will be an enormous elevator which can take a visiting state party, or an entire presidential group, limousine and all, to the grand ballroom level on the second and third floors. The main ballroom will accommodate three thousand people, with three smaller rooms up to one thousand in capacity.

There will be thirty-eight private dining-meeting rooms with capacities ranging from twenty-five to three hundred, a roof-terrace, and an all-season swimming pool on the twenty-fifth floor set-back.

The street floor will house an enormous exhibition hall, and off the main lobby will be two large restaurants, as well as a supper club, cocktail lounge, the ubiquitous coffee shop, a French-style terrace café, and a shopping promenade. The old-style hotel built as a castle for the sole purpose of hospitality and lodging is no more. One must seek and find them in Europe in solemn prestige. Every hotel must now have its quota of stores for rental income. At a cost of some $50 million, the Americana West will bridge the span from the twentieth to the twenty-first century. A towering structure, it will be built of honey-toned glazed brick, white Vermont marble, and stainless steel. It is described as "crescent shaped" by its designer, Morris Lapidus, of the architectural firm of Lapidus, Kornblath, Harle and Liebman, which has created plans for the Americana East, the Americana at Bal Harbor, Florida, and the famed Eden Roc and Fontainebleau of that State. Replacing the familiar old Loew's Theater on Lexington Avenue at Fifty-first Street will be the companion hotel, Americana East, a twenty-one story structure estimated to cost $25,000,000. (Recently I noted that the name had been changed to The Summit in the sign announcing its construction.)

These new hotels will incorporate the latest science and industry have to offer to future progress in the hotel and restaurant industry. Rooms are certainly needed for the flood of business and other visitors to New York, where it is presently almost impossible to obtain quarters without advance reservations. It will be interesting to see if the cause of the culinary arts is benefited, as well.

CHAPTER

 25

The Future of Gastronomy

"Let thy provision be solid, and not far fetched, fuller
of substance than art; be wisely frugal in thy prepara-
tion, and freely cheerful in thy entertainment: if thy
guests be right, it is enough; if not, it is too much;
too much is a vanity; enough is a feast."
—Francis Quarles (1592-1644)

The first book about taverns was written by Hammurabi, King of Babylon, who was a lawyer in the Valley of Euphrates some 4,000 years ago. He was concerned for the quality of the inns of his day, the cleanliness, quality of food and wines, and laid down laws for their control. The first institutions established with the colonization of America were places for refreshment. The first holder of a license to operate a place of food and drink in the Massachusetts Bay Colony was Samuel Coles, who was the Deacon of Boston's First Church. This was called Cole's Ordinary. He became a leading business man and was appointed Steward of the newly established Harvard University in 1632. In New York, the Stadts Herrberg —or City Tavern—was licensed by Governor Wilhelm Von Kieft and this became City Hall after serving some ten years as a tavern.

Today there are two urgent problems: feeding and housing for necessity, and housing and dining for pleasure in casual luxury. Mr. Bernatsky, Director of the University of Denver's School of Hotel and Restaurant Management has prognosticated that in business areas hotels and restaurants will become more highly mechanized and the approach to service will be more scientific. Doormen, bellmen, elevator operators will disappear. Menus will be simplified. In many cases, food service will be self-service. Pre-cut meats, pre-cooked, pre-portioned food, ready cake mixes, will be standard in hotel kitchens. Hours will be regulated for maximum turnover and maximum productivity to offset high labor costs. In off hours, believes Mr. Bernatsky, vending machines will take over.

To offset this robot-like picture of what the future may hold in store in the way of shelter and food for strangers, the Denver School believes that hotels and restaurants in suburban areas, and private restaurants in cities, will become increasingly luxurious. Out-of-town hotels and restaurants will look more and more like country clubs. Color schemes, indirect lighting effects, and correct acoustics will be necessary requirements. Swimming pools, golf courses, and other recreational facilities will be standard equipment. In such places, a wide variety of fine food will be offered at high prices, and served with skill and personal attention. There will be a more artistic approach with emphasis on presentation and service. Whether or not it will be possible to revive the greatness of the old hotels is a moot question. Perhaps people are different, times have changed too much, and to each era its own. Nevertheless, the industry will have an unequaled opportunity for expansion coupled with prosperity, unless inhibited by economic cycles or other untoward influences.

There are indications here and there of realistic application of the doctrines of the modern frontier in the culinary arts. Joseph Wechsberg in the *New York Times Magazine* (December 4, 1960) warned the gourmets of France against the invasion of frozen foods. It seems that Paris was thoroughly shocked when Monsieur Raymond Oliver, a famous French chef and owner of the Grand Véfour in the Rue de Beaujolais founded in 1760 as the Café de Chartres, announced that he planned the building of "a factory for the mass production of frozen food." This meant beginning with three tons of food a day and advancing to some eighty tons daily, employing 800 people. This was tantamount, said Joseph Wechsberg, a long-time Epicure, to say Benvenuto Cellini was going into the costume jewelry business or

Antonio Stradivari had made it known in Cremona that he was setting up a factory for the mass production of fiddles.

His predecessor to go into the wholesale food line was M. Louis Vaudable, proprietor of Maxim's of the Rue Royale, which caters to airline passengers. About a year ago, Potel et Chabot, France's largest catering firm, went into the frozen food business after two years of experimenting. Deep-freezing equipment had to be imported from the United States. The machines were brought from New Jersey. Potel et Chabot sells its foods through twelve outlets in and around Paris and elsewhere in France in luxury grocery stores, with exports to Belgium, England, Switzerland and Africa of such choice morsels as *Supreme de Barbue Dieppoise, Paupiettes de Veau Richelieu.* "Our aim" declared M. Maurice Bataille, a director of the firm, "is to combine American technique with the high quality of French cuisine."

M. Oliver, whose father was a great chef, too, runs a fine restaurant and will not try to combine American technique with French *haute cuisine.* He knows it cannot be done. He will mass-produce dishes of the traditional *cuisine bourgeoise,* not the *haute cuisine.* "You can't go against progress. A man who once had a car will never want to ride a bicycle again." Mr. Wechsberg voices his displeasure with such false notions of progress. To him it is sacrilegious what Monsieur Raymond Oliver has undertaken. He feels there is a limit to such progress. He salutes other restaurants in Paris such as Lapérouse which follows the traditional gastronomic approach—no *cuisine congelée* there. "In the fine Paris restaurant, where the customers still know and care enough to be stern about their food, the waiters are still solicitous and the cuisine is still *haute.*"

At the School of Aviation Medicine experiments are being made with food in tubes—like those used for toothpaste-containing such items as beef, pork, peaches and tomatoes and macaroni. During space flights food will have to be squeezed forcibly into the mouth because, in a gravity-free ship in space, nothing will have any weight. Food not in containers would float in the air. ("The Space Guidebook," by William J. Weiser—Coward-McCann).

Though this may all be pure speculation, the problems of feeding and housing remain real and the demand is urgent. Automation must be considered either as a help or a necessary evil. Strides have been made in the combination of ideas, energy, talent, and finances between suppliers and consumers. Within the last decade, the press has done a magnificent job of education and promotion in bringing into the home, ideas of gastronomy once reserved for the traveled and wealthy.

Annually the press meets in congress from every part of the country. In October of 1960 they convened at the Waldorf-Astoria Hotel, where 162 Food Editors assembled from 98 cities of the 50 states, and four provinces of Canada. The power of the pen was obvious as these writers represented a combined circulation of 49 million.

As the meeting progressed, it was clear that everything was a miracle of "packaging," in the idiom of Madison Avenue. The Florida Citrus Commission hosted the Editors at a Latin American luncheon, with emphasis on Argentinian beef, at the colorful La Fonda del Sol Restaurant. The international Tuna Association gave a tea at a Japanese tea-house, The Nippon Club, a private club for Japanese businessmen. The H. J. Heinz Company presented its new Swiss type Cheese Soup in an Alpine Chalet set up at the hotel. The Tea Council showed tea customs around the world. The Metropolitan Museum hosted the Editors in a "Masterpiece in Food Dining," under the auspices of and financed by the National Broiler Council. The Danish Information Office spread a lavish Danish cold table. The Ralston Purina Company of St. Louis, Missouri, referring to themselves as the "Republic of Checkerboard," served a regal embassy breakfast to welcome fellow ambassadors of good food.

As spokesman for the future, Mr. Harold E. Comfort, President of the Borden Company, presented opinions solicited from home economists of the company. They were concerned, among other things, with the size of kitchens, the resurgence of the lunch-box in a gourmet-packed kit, tenderized meat, plumper fowls, irradiated sterilized foods, and the development of freeze-dried foods. One economist stated that freeze drying is the next major advance in food processing, which will be as important as canning, condensing, dehydration and freezing. Micro-wave cooking units will become common. The end of top-of-the-range cooking was predicted, together with the introduction of newer convenience foods suitable to electronic ranges. Tomorrow's kitchens will have fewer utensils, smaller refrigerators, dehydrated products for compact storing, disposable dishes, and disposable table-cloths.

Mr. Comfort cautiously concluded by saying that "any attempt to envision the kitchen of the future in the broad sense I have discussed here must take into consideration what might best be called socio-logical factors. The people who live in and from that kitchen will, of course, determine its composition." This holds true for any type of innovation, for acceptance depends on the public, and the persua-sive ability of advertising to shape public taste and opinion.

It is my own feeling that hospitality, courtesy, and all of the human qualities, coupled with perfectionist skill, will still be necessary in-gredients as time goes on. One must recognize that since distance has been conquered, it has accelerated the acceptance of many foreign cuisines. The modern conception of speed was pin-pointed in the recent announcement that London and Paris will be within two hours' commuting distance from New York within the foreseeable future. This startling statement was made by Alex Kartwell, Vice President of the Republic Aviation Corporation of Farmingdale, Long Island, in addressing the Aviation Space Writers Association gathered in the Promenade Room at Roosevelt Raceway.

One of the world's top men in plane research and development, Mr. Kartwell said that the crossing from New York to France and England will be made in 120-passenger airliners which will be pro-pelled at three times the speed of sound. He described planes with a 10,000 mile range, flying at 150,000 feet at a speed of 7,000 miles an hour. These planes, a by-product of military aircraft, are now on the designing boards and some will be produced within a year. In this new era of speed and luxury, I believe that more than ever before in history, "much will depend on dinner." We live in times in which the pursuit of happiness is overshadowed by the pursuit of greatness. As Walt Whitman said: "The past has been great and the future will be great." There are infinite possibilities right now for emphasis on the joy of living, which was so treasured by the ancients as opposed to the tyrannies of life. This is the time for optimism rather than despair in keeping with the vast advances made on many fronts. It is inevitable that more people will live longer and enjoy more. One day they will renew rather than retire. They will study the means of attaining soul-satisfying happiness. And the culinary arts will be of greater importance than ever before.

Recognition of their importance is given by many persons in high places. While President, Dwight D. Eisenhower made no secret of his love of cooking, concocting and roughing it gastronomically at times on his hunting trips. In retirement, his hobbies of painting, writing, cooking, among others, will serve him well as he assumes the role of elder statesman. The director of New York's Metropolitan Museum of Art, visited by four million people in 1959, is an enthusiastic chef with no mean talent. James J. Rorimer is proud of his culinary gifts and allowed himself to be interviewed by Craig Claiborne for the *New York Times*. Mr. Claiborne put it very neatly: "Since man first discovered that dining is a pleasure, cooking has been considered the eighth lively art." When a cultural leader such as Mr. Rorimer takes pains to give the ingredients of a favorite recipe, there is a message in the doing. People are looking for something beyond physical comfort and satisfaction. There can be adventure in the palate, knowledge, too, and point of view. "Life without inquiry" said Plato "is not worth living."

It was with Mr. Rorimer's consent that for the first time in the history of the august Metropolitan Museum a ball was given in December, 1960 in the great hall. The block-long room was filled with the sound of dinnerware and dance music as, beneath the gaze of an Egyptian sphinx and under medieval gonfalons, elegantly dressed New Yorkers enjoyed the first banquet and ball ever held there. Leaders of the New York fashion industry held a benefit for a cause close to the Museum's heart: The Metropolitan's Costume Institute. Events of this kind foretell the future of gastronomy, I believe.

It is interesting to note that when the name *Gourmet* was selected by Earle R. MacAusland, publisher of the now well known magazine when it was initiated in 1941, it was because this particular word is a synonym for the honest seeker of the *summum bonum* of living.

The premise was that "the art of being a gourmet has nothing to do with age, money, fame, or country. It can be found in a thrifty French housewife with her *pot-au-feu*, or in a white-capped chef in a sky-scraper hotel. But wherever this art exists, its practitioner will have the eye of an artist and the imagination of a poet.

"Good food," continued Mr. MacAusland's credo "and good living have always been an American tradition. At our very fingertips lie an abundance and variety of foods unequaled anywhere. And our native, unquenchable thirst for discovery is now leading us daily into new and exciting channels of exploration in the realm of fine food and drink. Today (he wrote two decades ago) the mad hurly-burly of our modern daily existence forces us all to catch hold of the charged wire of noisy, strident living. It is a wise person who makes the satisfying of his palate a time for exciting, stimulating adventure, a time when he completely disassociates himself from the discordance of the world and recaptures the mellow moods and manners of a bygone day ... good food, good drink, fine living ... this is the universal language of the gourmet."

Eating and dining in public places has been going on for a long time and will continue to do so along the bright paths of the gastronomy of the future. It is a heartening thing to note the interest in food history taken by our leading columnists. One who often pauses to dip into the past, and to serve up a choice bit from the ancients, is Louis Sobol, whose *New York Cavalcade* has had a devoted following for the *New York Journal-American* for many years. Here is a classic example from his column: "For the records, the first 'Business Man's Lunch' was introduced in Rome as far back as 40 B.C. by one Segius Locates, an innkeeper, for the accommodation of ship brokers too busy to go home. A good chef in those days was an important personage— and still is—in fact, Mark Antony once gifted a chef with an entire town because his dishes had elicited glowing praise from Cleopatra."

René Bouché, the portraitist of international beauties renowned for loveliness of face and form, has put it this way: "There is an awareness today of the eternal invitation to elegance which is being recognized as an American characteristic." While this country is the youngest of the world's major nations, it stands on the threshhold of a way of life in which elegance and refinement are sought after and expected. I feel there will be an increasing interest in dining, aside from its gustative delights, for dining has long since been acknowledged as one of the most important of social factors in shaping lives and events. One can never know enough about such a fascinating subject.

This book—which has been a labor of love—was finally completed at Christmastime, the last paragraphs put in place on Christmas day in fact, when we found a quotation from the writings of Charles Dickens, who loved good food, good drink and its literature. It seemed a fitting fare-thee-well: "It was" he wrote "the season of hospitality, merriment and open-heartedness. The old year was preparing like an ancient philosopher to call his friends around him and amidst the sounds of feasting and revelry to pass gently and calmly away." This morsel was topped by a *petit four* from that old master himself, William Shakespeare, holding forth in his "King Henry V": "A good leg will fall; a straight back will stoop; a black beard will turn white; a curled pate will grow bald; a fair face will wither; a full eye will wax hollow; but a good heart, Kate, is the sun and the moon; or, rather, the sun and not the moon; for it shines bright and never changes, but keeps his course truly."

BIBLIOGRAPHY

Adams, Leon D., *The Commonsense Book of Drinking,* David McKay Co., New York, 1960.

Adams, Samuel Hopkins, *Tenderloin,* Random House, 1959.

Andrews, William Loring, *New York as Washington Knew It After the Revolution,* 1905.

Asbury, Herbert, *The Bon Vivant's Companion, How to Mix Drinks,* Prof. Jerry Thomas. Alfred A. Knopf, New York, 1928.

Barnes, Harry Elmer, *Society in Transition,* Prentice-Hall, Inc., 1939, 11th printing, 1950.

Beebe, Lucius, *Snoot If You Must,* D. Appleton-Century Co., N. Y., 1943.

Berger, Meyer, *About New York,* N. Y. *Times,* May 29, 1953.

Bird, William, *French Wines,* Centre National du Commerce Exterieur, Paris, 1955.

Botkin, B. A., *New York City Folklore Treasury,* Random House, N. Y., 1956.

Brown, Henry Collins, *From Alley Pond to Rockefeller Center,* E. P. Dutton & Co., New York, 1936.

Browne, Junius Henri, *The Great Metropolis, A Mirror of New York Life and Society,* American Publishing Company, Hartford, Connecticut, 1959.

Burke, Thomas, *The English Inn,* Herbert Jenkins, Ltd., 3 Duke of York Street, St. James's London, S.W. 1, England.

Collins, Frederick L., *Money Town, Story of Manhattan,* G. P. Putnam's, 1946.

Collins, F. A., *The Romance of Park Avenue,* Park Avenue Association, New York, 1930.

Crockett, Albert Stevens, *Peacocks on Parade, Unique Period in American Social History,* Sears Publishing Co., New York, 1931.

Early, Eleanor, *New York Holiday,* Rinehart & Company, 1950.

Bibliography

Ellis, Aytoun, *The Penny Universities, A History of the Coffee Houses,* Secker & Warburg, London, 1956.

Footner, Hulbert, *New York, City of Cities,* J. B. Lippincott, 1937.

Fortnum & Mason, *The Delectable History of Fortnum & Mason,* Piccadilly, London, England, 1957.

Greneker, C. P., *With the First Vanderbilt,* Railroad Man's Magazine, Vol. II, Feb., 1910, No. 1, Frank A. Munsey Company, N. Y.

Grossman, Harold J., *Guide to Wines and Spirits,* Scribner's, 1943.

Hart, Smith, *The New Yorkers: A Story of a People and Their City,* New York, 1938.

Klein, Alexander, *The Empire City, a Treasury of New York,* with a Preface by Meyer Berger, Rinehart and Company, 1955.

Lawrence, D. H., *Etruscan Places,* Viking Press, New York.

Melville, John, *Guide to California Wines,* Introduction by Joseph Henry Jackson, Doubleday and Company, Garden City, New York, 1955.

McCarthy, James Remington, and Houghton, John, *Peacock Alley, the Romance of the Waldorf-Astoria,* Harper & Bros., New York, 1931.

Pratt, Fletcher, *A Man and His Meals,* Henry Holt and Company, New York, 1947.

Rogers, W. G., and Weston, Mildred, *Carnival Cross-Roads, Story of Times Square,* Doubleday and Co., New York, 1960.

Sandeman, Patrick W., *Port and Sherry, The Story of Two Fine Wines,* George G. Sandeman Sons & Co., Ltd., London, England, 1955.

Schoonmaker, Frank, *The Wines of Germany,* Hastings House, New York, 1956.

Walker, Danton, *Danton's Inferno,* Hastings House, New York, 1955.

Walker, Stanley, *Night Club Era,* Frederick A. Stokes Co., 1933.

Wecter, Dixon, *The Saga of American Society,* Scribner's, New York, 1937.

Wilson, Rufus Rockwell, *New York Old and New, Its Story, Streets and Landmarks,* J. P. Lippincott, 1902.

Worden, Helen, *Here is New York,* Doubleday, Doran & Co., New York, 1939.

INDEX

Index

Index

Index

Index